To Lawra with Love

To Lawra with Love

THE TRUE STORY OF ONE WOMAN, TWO VILLAGES, INFINITE OPTIMISM AND THOUSANDS OF LIVES CHANGED

Sarah Annable-Gardner and Michele Carlisle

BROWN
DOG
BOOKS

Published under licence by Brown Dog Books and
The Self-Publishing Partnership Ltd, 10b Greenway Farm, Bath Rd,
Wick, nr. Bath BS30 5RL, UK

www.selfpublishingpartnership.co.uk

ISBN printed book: 978-1-83952-697-8
ISBN e-book: 978-1-83952-698-5

Cover design by Andrew Prescott
Internal design by Andrew Easton

Printed and bound in the UK

This book is printed on FSC® certified paper

For Aviella, Bie and the children of Lawra

– may you know you are loved

Nearly time to go ...

Ramsbury, UK

Feb 11, 2012

Tomorrow I will be leaving the delights of beautiful, snowy Ramsbury and setting off on my adventure to Ghana. Its 30 degrees there, slightly different to the -8 it is here tonight. I think I may melt.

It's hard to believe that this time tomorrow i'm going to be in Accra, a very scary thought. I'm hoping by then i may be vaguely excited ... Or at least slightly less terrified.

I'm dreading the thought of having to transport my luggage ... roughly 57 kilos, about 30 kilos more than i can comfortably drag. Hopefully I'll be aided by a well-muscled African.

Going to try to get some sleep – doubtful, i know. Wish me luck!

I went to Ghana full of assumptions, the first being that when you *go on an adventure*, you must write a blog. It's hideously embarrassing, not least the atrocious grammar, which I put down to sheer panic (and no autocorrect), and the racist stereotype, for which I have no excuse. However, it is honest, and on the odd occasion someone tells me what I've done is brave, I remember the person I was when I wrote that blog and how far they are from the truth.

The truth was, I was a 'normal' girl with a comfortable if rather sheltered life, a broken heart and the hazy notion of a big old world in which I should *have an experience*.

In the end, though, I did more than that. And not just me.

Hundreds of us – from my new home of Lawra, in challenging, distant Upper West Ghana and from my old village of Ramsbury in leafy, English Wiltshire – who worked together to achieve something we're all proud of. And whilst we got some things wrong, we got lots of it right, and children are now eating and learning, weavers have looms, farmers have seeds, disabled children sing and thousands of lives have changed for the better.

And I've changed too. I've had to question many assumptions, about myself and the people I thought I was meant to save. I've learnt a lot — they've taught me, shown me, so much — and I want to share that with you.

My collaborator in writing this book has been the talented and ruthlessly forthright Michele Carlisle, whose friendship I treasure and who genuinely doesn't let me get away with anything. The result, I hope, is a candid, fair, unvarnished telling of an extraordinary decade, warts and all, highs and lows. All the bad bits, the malaria, hungry, desperate bits, the feeling powerless and being lonely, the shameful white saviour bits. And the amusing bits (mostly involving me being ridiculous) and the stuff you never hear about Africa, which show it really is a small world and we all like sharing a beer or dancing 'til dawn, and people are as funny and clever and hardworking as they are anywhere else.

This is a tale of two villages, thousands of miles and unfathomable privilege apart, where the similarities make you smile, the inequalities make you sob and ordinary people are brave every single day. Of course, those people have lived a life enough to fill their own book, though none of those books will probably ever be written. That's why, in telling my story, I want to use my platform to tell you some of theirs.

You've never heard of Lawra (few have, even in Ghana) yet through my stumbling journey you'll discover why a part of my heart lies there.

Sarah

ONE

SMALL WORLD

If I'd had a mirror I would have been admiring myself in it. Instead, as I stood in a remote concrete house in the heart of the scrub, I could only imagine how fabulous I looked. I'd gone full safari (thank you, Primark) and in my baggy cream trousers, loose white shirt and neat pumps I felt I'd struck the right note. All very colonial. What a total fool I was.

It was a week since I'd arrived in Ghana, forsaking a near-perfect existence in the quintessential English village of Ramsbury in Wiltshire. Ramsbury is the kind of place chocolate boxes were invented for. The high street rings with the sound of nice people wishing each other good morning and the village pub has been thoroughly Farrow and Balled. Richard Curtis would definitely approve. I approved too. But I was twenty-eight and I needed a change.

It's not that I didn't appreciate how lucky I was. Life was fun, full of friends and family, and I was incredibly loved. I'd drive each day to my fantastic job at The Winchcombe School in Newbury and then home to Ramsbury for glorious countryside walks and nights in the pub, where there was always a friendly face.

Of course, there were downsides. In a village, you can't get away with anything. If you change your hairstyle, word gets round. If you have a problem, everyone will hear about it. And if you want to sneak a BMW-driving six-foot-four black man into your flat without anyone spotting him, you won't be able to. Believe me, I tried.

So (and not unrelated to that) I'd decided to take a year out, to leave Ramsbury and do something different – maybe even *make* a difference. I'd already been to The Gambia a couple of times with a teaching group and had found it inspiring, eye-opening, a beginner's guide to Africa that made me want more. And when I told Mum I was heading off with my backpack she suggested VSO, Voluntary Service Overseas. They send professionals with skills to marginalised communities to help fight poverty. *I've got skills*, I thought, *I like communities, I'm against poverty*. Yes, I thought all those things. Though mainly I thought, *that will show him*.

Ah, him. The six-foot-four elephant in the room. The love of my life (maybe) and unlike anyone I'd ever met, he *represented* bigness, the bigness of the world.

But I was a village girl and he wasn't attracted to the me that was small-town. After six months, he broke it off and I felt I couldn't survive, not in Ramsbury, not in the same place, doing the same things. We'd often talked about international development and Africa, and he'd made me realise there was so much world out there and perhaps I could do something in it.

Suddenly, I was filling in forms and heading to London for an interview. Not with a burning desire to do the work, more a burning desire to escape. A one-year sabbatical, a line for the CV, and VSO pay your costs and a small allowance. It was a safe way to do it, to get away, to do something worthwhile, to take control.

A few weeks later, I landed at Accra Airport, decided I *loved* the heat and even carried my own cases. My adventure, as they say, had begun.

Exploring the City

Accra, Ghana

Feb 15, 2012

Its been fantastic to get out and about in Accra. The city is a vibrant, exotic, noisy place where you sweat constantly and get covered in dust. I FINALLY feel like I am in Africa.

We travelled on a 'Trotro' which is a minibus with 23 people crushed onto it, swerving traffic on the very busy roads. Our destination was a large market, which sold many things, including colourful fabrics. I plan to have lots of traditional Ghanaian outfits made. The women all look so bright its hard to resist following their fashion.

After shopping, I experienced my first 'street' meal. The woman was cooking over an open fire, behind her drink stall. It was ridiculously cheap (about 40p), and consisted of noodles, with cabbage and eggs. It was fantastic.

I've had my first mosquito bite, but no malaria so far. We had an alarming health talk – did you know you could still get cholera/hep A/ typhoid/meningitis despite having had all the vaccinations?!?

Also, apparently I'm vulnerable to hippo attacks in my area ...

There's a salsa night in Accra tonight! Woohoo!!!

In-Country Training started well, mosquito bite and continuing poor grammar aside. After all, I was fine in an ex-pat, trip to the market, salsa night kind of way. As the week went on, though, I had a creeping sense of dread.

My fellow volunteers knew so much more than me, were cleverer, more together, more intrepid. My impressive room-mate Leela – who'd already travelled practically half the world

– would spend the lunch break talking seriously with the others about development, while I'd be in a bikini, not understanding why they weren't topping up their tan.

I struggled in the language classes and some of the sounds in Dagaare (one of the languages of north west Ghana) don't exist in English, so I couldn't even write the words phonetically, and teaching phonics was my thing. Apparently, I needed to be more nasal. I just about got my tongue around kommie (tomato), daa (market, wood or push) and Naa Yiri (Chief's Palace) – hardly the basis for meaningful conversations – and I hoped people would speak English.

Still, despite the language difficulties, a bout of food poisoning, some hot sleepless nights, an endless battle with Vodafone over buying a dongle for internet access and the terrifying realisation I hadn't got a clue what I was doing, I tried to persuade myself it was *part of the experience.*

Then I discovered where everyone was being sent. Leela was in a big group of volunteers going to Bolgatanga, a relatively well-developed town in the Upper East. I was going to Lawra in the Upper West. On my own.

At 6 am, Accra bus station was a scramble of activity, with industrious women balancing huge plates of bananas and pawpaws on their heads and agitated men running around with outsized luggage, the coach being the only way to get, say, a fridge, up north. At least the bus was air-conditioned and I sank into a surprisingly well-proportioned seat ready for my sub-Saharan expedition.

I wish I could tell you about that journey, through the heart of Ghana towards the border with Burkina Faso, heading through the lush, green jungley south to the stark, red, blah, blah, blah but I'm afraid I pulled a sarong over my head and slept nearly all the way, exhausted from a week of training, vomiting and freaking out. Seventeen hours later, I emerged in Wa, capital of the Upper West region, the blazing night air hitting my air-conditioned skin like a blow torch.

Next morning, a car collected me for the two-hour jolt to Lawra. We bumped down rutted crimson-dust roads, through scrubland, past laden-down trotro minibuses stuffed with people and goats and rolls of carpet. Children carried water from pumps, women took tomatoes (kommie) to market, families minded roadside stalls selling barely anything, people slumped under trees. There was life here, and it looked hard and slow and hot.

On the outskirts of Lawra, we drew up at my red-orange concrete home. It was isolated, in scrubland on the edge of the grounds of Lawra Secondary School, with a few mud structures – the community of Tuori – in the distance.

'Welcome to Lawra,' said Izzy, the volunteer I was replacing. It was sweltering, yet she looked amazing, suntanned, no make-up, relaxed in her own skin. Even once I'd washed my epic journey away (dare I expect running water?) I'd never glow like that.

'Ignore them.' She nodded towards a meagre tree about a hundred metres from the house.

I glanced over. A flash of torn clothes and tiny flip-flopped feet.

'Don't interact with the children. You'll never get rid of them.'

The mosquito frame banged behind us as we walked into the dark, cavernous lounge. A weak electric light did little to brighten the room, though I could see it was simply furnished with a wooden sofa, a cushion and a map on the wall. Of course, compared to the mud dwellings, this was luxury. Izzy went to the fridge freezer (thank you, VSO) and took out a couple of the plastic pure water sachets that are popular in Ghana, if you can afford them.

'Shall we go for drink?' She bit the corner off her sachet and sucked. 'There's a spot in town.'

'Spot?'

'Drinking spot, a bar. Grab a wash and we'll head out.'

Joy. There was a bath. OK, the taps didn't work, but the blue container of sun-warmed water beside it was full and I had a refreshing bucket bath. Even more joy, toilet, though I had to flush it with another bucket of water. The soiled paper went in a bin (like Greece) to be burned outside (not like Greece).

My room was large and airy. The double bed looked comfortable, grand even with its four posters from which the mosquito net hung. There was a ceiling fan and, although the doors were hanging off, there was a built-in wardrobe for my baggy clothes. Traditional fabric shrouded a couple of wobbly bookcases, yet everything was covered in dust. And there was no mirror, which was possibly a blessing. I smoothed down my linens and went for a drink.

We cycled to the spot, circumventing straggly trees, piles of smouldering rubbish, various pigs, goats and chickens and the odd, inquisitive youngster defying Izzy's no child zone. Even the main tarmacked road into Lawra was an obstacle course, with deep craters that had been badly filled and then washed away in the rains. Each passing car swirled up a great russet cloud, much of which landed on me.

'You OK?'

Izzy, in skimpy top and jeans, was somehow clean. I had

swathes of cream linen billowing round my ankles and the dust was sticking to my sweat.

'Fine, thanks,' I said, realising my first email home would be an urgent request for my sister Karen to send some normal clothes. Everything I'd packed was wrong, on so many levels.

The spot was painted a vivid green with a few plastic chairs outside. Izzy headed to a table occupied by a couple of well-dressed men and when one of them clinked two beer bottles together, a waitress appeared.

'Would you like a Club?' The man looked at me.

I'd never been a beer drinker – more a Sauv Blanc kind of girl – but I went with the flow. It came in towering bottles, about two-foot tall. Yet, in that heat … after that ride … and that journey … God, that Club tasted good. And sitting there, in the dying sunshine, drinking a beer in stimulating company, I felt utterly alone.

How could I be friends with these people? I was a humble primary school teacher and they had senior government jobs at the Ghana Education Service. They were part of a world I didn't understand, well-connected, arguing loudly about that year's general election, effortlessly showing me traditional hospitality by ordering more beer before I'd finished the one I was on.

I'm not sure how many large Clubs I had that night (three? four?), and I sat there feeling sillier and sillier, intimidated by these important men and this assured woman, mozzies flying up my flappy trousers, my bladder filling with fizzy beer until I was squatting in a three-sided, roofless urinal near the spot with my Nokia in my mouth and the torch on, trying to aim at the gulley that ran down one side, wee seeping into my cream linen. I bet Izzy never weed on herself.

Over the next few days Izzy dragged me round town, introducing me to people and showing me where everything was, until the whole week blurred into one scorching, sticky panic, with me cycling breathlessly behind her, cross-country, in thirty-odd degree heat, marinated in sweat and pebble-dashed in scarlet, thinking, *remember where you're going, remember where you're going.* I was constantly lost, in all senses of the word.

She showed me the trotro station (as if I'd ever have the courage to use it), we went to the general shop (it took me a week to find it again) and we bought bread at the market (I forgot where the stall was).

On day five, she went, leaving me with an overwhelming sense of fear and some skimpy clothes that didn't fit. I waved goodbye from the veranda and ran inside, trying not to catch the eye of any of the children hanging around in the distance. And then it was just me, in that house, on my own, like an abandoned kid on a messed-up school outing in Upper West Ghana.

By 6.30 it was dark, pitch black, no light from anywhere. I seemed to be the only person in the neighbourhood who even had electricity. I checked the doors were locked, and checked again. This was not what I'd signed up for. Those jaunts to The Gambia were nothing like this, with their beaches and bars and swimming pools brimming with volunteers having a laugh. I imagined Leela and the crowd in Bolgatanga, drinking beer, chatting over events of the day, and felt even lonelier.

For want of something to do, I examined the large world map on the living room wall, put there by a previous volunteer in an attempt to cheer up the place. Over the following months, I spent hours staring at that map. The day I clocked how vast Canada was, that was interesting.

But that night, that first night on my own in Lawra, all I could think was I'd left a home, a family and a job in order to impress a man and see a bit of the world. And standing in front of that map, in that dim room, with the doors locked, on the edge of a town full of children I wasn't supposed to speak to and work colleagues I didn't know how to, it struck me that my world had got a whole lot smaller.

TWO

RUBBISH

I hid behind my front door, peering through the louvre slats of the windows, assessing how many children were nearby and how quickly I could dispose of my festering rubbish. About fifty youngsters lived in the neighbourhood, and I'd watched them over the weekend, gangs of them with catapults hunting birds to eat, climbing trees to grab fruits, tending animals, running errands for their parents, nosing round my veranda. Despite Izzy's rules, they were curious about the new white lady. I, however, had stayed indoors.

Now, I made a dash for the tree where Izzy dumped waste for the goats, deposited banana skins, egg shells and stale bread crusts and legged it back. A few moments later, floppy hat topping off my development worker chic, I pushed the bike down the steep slope from the garage and cycled off for my first day at work.

As I did, a couple of boys, six or seven years old, crouched under the tree and picked their way through my rubbish, eating my crusts.

I live in a sauna

Lawra, Ghana

Feb 24, 2012

My commute to work is my favourite time of the day. I see many animals – new piglets (born this week – adorable!!!), goats who constantly lose and find their bleating kids and noisy cockerels. As well as this menagerie, I normally pass several naked young men from the school campus who are either crouched down to go to the loo (!!!!) or taking a shower with a bucket. I pass through a little village where I say good morning to what feels like hundreds of people, and then turn left at the Pawpaw trees to join the main road which leads me to work. This takes about 6 minutes, in the sunshine, I love it.

I bloody hated that ride. It was boiling and dirty and dangerous, cars coming from all angles, beep beeping. And lots of bare bottoms. Evidently, the boys from Lawra Secondary School went into the scrub for their morning poo. It was, I'd heard, acceptable in Lawra to defecate in the open, though when I saw one boy use a piece of exercise book to wipe his bum, I looked away.

'Good morning,' shouted a red-dressed lady from a packed nyaaba, a taxi made of a trailer bolted to a motorbike. She had a goat on her lap.

'Good morning.' I scoured my mind for the Dagaare.

'Good morning,' the nyaaba passengers waved. Then it came to me.

'Fo angsoma. Fo angsoma.'

It reminded me of home. Everyone in Lawra said good

morning and Ramsbury is also a very good-morningy place, so there were parallels. Not the pooing, obviously.

Then a lorry sped past, coating my pinstriped shirt in hot orange grit. Not the best first impression, but at least I found my way to the offices of Ghana Education Service, where I was to be based.

The GES office didn't impress me either, though I'm certain it was meant to. An imposing three-storey building oozing colonial grandeur, it shone incongruously in the dust. Out front, a flashy jeep glinted in the sunlight, a perk, I later learnt, for the Director. Inside, civil servants sat in chilled offices, drinking chilled bottled water, no doubt wondering why a fool in a floppy hat had just turned up.

'Hello. My name is Sebastian.' He was a GES Circuit Supervisor and the first person to speak to me in three hours.

I was seated in a fat leather chair behind my expansive desk, having spent the morning attempting to get on Facebook, fiddling with the air conditioning and hoping someone would tell me what to do.

'I am going on a school visit to Bagri. Care to come along?'

We drove on his motorbike through Lawra town (population 6,500) to one of the villages that made up the wider Lawra District where another 50,000 people lived in basic, rural conditions. Eighty per cent of people survived on subsistence farming, Sebastian told me, scarcely able to grow enough for their own family, with little surplus to sell or save for leaner times. Everyone else was either a lucky public sector worker (a job for life), a trader or skilled, like a plumber or seamstress. There were no private companies. In Bagri, where the village runs along the banks of the Black Volta River, the locals mostly fished or farmed. Though, in dry season (as it was then) there was little sign of either activity.

'Bagri Junction is not one of the better-funded schools,' said Sebastian, as we pulled up outside a faded yellow building.

He wasn't kidding. We walked along a veranda, past dilapidated classrooms. Doors were no more than holes in the wall, windows were falling apart, floors were falling apart. And the children …

God, the children …

How they'd managed to stagger in to school at all was a wonder. The ones who'd made it – some, according to Sebastian, walking for two hours – looked hungry and totally spent. A few wore raggedy school uniform, the rest were in grimy, ill-fitting T-shirts and torn shorts, or shabby ripped dresses (charity bin donations, presumably) and no shoes.

We stopped to watch some lessons, the pupils taking notes on scraps of paper, sharing pencil stubs. One teacher tried their best as a dozen children huddled round a single maths textbook.

'We have no resources,' shrugged the head teacher. 'How are the teachers supposed to teach?'

In the next classroom, there was no teacher, only children slumped among broken desks, asleep.

'It can take months for teachers' pay to come through. They run businesses on the side to survive. They are not always here.'

The head was dynamic and smart, and I could see, in different circumstances, he would have run a successful school. But what could he do with classrooms of malnourished pupils, no-one to teach them and no books? What could anyone do? I was still in shock as we rode to nearby Bagri Baptist School (run in partnership with Savannah Education Trust, a UK charity). And it was the complete opposite. Students were provided with lunch, they wore school uniform, they were learning. They smiled. It should have been cause for optimism, yet all the way back I couldn't shift that picture of stereotypical Africa, of poverty, misery, negativity. Unfairness.

Home, and another supper from the food Izzy bought before she left, bread and groundnut paste (like peanut butter, but better). Outside, as ever, hungry children waited for my scraps.

In Izzy's time, they'd stand silently at the door, knowing they weren't allowed in but still hoping she'd give them water or something. Although the borehole was a long searing walk away, she stuck to her rule, ignoring them or shouting until they ran off. One afternoon in the crossover week, I'd flouted the ban and ventured out to talk to some girls, and then I got yelled at too.

'Trust me,' she'd said, 'it's for the best. Give them anything and you'll make a rod for your own back. Did I mention that Peace Corps volunteer, the one who kept a stick by her front door?'

I was appalled, but had very much got the message, from Izzy, the GES guys, VSO and anyone in the development community I met. Do not make relationships with the children. *Whatever you do.*

So I spied on them through the louvres, watching a group under a tree, sharing food from a large tomato tin. Begged leftovers from the senior school. Tonight, at least, they dined on something other than my rubbish.

I spent the next two days rattling round my echoey office, daunted by both my surroundings and my task as Teacher Support Officer – *to raise standards of teaching literacy and numeracy across Lawra District's ninety-six primary schools.* I then decided to decamp to the Teachers' Resource Centre (TRC) over the road, which (in theory) I was supposed to manage.

I had high hopes for the TRC. *The people there are really excited about you coming,* Izzy had written in her handover email, but when I walked in, that hope died. Thousands of pounds' worth of teaching guides, picture books, books in Dagaare, maths equipment and English equipment were mummified in the thickest layer of dust, untouched and unloved.

Off the main room, my office also served as the technology centre, with eight computers draped in pieces of patterned cloth. I tried each filthy machine and not one of them worked. I tried the ceiling fan and that didn't work either. I heard chatter from the next room.

'Fo angsoma.' I walked through to another office and summoned my cheeriest smile. 'Hi, I'm Sarah.'

'Good morning, Sarah, you are welcome.'

Rena and Martha were employed by GES to do photocopying and typing for teachers that used the centre, though clearly few did, and if they did the photocopier would probably not be functioning and, if it was, Rena and Martha might well not be. Contrary to Izzy's email, they did not appear excited by my arrival. That afternoon, as I tried in vain to tidy up, I could see them outside, under a mango tree.

Abandoning the cleaning, I focused on identifying a cluster of schools that were particularly in need, and I failed at that too, having no idea where to start, no list, no map and no budget.

Actually, someone told me there had been a budget, but it had been spent on something else. My leather chair, possibly.

I'm not sure what I did all day. Sat there sweating, mostly. I borrowed a modem from GES, and got online long enough to upload a blog so breezy no-one would realise quite how mundane and unimportant my adventure was proving.

On the first Thursday, I went shopping. I'd run out of food and was now on the emergency cereal bars my thoughtful Ramsbury friend Laura had popped into my suitcase. That morning, through the louvres, I could see a lot of traffic in front of my house. Women with basins of eggs on their heads, children lugging sacks of groundnuts, men on rickety bikes with live chickens dangling from the handlebars all trooped by, slowly, purposefully. It was market day in Lawra.

As I cycled over the scrub, praying I would remember the way, I passed a willowy twelve-year-old girl in tiny shorts, a strappy top hanging off one shoulder, a plate with a few half-rotten kommie on her head. I'd noticed her before and (as instructed) had stayed aloof.

'Hello, Sister.'

Instinct and manners kicked in. 'Hello.'

'My name is Celina. What is yours?'

'It's Sarah,' I replied and sped off. A few words, yet all the way to market I panicked about what I'd done.

The market, in the end, was easy to find because *everyone* in Lawra was going. It came to town every six days, and, after a week of groundnut paste on toast, I was craving fruit and veg.

It was massive, labyrinthine, with hundreds of stalls selling clothes, kitchenware and food, though, it being dry season, that was in short supply. I wandered around, trying not to tread on animals (dead and alive), overawed and almost overcome in over forty-degree heat at the heart of the market.

When I ventured to buy something, it was easier said than done. Most stallholders spoke only Dagaare and my smattering of mispronounced words got me nowhere. Even sign language let me down, as I repeatedly displayed four fingers while the woman sold me four *bags* of bananas.

I handed over a ten cedi note (GH¢10, about £3), crisp from the currency booth at Accra Airport, and the woman walked, unhurriedly, from one stall to the next, collecting change. Another lesson learnt, bring small notes.

Two hours later, overheated and dehydrated, I was done. My backpack bulged with bananas and I wedged half a dozen eggs – sold loose, in a plastic bag – into the bicycle basket for the bumpy ride home. In the end, one egg survived.

I ate a tiny omelette and enjoyed the sunset from the kitchen window. It was a pleasant, pastoral scene, people lounging under mango trees, boys and girls chasing goats, a few young men, stripped to the waist, going through their paces at a makeshift gym. Then there was a power cut, so I lit a candle and had an early night, diligently sleeping under the mosquito net even though it was suffocatingly hot without the ceiling fan. And such was my thrilling new life in Lawra.

On Friday, the electricity was back on at the house but not in the Teachers' Resource Centre. It was my best day so far, having been invited to a church choir by Izzy's friend, Benjamin. In Ramsbury, I had loads of hobbies (choir, Ceroc dancing, anything musical) so the prospect of weekly practice and

Sunday service was promising, a first glimmer of how things could work for me in Lawra.

Next, this GES guy, Derrick, came into the TRC and suggested we collaborate on a project. I was pleased someone had reached out and we put our heads together, going through lesson plans for inspiration until I couldn't stand the heat any longer.

'Why don't we go to mine? I've got fans and my electricity's on, we can work there.' Needless to say, he readily agreed.

I suspect you're ahead of me on this one. But I was so desperate to forge any kind of relationship that I was genuinely surprised when he forcibly grabbed me and lunged for a kiss. I pushed him away and he instantly backed off.

'Sorry, I thought ...'

'Just leave, please.' I was shaking.

I didn't have any supper on Friday night and went to bed as soon as it got dark.

I awoke on Saturday to the warmth of morning sunlight, and it washed away the horrible memory of the day before. Gazing up towards the barely netted window, I saw several pairs of eyes staring down.

The children had been getting bolder, creeping up the veranda steps and peeking in through the mosquito net. Now, they were hanging on the window bars, trying to glimpse the foreign lady, wishing she'd give them something to eat or drink. Izzy would never have allowed it, but I couldn't shout at them, it wasn't my style. I snuck out of the bedroom and skulked in the kitchen, hoping my hungry neighbours couldn't see me having breakfast. What with Derrick and the children, I felt under siege. The one bright spot was my invite to the church choir.

I got up at 5 am on Sunday, braved a bucket bath (the water was *not* warm so early in the day) and put on my church clothes. I'd been told to wear a long frock and, as I went outside, it felt nice to be dressed up and with somewhere to go. I'd never been properly on the veranda, not scurrying in and out and praying no-one would catch me, just quietly standing there, taking it all in. And at that hour, it was breathtaking. The sun, rising above the hamlet in the distance, was enormous, cocks crowed, goats gambolled and, briefly, I could forget my troubles and the troubles of the people around me, and believe in the wonder of life.

Of course, Benjamin never came. I waited for over an hour, but he never came. And my glimmer faded. Standing alone on the veranda, it dawned on me how hard it would be to achieve anything or connect with anyone in Lawra, and how easy it would be to waste the opportunity and the money spent on me and a year of my life. Then I noticed some children emerge from one of the buildings and rushed back indoors.

That afternoon was a scorcher and I hid inside from the sun and from the children and from the men and from everything. This was the hottest part of the year, with the weather not due to break until April or May when rainy season began. Would I even last that long?

'Sister Sarah, I will drink the water.' It came from the veranda. I assumed my position by the door and squinted through the louvres. Half a dozen children had gathered, including Celina.

'Sister Sarah, I will drink the water.'

And in that moment, I made a decision. I knew why Izzy had

warned me, why VSO told me to keep my boundaries. Almost, in a way, why that Peace Corps volunteer kept a stick by the door. But it was not how I wanted to do things.

'Sister Sarah, I will drink the water.' I went to the fridge, took out a bottle and found a few cups on the draining board. Outside, I poured the children some water. I mean, how can you not give a child, a thirsty child, something to drink?

As the children drifted away, a couple of little boys hung back, all distended stomachs and snotty noses. I grabbed a couple of bags of bananas and handed them over, pointing across at the others. They ran off and shared them out.

I knew I'd broken the rules. That everyone would say I'd made a rod for my own back. Yet, for the first time since I arrived in Lawra, it didn't feel rubbish any more.

THREE

SMILE, PLEASE

Feb 24, 2012

My project for the week is to make friends ... suggestions on how to do this would be welcome! My plan is to hang out in town and smile at people. I'll probably get a reputation as The Crazy White Woman Who Smiles For No Reason. Wish me luck!
xxx

In Ramsbury, I had lots of friends, I was the one who held the parties, life was fun.

In Lawra, not so much. At work, the obvious place to connect, the best I got was a lazy wave from Rena and Martha as they reclined under the mango tree. I couldn't go to a spot on my own (women rarely ever went to them), my VSO colleagues were miles away and I was still, more or less, keeping my boundaries with the children. So, other than *good mornings* from passers-by and *thank yous* for water and bananas, I often went days without any contact. My friend Owen had compiled a mix tape of our favourite songs and I played it constantly those first weeks because it made me feel close to my friends. In reality, though, I was alone. Hence, the Crazy White Woman Who Smiles For No Reason. When you're a foreigner you can get away with all sorts.

Checking the coast was clear, I set off into town for a morning of errands, smiling as I cycled by women grinding maize under a tree.

'Good morning, Sister,' one of them called.

'Morning,' I replied and rode on, wondering how I'd ever get past *good morning*. Preparing food or washing clothes, that's how women made friends in Lawra and no amount of smiling would get me there. And what would we even talk about? My broken heart? My frustrations with a (relatively) well-paid job? My patchy new tan?

Or we could talk about them. We could talk about the lack of food and the half-hour round trip to the borehole or that many of them had low-level malaria really quite often and not everyone had health insurance. Though, I don't suppose that's what they talked about, under the tree, grinding maize. People don't, do they?

In the Post Office, I beamed idiotically at the clerk and because he was kind, he paused his examination of a sachet of dehydrated pasta and cheese and beamed back. The pasta was from Laura, alongside antibacterial wipes, antibacterial spray and J-cloths. I laughed. *If she could see the way I live.*

The clerk rummaged through jeans and T-shirts sent by Karen (at last, I could stop looking like an extra in a period drama) to discover a carefully wrapped can of gin and tonic.

'There is duty to pay on these items.' He handed me a form. 'Please go to the Customs Office.'

I suspected there was *always* duty to pay, regardless of it being settled in the UK, and decided to ask people to label their next parcels *Feminine Hygiene Products*. I handed the clerk a precious bag of Skittles and got a smile.

After the Customs Office, I waved at the lady selling boiled eggs at the roundabout, visited a seamstress to be fitted for an appropriate dress and went to the general store. Smiling all the way. No-one could say I didn't try.

Then, something extraordinary. A young man walked over,

amused grin on his vaguely familiar face.

'You are the lady.' He grinned again.

'Hi, I'm Sarah.'

'You are that lady.'

'Sorry?'

'That lady. The one who watches.'

He raised his arms, flexed his biceps and the penny dropped. With his clothes on, I hadn't immediately recognised one of the youths who frequented the gym behind my house.

'Yes.' I hung my head. 'I am that lady.'

Later, as the grunt of people exercising drifted across the scrub, I crouched on the kitchen floor so they couldn't see me and ate rehydrated pasta and cheese. Then I dug out the trusty recorder a primary school teacher *never* travels without and sat there, playing to myself, in the dark.

I had a visitor. James (a VSO volunteer based four hours away) came for the weekend and it was like a miracle. Someone to talk to, to giggle with when the electricity went off and candles drooped in the heat, to drink sangria with by the lights on our phones. To feel normal with. He took some wonderful photos – bendy candles, the spot with a passing herd of goats, me, slim in a new blue dress, reading with my young neighbours.

I loved that photo. I loved it so much I put it on my blog. Yes, we need to talk about that photo.

Mar 6, 2012

I'm getting a lot of pleasure from the children. Today I had 16 of them on the veranda; drawing, talking and, hopefully, learning. They are delightful, and live in absolute poverty. These resilient little people are bloated, barefooted, dirty, mostly not enrolled in school and some look very ill. I'm so enjoying getting to know them.

I've totally nailed making hummus - it's amazing! I've got 3 Peace Corps volunteers coming for lunch tomorrow, so I'm making a huge batch.

The things you can achieve when you have a bit of time and motivation!

It just wasn't true. Actually, I *had* nailed hummus. But that image, me in the blue dress, with the children, wasn't true. It didn't represent something I was doing, other than on that day, for that photo. I'd even found my camera so James could record it for posterity, the nice lady reading a story, learning a few names, feeling good about herself. Knowing she could close her door and disengage.

Though I'd never heard the term back then, I plainly had a whiff of white saviour about me. And I've got the photo to prove it.

It was 6.30 in the morning and I was in the middle of Lawra, alone.

I'd been invited to the Schools March on Independence Day (it was fifty-five years since Ghana gained independence from Britain) and though I felt honoured to be included, I wasn't quite sure what I'd agreed to or where everyone else was. Then I recalled a recent bit of advice – *the only way you know a meeting is going to happen in Ghana is because you are in it. Until then, it's a maybe* – found myself a shady mango tree and waited.

At about nine, they came. Hundreds, thousands possibly, on

foot, in trotros and nyaabas, whole families on one motorbike, legions of children from those ninety-six schools I'd been tasked to improve. Though no-one could have improved on their performance that day, marching in a straight line, in unison, in their many-coloured uniforms scrubbed until they gleamed. Proud parents in their Sunday best long dresses and traditional smocks cheered them on until, in a moment of solemn ceremony, everyone saluted their flag.

I was put on the judging panel for 'Best School' and immediately promoted (or perhaps demoted) to secretary, compiling the scores and ranking the schools. After feeling so useless at work it was gratifying to do something with purpose, even if it helped me more than I helped them.

'Hey, Small Girl, get me groundnuts.'

Beth, a Peace Corps volunteer, handed over a few coins to a young woman who, for the past ten minutes had been patiently holding her rucksack. As the girl skipped off on her errand, Beth turned to me. 'They like to do stuff for you.'

I wouldn't say Beth was my new best friend, but in the absence of anyone else, I'd leapt at her invite for a day on the river. Exuding confidence, she was perched on the bonnet of her boyfriend's red jeep while he bought provisions in the general store. Outside the adjacent police station, officers in dark blue sat around, AK-47s slung over their shoulders. It was all very different from hiding in my house.

The boyfriend, Dan, emerged from the general store, another man in tow.

'Here they are. Sarah, meet Felix.'

Felix was a policeman, and I was almost disappointed he

wasn't in uniform because I guessed he'd look rather good in it. He shouted to a young skinny guy in a faded T-shirt, sending him off with some money as we climbed into the jeep. Soon, snacks began arriving through the windows, fried plantain from the skinny guy and roasted groundnuts from the *small girl*, who kept a bag for herself. I wasn't sure what was going on, but it seemed the way of things in Lawra.

A day out was what I needed. We took a canoe across the river to Burkina Faso (the French-speaking country north of Ghana), and I searched for hippos and crocodiles in the murky water and flirted with funny, interesting Felix, a fellow 'immigrant' in Lawra (he was from the south). On the riverbank, men panned for gold, giving shouts of excitement if they found some.

They weren't the only ones to strike lucky.

'Fancy a game of cards?' When Beth and Dan dropped me off, I invited Felix in.

I know. Except he *was* Beth's friend, so I thought it would be alright and I fancied a game of cards and a game of cards is what I got. Over the next few weeks Felix took me for the occasional drink, sent texts, dropped by with a bag of fruit. It broke up the daily grind.

'You like Ghanaian food?' He was cooking.

'I'm not sure.' I'd been in the country for a month and had eaten groundnut paste and fried eggs for a lot of it.

We were in his basic government lodgings – bed, TV, two-ring hob – and he was filling a rice cooker and stirring some kind of tomato and greens stew (kontomire, very tasty). In the corner, squatting by the wall, was the skinny guy, the fried plantain guy, mending a plug.

This became the pattern. Me and Felix, along with Nasir

(as he'd quietly introduced himself), who would stay in the background, running errands, Felix's *small boy*. We'd often hang out at the police station, where groups of officers played cards and ranted politics. Occasionally, someone came with a dispute that couldn't be resolved by traditional leaders and the whole family would get involved, Felix in the middle, with his uniform and his big gun, completely in charge. Having been disempowered for weeks, it was a relief to feel that somebody was.

One day, I was in the Teachers' Resource Centre wondering what to do with myself when I heard the door bang, which was odd because Rena and Martha were under their mango tree and we never had callers.

'Good morning, Sarah.' It was Nasir, with a carton of juice. 'This is from Felix.'

'Thanks,' I said. And, awkwardly, we smiled.

FOUR

TWO STEPS FORWARD

'May I carry your bag?'

She was a strong, beautiful woman in a vivid green dress, a different version of the muscly African I'd once envisaged and I couldn't have been more grateful. I'd just hauled my wheelie cross-country to the main road and definitely needed rescuing.

'My name is Olivia.' She deftly tied the suitcase to her bicycle. 'Where are you going?'

'Trotro station, thank you so much. I'm Sarah.'

We chatted as we walked and I discovered she was, like me, a teacher. Though, I suspected, far more capable.

'Do you live over there?' I glanced in the direction she'd come.

'Sometimes I live there and sometimes I live there.' She indicated the other way. 'It's complicated.'

I found out later quite how complicated. For now, I was glad to be talking to someone I liked, and when she dropped me and my case in town I knew I'd made a friend.

Bolgatanga, Ghana

Mar 14, 2012

I'm in Bolga for motorbike training. It has been the most terrifying week of my life. The rural roads are sandy, holey, stony, unfinished and so so dusty. Animals and children run out at you, as if from nowhere and in some places the sand is so deep it's practically impossible not to skid and fall. In town, it's utter chaos, bikes and cars come from all directions. People drive/ride wherever they like and stop for nothing – including red lights. It's scary.

We had a talk from some policemen today. These are some of the things I learnt:

- *'If you overtake in dust, you will die.'*
- *'If you don't wear a helmet, you will die.'*
- *'If you go fast, you will die.'*
- *'If you carry 3 people or more on your bike, you will all die.'*

When I pointed out no-one in Ghana wore helmets, everyone overtook on the dusty roads, travelled with up to 5 on a bike and went very fast, he said that they will all die. We've had several crashes this week, nothing too serious. My worst incident was driving straight into the side of my friend. I'm having trouble remembering to use my back brake.

Wish me luck! x

I returned to Lawra with my shiny new license around the time permission came through for my first official visit to a school. After six weeks, several cancelled meetings and three lunches with GES officials, finally, the work could begin.

Even getting the motorbike out of the garage was a struggle. It was a hefty old thing, a Yamaha DT dirt bike, kick start and no handbrake, so I had to straddle it and slowly, slowly edge down the slope with the foot brake on. And then I was off. I was possibly the only person in Upper West Ghana wearing a helmet, but I felt liberated as I rattled my way over the scrub to Karbo Primary.

I was met by Mary Karbo, the head teacher, who led me across an imposing courtyard, past a sprawling mango tree, towards a large yellow building. 'This was a boarding school in colonial times.' She pointed to some dilapidated outhouses. 'Those were the dormitories.'

'And you're Mary *Karbo*. Any connection?'

'The school was named after one of my ancestors, a hundred years ago. You'll hear the name everywhere, chiefs, politicians, even head teachers.' She raised her eyebrows and I sensed the potent Karbo blood pumping vigorously through her veins. 'Now, what can I do for you?'

'I'm here to train your teachers.'

'Really?'

We'd stopped outside a classroom and I peered through the window to see about sixty children reciting vocabulary.

'The weather is sunny,' droned the teacher, prodding each word on the blackboard with a stick.

'The weather is sunny,' the children repeated, monotone, detached.

The weather is sunny.

The weather is sunny.

No wonder three out of four children skipped school. My own neighbourhood was in the catchment area, yet I didn't recognise any of the pupils. Then I spotted someone, a girl I knew had been doing chores since six that morning.

'The weather is windy.'

I turned to Mary. 'I can make these lessons more interesting. I use phonics, breaking words into sounds. It's better than repetition. And it's fun.'

'You are a nice girl, and I'm sure your phonics is very clever.' She put her hand on my arm and I felt the *but* coming. 'But why are they sending people to train teachers when the children are hungry?'

It was a good question – life-changing, as it happens – and I had no answer.

'The weather is rainy.'

I wanted to scream. I mean, I know I'm English, but enough about the bloody weather. Then, as we approached the next classroom, a familiar sound. Children singing.

'One, two, three, four, five. Once I caught a fish alive ... '

And there she was, my friend from the roadside, my suitcase saviour Olivia, encouraging children to clap and sing their numbers in a perfect example of interactive learning.

'She's one of my best teachers. Is this more your style?'

I nodded eagerly, my instincts about Olivia confirmed.

'Splendid. Now, what can we do with the others?'

We arranged phonics training three times a week, agreed a start date for after Easter and I left, buzzing with ideas. None of them, of course, got to the heart of the matter. How *can* you teach a hungry child? Maybe I thought my lessons were *that* mind-blowing and the other issues were someone else's problem. Either way, I was just happy things were moving. And when I was happy, I always threw a party.

Music blared from the house as I sat on the roof of Dan's jeep, watching Felix play a bongo drum to the delight of the neighbourhood children.

I was surprised by how many people I knew in Lawra, even if the guest list was a bit random: Felix and his police friends; Beth and Dan; Leela and some volunteers from further afield; Sue, an American missionary everyone called Makum ('Grandmother'); and half a dozen Chinese workers who'd never been to a party before and who didn't mix with anyone in Lawra even though they'd been there for months erecting electricity poles. I'd struck up a conversation with one of them during my Crazy-Woman-Smile phase, and he'd rung that morning to ask what to bring (*booze!*) and what to do (*dance!*). They came with a generous crate of beer and spent the evening huddled together in a corner.

The Ghanaians had a ball, drinking and dancing azonto, a rhythmic blend of gestures mimicking everyday activities like washing or praying – lots of pointing – and I must have looked very awkward, very foreign.

'Let's have Britney Spears,' I shouted to Nasir over the upbeat Ghanaian High Life party music pumping from the large speaker he'd brought along. 'I feel so stiff with your music.'

'Sarah, I think you dance well.'

He was being nice and I appreciated it. Dancing, mixing cocktails of ginger gin and Sprite, handing round my famous hummus to an appreciative crowd, it all reminded me of my happy days in Ramsbury and I felt young, vibrant and that I was building a life.

That feeling continued at work, with a meeting booked to discuss phonics training at Bagri Junction Primary, the school that shocked me on my first day. It was pleasing to make the journey under my own steam and I arrived on the Yamaha oozing positivity.

But some things hadn't changed.

'Where's Madam?' I asked a sleepy class of children. A boy at the front raised his head from the desk where it had laid.

'Madam is not here today.'

I turned to leave, frustrated, indignant for the dozen children who'd dragged themselves to school in thirty-degree heat, with no breakfast and no shoes.

Then I had an idea. I rummaged in my backpack for a picture book, asked the children if they'd like a story and a few minutes later, I was going for it.

'Not by the hair on my chinny chin chin.'

I couldn't have been further from The Winchcombe School, yet standing in front of that depleted class of determined youngsters, I felt as if I'd come home. And although they were weak and tired and couldn't understand my accent, they were engaged.

'I'll huff and I'll puff and I'll blow your house in.'

While it wasn't an answer to Mary Karbo's question, it was all I had. And after that (with permission from the head) I was a regular at Bagri Junction, on the off-chance a teacher was absent, which one usually was. I'd do accessible stuff, reading a story and getting them to retell it or draw a picture. It was a way to spend a nice hour – nice for me, definitely, and, I believe, for them.

'And they lived happily ever after.'

Of course, even naive me didn't suppose it would change the world. I knew the challenges in Lawra were endemic and complex. But making lessons fun, giving children attention, noticing tiny, tiny improvements, gave me enough hope to keep going and enough go to keep hoping.

I popped a box of red wine in the fridge (at room temperature, it was akin to soup), checked my candles were vertical and pressed play on the mix tape.

'Hello, Sarah.'

I'd been expecting Felix for dinner, but it was Nasir at the door, carrying bags of food.

'Excuse me. Felix sent me.' Always polite. 'Please, Sarah, I will come in.'

'Thanks, just dump it on the table.'

Across the scrub, children wandered in my direction and I hastily closed the door. Nasir was already chopping onions.

'There's no need. I'll make it.'

'I think this will be better.'

He was right. Nasir was an excellent cook and I wouldn't have known where to start with the ingredients, a spinachy dried leaf and bean flour pancakes, from which he made delicious sen sen. It was the first of many agreeable evenings, Nasir showing me how to cook, Felix coming later to eat with us.

'Maybe we could go to Wa tomorrow?' I said to Felix. 'Have a look around the market?'

'Take Sarah to Wa tomorrow,' he told Nasir, which was not quite what I'd had in mind. But in Lawra, apparently, that was how it worked. There was virtually no task left undelegated, seemingly no pleasure from doing something for someone else. Everyone was a manager, managing the people below.

'Doesn't matter, just an idea.'

Felix and Nasir *were* friends, but I could see it was essentially a transactional relationship, based on Felix, with position and a government salary, getting Nasir to run around for him in exchange for food or use of his motorbike or a handful of change. It made me uncomfortable though, if I'm honest, it worked for me too, because I liked spending time with Nasir and didn't need to give him anything in return.

Apr 12, 2012

Today is the 2-month anniversary of my arrival in Ghana. Sometimes I look around and feel like a complete stranger, in other moments, I forget I'm an outsider and think I've been here forever.

How can I explain? You're very in it, it's all-consuming and hard to conceive of being anywhere else. Imagine a mirror on the horizon and nothing to see but yourself coming back, no world beyond. I'm saying this badly. Put it this way, it was intense. Intense and hot.

Would the heat ever end? I'd taken to sleeping under a wet sheet because it was the only way to be cool. In school, classes were dwindling. In the market, fresh food was scarce and expensive, though once Nasir popped round with a bag of mangoes Felix had sent him to Wa for, and I shared them with the children. Everyone was waiting for the rains.

Then, one evening in April, after a stifling couple of hours outside the police station, I was cycling home and the heavens opened. Within seconds, my dress was drenched. And I remember riding down the no-longer dusty track, spotting a few faces peeking out from their dwellings, thinking, *it's going to be alright, there's hope. There's life.*

I changed into jeans and my cosy pink Superdry hoodie and went to the veranda with a can of gin and tonic from my sister. Soon, Celina and a couple of other children defied the weather and I poured them cups of water. And we sat there, staring at the rain, and it was beautiful, really beautiful.

Things were looking up. The seasons were changing. I was teaching. Phonics lessons were planned. I had friends.

A week later, I also had malaria.

FIVE

SICK

It started while I was playing nursemaid to fellow volunteer James, who'd ridden cross country to visit me and fallen off his motorbike. His leg was a mess, so I looked after him, cooked for him and assumed all that running around was why I was shattered. Then I felt sick. Then I *was* sick. Maybe it was the heat. That downpour had not heralded rainy season and it was scorching again. I focused on my patient and tried to ignore my own troubles.

I was still trying a week later, when a limping James and a grey-faced me climbed onto a bus in Wa. The Bolga crowd were throwing a party and youthful enthusiasm meant it hadn't occurred to us not to go. The big orange Metro Mass Transit was packed and – for seven hours – we had to stand. I felt awful, and put it down to travel sickness.

I've never been a quitter, and there are some brilliant photos of me at the party (in one, I'm dancing on a chair) and I suppose I just thought I wasn't that ill. Little did I know that a parasite was inside me, infecting my red blood cells, giving me a few hours off before releasing a new wave of parasites into my system.

Next morning, I strolled round the market, breakfasted on pineapple and chocolate, went to the bus station and boarded the trotro for Lawra. And then I began to feel *really* sick. As in can't-lift-my-head-up sick. Someone carried me from the trotro to a volunteer's house and put me to bed.

We're popping out for a couple of hours. Will you be OK? they may well have said, it's a blur. All I know is I deteriorated fast, agony searing through my neck, paralysis creeping down my arm. My phone rang but I couldn't answer because my hand had become a claw.

By the time they got back, my neck was so painful I couldn't move. They bundled me into a cab, first to a private clinic that had run out of malaria tests, then to the regional hospital.

'I'm in agony,' I whispered. 'Help me, I'm scared.' An efficient doctor promptly admitted me, pumped me full of drugs and that's basically the last thing I remember.

I floated in and out of consciousness … a busy ward … staff in green uniforms … a nurse with a long needle. When I came to properly I was in a private room, my leg soaked from the rain blowing in through an open window, a drip skewered into my hand. I was exhausted, but the excruciating pain was gone.

My phone rang.

'Hi love, you're alive,' said Mum, and it hit me that I might not have been. 'You've got malaria, you've been in hospital for three days. How are you feeling?'

How was I feeling? Stiff, achy as never before, and still a bit nauseous. But whatever the hospital had done, I was a million times better.

'I'm alright,' I bellowed. 'Sore.' Why was I shouting?

'Good. We're getting you out of there.'

My uncle had pulled strings with a contact in an African gold-mining company and had arranged an emergency evacuation. The cavalry was coming. I glanced at my wet leg and the mattress that had no sheet and the same floral skirt I'd been wearing since I'd come in, now soiled with my own faeces, and realised I was too sick to care about the mess or the bare mattress or even the cavalry.

We cancelled the airlift and I stayed put. I was past the worst and what I needed most was rest. A VSO friend brought in a bucket of water (there was no running water on the ward) but I was too knackered to wash. With no toilet close by, I may have used the bucket for that. I can't recall and I don't want to.

'That hurts.'

'Sorry, my dear.' The nurse administered a jab to my buttock. 'I am afraid our needles are blunt.'

Was she telling me it was a *used* needle, I wondered, and vowed to get an HIV test at the earliest opportunity. Despite limited resources, though, when it came to malaria, the staff were experts. They'd diagnosed and treated me quickly, cared for me kindly, cleaned me up and, in the case of one gentle nurse I'll never forget, held my hand as I sobbed.

I was there for another couple of days, one of millions of people who would contract malaria in Ghana that year, lucky because my illness had been relatively mild, lucky to have been in reasonable health before it struck, lucky because one of my friends came in each day to pay for my treatment, lucky not to die.

I was weaker than I'd ever been, ravaged from days of fever and chills, and unable to travel. Thankfully, in the absence of any official VSO support, Ellie, a Bolgatanga volunteer, generously took me in. I couldn't eat, I couldn't hear (the quinine medication wiped out forty per cent of my hearing) and, as I collapsed onto Ellie's spare bed, I caught sight of my bum in the mirror and it was black and blue from blunt injections.

My body needed that week in Bolga, but my head was all

over the place. One night, we sat on Ellie's roof terrace, a few volunteers chilling, playing cards, having a laugh. I watched, too tired and too deaf to join in, and all I could think about was my empty house in the middle of the Lawra scrub and the dreadful isolation awaiting me. It reminded me of a project I'd read about, in which rural Ghanaians were given a TV and access to Nigerian films, many set amongst the upper classes. Sometimes, it's easier not to know how the other half live.

I found the strength to text Felix, and received a message from him and one from Nasir, which was sweet. The following day, Felix showed up and someone from VSO drove us to Lawra. Now I understood why so many people languished under trees along the roadside. Of course, some were having a snooze, but many had malaria – everyone got it, often several times a year – and when you've got it, aside from fighting for your life, you're incapable of actually doing anything. *I know what you're going through*, I thought as we bumped along, except, of course, I didn't, because I was in a car heading to house with a ceiling fan and a fridge, while they were laying under a tree.

It was dark when we arrived in Lawra and with no children around, Felix snuck me in and shut the door. I was in my concrete prison once again, physically and mentally absolutely destroyed.

I don't think I'd ever been quite so vulnerable. Life in Lawra was tough enough and now I was fragile and afraid, it felt insurmountable, even with a little help from my friends. I was indebted to Felix and Nasir, who supplied food I was too weak to eat, and to thoughtful Olivia, who'd somehow procured a watermelon, though I had no strength to chat and she left me sucking on a slice, laid in bed.

On the upside, I could, at last, fit into Izzy's left-behind combat trousers. Truthfully, I was too thin, anaemic, my acne had flared up and two weeks later, when I set off for my first day back at work, I looked a wreck. Inevitably, the heavy motorbike fell on me halfway down the slope and I lay there, leg trapped, bleeding, desperate for someone to save me until I managed to drag myself free. After that I used the bicycle, though I couldn't even last an hour at the Teachers' Resource Centre. I postponed the phonics classes and the humble progress I'd made disappeared.

I kept away from the children, not just because everyone said I should, I was simply too drained to do anything else. No-one even realised I was there for a couple of days, but now I had people banging on my door all the time, *help me, help me, I'm hungry, I'm thirsty, I need school uniform, my mother's sick, my father's sick*. It was constant, and I could do nothing.

'Sister Sarah, you help, you help.'

It was dusk and I was crashed out on the bed, *Modern Family* washing over me.

'Sister Sarah, Sister Sarah, my brother is sick.'

I dragged myself to the door. My caller was a girl of about twelve, and I recognised the child draped across her back as one of the small boys I'd given those first bananas to. His name, I thought, was Kojo, and he didn't look well.

'Sister Sarah, you take us to hospital.'

I did think about it. But the idea of me and two children on the back of that unwieldy bike, even if I could get it down the slope, and start the engine and drive it at night, which I'd never done before, all seemed like an accident waiting to happen.

'I'm sorry, it's not safe. Can your family take him?' She shrugged and retreated into the dusk. 'Sorry.'

I *was* sorry. Though, by then, she was just another person knocking on my door that I couldn't do anything for. I flopped onto the bed, too tired to eat, too tired to undress, too tired to watch *Modern Family*, until I dozed off.

Next morning, a subdued Celina was on the veranda. She suppressed a sob. 'It's about the boy. Kojo.'

My heart went cold.

'Last night he died.'

I was devastated.

A boy had died. A little boy who loved bananas, who loved his friend, who needed help. A little boy, a wasted life.

I felt utterly guilty. Because although, in the moment, I'd done what I thought was right – and maybe if I'd taken him it would have been too late or we'd have had an accident on the bike and died on the way to hospital – I knew, on some level (lots of levels, actually) that I *was* guilty. And not only me, the world.

After all, when *I'd* been sick, someone took *me* to hospital. And if I knocked on any door – in Lawra or Ramsbury – and said I needed help, someone would help me. People were ready to scramble a plane for me. It was horrendous and so, so unfair.

Until then, and it's terrible to admit, I'd seen the poverty around me as a kind of project, part of my adventure, a vessel for *my experience*. Now, that stopped. Now, I was angry, angry with myself, angry about what happened, angry that I had no answers.

I went to the family's house. The sister was there, crying. And I gave Kojo's parents a couple of bags of food. It was the very least I could do.

A few days later, a little stronger and no less devastated, I sat on the veranda with a story book, a coffee, a bottle of water and some cups. It was a conscious decision, to open up myself and my home, not half-heartedly but wholly and meaningfully, and not for a photo or to make myself feel good (though it did) but because they wanted it. They'd been telling me what they wanted all along. A cup of water, a banana, someone to notice them.

I got paper and pencils, read stories and ran phonics lessons with the children from my neighbourhood. And when it stopped being such a novelty and they no longer had to shout about being hungry and thirsty to get my attention, they would pass by, stop for a chat and move on. Older boys would push my hulking bike up the ramp each evening. When I had a scorpion in my bathroom, Celina came in and we got rid of it together.

It became a symbiotic relationship, pleasant and beneficial to all. Surviving in Lawra wasn't easy and with so few systems to make it easier, you needed people watching out for you. That applied to the children and it applied to me.

Kojo dying was *the* turning point. I just thought, *fuck it.* Fuck them all. All the people who said *keep your distance, build walls, don't connect.* And that's when I let the children in and became ready to let in anyone who wanted to build a real, true relationship. Because isn't life all about relationships? That's all life actually is.

SIX

AS IF BY MAGIC

'How do you do?'

A boyish hand with a filthy cloth wrapped round the thumb extended itself hopefully.

I tentatively reached for the ends of his fingers and – undeterred by whatever lurked beneath the cloth – he gave me a bold and positive hand shake.

'How do you do. What's wrong with your thumb?'

He was a cow-boy and I'd noticed him before, in his torn T-shirt, shorts and flip-flops, as he directed thirty-odd scrawny cattle past my house, tapping their bottoms with his cow-stick, pushing them where he wanted them to go. I guessed he was about eleven.

'This is small, small. I cut my hand and my uncle has given me medicine.'

'Is your uncle a doctor?'

'No, Sister, but he has the medicine. My name is Jeremiah.' He waved his stick towards the cows. 'And this is my herd.'

'What are you reading?'

I glanced up from *The Other Boleyn Girl* to find my studious neighbour from Karbo Primary on the steps of the veranda.

'Actually, I've finished with that.' I picked up *Little Red Riding Hood* from a pile of children's books I'd left prominently on the table. 'Shall we try this? What's your name?'

'My name is Judith. And you are Sister Sarah.'

As I opened the book, Judith ran her finger along the words and began to read. 'Once upon a time, there was a little girl ...'

I was kicking my outside tap (the mains supply had been switched off, yet again) when I spotted a disrobed shoulder heading my way.

'Do you need some help, Sister?'

It was Celina, and she looked tired, like a child who'd been working since dawn on an empty stomach, which I imagine she was.

'Probably, thanks. Want some rice?' Whilst Celina did all the cooking for her family, I knew adults usually ate first in rural Ghana and there wasn't always enough to go round.

'Please, Sister Sarah. Then I will show you the borehole.'

Jeremiah, Judith and Celina became my friends. The girls often came to market with me, and we'd lug bags of rice and groundnuts and water. Jeremiah would pass by with his cattle and we'd sit in veranda shade, chatting. Though he rarely attended school, his parents had encouraged his social skills, hence the hand shaking, which we did every time we met. I continued giving bits of food to the other children in the neighbourhood and reading with them on the veranda, but those three were the ones who came inside, who I cooked and ate spicy jollof rice with, who I trusted and who trusted me.

'Who is this lady?' asked Jeremiah. We were sitting at my kitchen table one evening in May, browsing through photos on my laptop.

'That's my mum.' And there she was, with me and my sister and glasses of Prosecco, in our lush-green Ramsbury garden.

As we scrolled through more snapshots, of healthy faces at barbeques and fancy dress parties and Christmas, I'm almost sure I caught Jeremiah studying me, as if to say *if you have all this, what on earth are you doing here?*

It would have been a fair question. Because – beyond the broad assumption I was *helping people* – the children had no idea what I was doing there. To them, I'd turned my back on an easy, enviable life and randomly come to their town to catch malaria and fall off my motorbike.

Watching their faces huddled round the laptop, I wondered what their own lives might have been if fate had landed them in Wiltshire rather than the Upper West. Kind, responsible Judith might have become a nurse or a teacher – and maybe she still could, they're desirable, get-able jobs in Ghana. Star-quality Celina might have found a career as a beautician, singer, even a TV personality. Jeremiah, with his gift of the gab, would be a natural car salesman or estate agent or politician.

He flicked onto another picture, thumb resolutely wrapped in the same dirty cloth.

'That should be healed now. Can I see?'

Cautiously, I unwrapped his hand to reveal first a layer of green sludge – whether pus or just leaves from the traditional poultice, I couldn't tell – and then a rancid, gaping wound. He said it looked nastier than it was but after Kojo, I was taking no chances.

'We need to get you to hospital.'

He stared at me as if I was mad. 'It's OK, Sister. I am sure it is improving.'

I was torn. In England, his parents would have been straight to A&E, but in Lawra, where cow-boys got injured all the time and not everyone had health insurance, local medicine was many people's first choice and it did often work.

In the end, we agreed to check again in a couple of days, he re-wrapped the stinking wound and they all raided the freezer – their favourite thing in the entire property – grabbing solid bags of pure water and biting off the corners. Soon they were sucking contentedly on the sofa, watching *Modern Family* and goodness knows what they made of that.

'Too cold for you?'

I was in the house of missionary Sue (aka everyone's grandmother, Makum) and, yes, it was too cold.

'I'll turn the air con down. Diet Coke?' She headed to her American-style fridge.

I was in heaven. Makum's place was an oasis, filled with luxuries (comfy sofa, freezer full of cheese), not to mention Makum herself, so spirited and resolute and an indispensable support from the moment we'd met.

We'd dined well on macaroni cheese topped with cornflakes and Makum was now rolling back and forth on her rocking chair as I flicked through photos on her laptop. They couldn't have been more different from my own slideshow a few days earlier. Children, many profoundly disabled, laid on dirty floors, dead-eyed, defeated, lost.

'I mean, living in the Upper West is not a walk in the park, right? For these children and their families, it's virtually impossible. And no-one's doing anything for them.' She pulled herself out of the chair and leant over my shoulder as I opened another photograph. A girl, her pretty face etched with fear. 'This child is deaf. Should be manageable, but her parents hide her away. They worry if people know, they won't buy their groundnuts.'

Another photo. 'This child, teenager really, is severely disabled. He lives on the floor, in a corner. Even if his mother wanted to take him out, how could she? She can't carry him, he's huge. When he was born, his father's family said she'd given birth to something not human. They told her to go to the river and drown him.'

'My God … sorry.' I'd forgotten I was with a missionary.

'It's fine. It is upsetting.'

Another picture, a mum and a toddler whose eyes didn't quite focus.

'She's mentally impaired, poor thing. Mother likely had iodine deficiency during pregnancy. And here …' Makum pointed to the mum, who had a lump on her neck and bump in her stomach. 'Goitre, a sign of lack of iodine, and she's pregnant again. She sells pito, local hooch, but who's going to buy it now? Could you blame her if she left her baby at the orphanage?' Makum was a volunteer at a local orphanage. 'I swear half the children there aren't even orphans.'

She slumped into her chair and rocked furiously.

'People don't understand the medical reasons for these disabilities, or the role poverty plays. They don't know that deafness and epilepsy can be managed. Families are isolated, told they've been cursed or must be wicked or dirty to bring it on themselves.' She took a deep breath. 'So, what are we going do? You're a teacher, got any ideas?'

It sounds awful, but I was excited. At last, someone wanted my contribution, and what's more, I felt I could give it. Hideously naive, of course. I mean, how could I solve a deep-seated problem bound up in mysticism, poverty and ignorance? Wave a magic wand?

'We could hold a workshop.' It wasn't my best idea ever, and yet it became the beginning of something.

A couple of days later, when I spotted Jeremiah's mother on her way to work at the flour mill in town, I ran after her.

'How do you do,' she said, offering her hand.

'How do you do. Can we talk about Jeremiah?'

She was an intelligent, decent woman and politely agreed to indulge the anxious foreigner with a thumb obsession by giving me permission to take him to hospital. Jeremiah dutifully arrived with his precious insurance card in a clear plastic bag, slipped it into the pocket of his shorts and helped me get the Yamaha down the slope.

After Kojo, I was adamant the motorbike must be an asset, useful in an emergency rather than sitting in a garage. I'd been practising with a nervous Felix, him wearing a helmet he'd found in the house because he didn't trust me, and now I handed that helmet to Jeremiah. I'd seen him and several siblings hanging off his uncle's bike so I knew he was humouring me by putting it on and I didn't care. I hated riding that bloody bike and carrying a child was scary.

Lawra Municipal Hospital was grey, uninviting and smelled of disinfectant. The second we walked into Outpatients, the green-uniformed health assistants at reception snapped to attention only to immediately unsnap once they realised the patient was not the white lady but the black boy with the dodgy thumb. Though I don't suppose Jeremiah expected anything else, it made me feel ashamed.

There was a load of paperwork for the insurance. The Ghana National Health Insurance Scheme is subsidised by Government and offers basic health care for GH¢12 (about £4) a year. It doesn't cover special treatments like cancer or X-rays (not that Lawra Hospital had an X-ray machine) but includes emergency care, immunisations, maternity care and, thankfully, sore thumbs. Of the people waiting to be examined, we had the most trivial complaint.

Many of the others appeared seriously ill, presumably having delayed their visit to hospital because they didn't have (or couldn't afford) insurance or they'd first tried traditional medicine or the juju man (a sort of mystical priest who provides potions and spells in exchange for chickens or booze). As I looked around the waiting room, I feared not everyone would make it.

Eventually, we saw a physician assistant who barely glanced at Jeremiah, gave him an injection in his bottom (perhaps for tetanus, he didn't say), handed over a prescription for antibiotics and nodded for us to go. He didn't dress the wound. He didn't even wash it. That's the Ghanaian Health Service, you don't ask questions, you don't get answers, they give you drugs, you depart. Whatever 'status' my whiteness conferred at reception had faded fast and poor Jeremiah, stripped of his usual social aplomb, was unable to muster even a single *how do you do*.

After an hour's wait to collect the drugs (which came loose, in a plastic bag), I drove Jeremiah home and we sat on the veranda sucking bags of frozen water, the poultice still on his hand. For once, though, maybe I'd accomplished something because after a week the wound was nearly healed. Jeremiah told me his uncle was most pleased with his treatment.

The following afternoon, Makum came to prep for the workshop. With guidance from my friend Nicola, a speech therapist, we'd decided to make 'communication fans', creating decks of cards for children with no language to indicate their essential needs and feelings. *Happy, sad, hungry, thirsty, sick* and *defecate* were represented by hand-drawn images of smiley face, sad face, bowl of food, tap, stick man vomiting and stick man pooing.

The VSO house was a treasure trove of resources, bequeathed by generations of earnest volunteers who'd bought paper, pens and science kits that were gathering in my spare room. Makum and I put some glossy A3 card and pens to good use and I felt purposeful, motivated, smiley face.

May 12, 2012

Today, Sue and I worked on our 'Communication Fans' for our workshop next week. We have to make and laminate 45 fans, each with 6 pictures accompanied by a word in English and Dagaare. Never have I had such appreciation for the resources in my old classroom (specifically the paper-cutter, I have a blister from the scissors). It's a treat to have somebody to work with, sharing ideas and expertise leads to far more productivity.

Saying I was achieving something made me feel I actually was achieving something and then, out of the blue, I did. Off the back of the blog, Rhona O'Neill (a valued colleague from The Winchcombe School) sent £50 towards the costs of the workshop. Without meaning to, I'd done my first fundraising and a genuine connection between my two homes, in Ghana and England, began.

Over the next few days Makum and I attacked our fan-making with renewed vigour. We were halfway through 'laminating' the cards with Sellotape and fixing them together with pipe-cleaners when Nasir called in with some juice, courtesy of Felix.

'This is wrong.' He flicked through one of the completed fans. 'This is not the correct Dagaare word for shitting.'

I gazed at our pile of finished masterpieces. Much as I excelled at laminating, there was no way I was doing them again. I held the reel of Sellotape towards Nasir. 'I think we'll have to live with it. Fancy giving us a hand?'

We chatted as we worked, ignored by Makum, who focused on her laminating, and spied on by a couple of children who peered in through the window where the mosquito netting was loose. I was struck by how open-minded Nasir was about working with disabled children and despite the stigma, despite the widely held belief you'd catch something or be cursed, despite the stick men and the self-lamination and the bad Dagaare, he embraced the project.

And he wanted to talk. After weeks of half-hanging out with Felix, it was fascinating to get to know Nasir and discover he was so much more than Felix's *small boy*.

'I went to the south, and there were many days without food. I found work in an electronics shop in Accra, sleeping there in the night to keep guard. The boss man knew everyone was stealing from him and I was the only one he trusted. I would have made more money if I had stolen from him, like the others.'

He was in his early thirties, with a baby son, a partner and a large speaker, bought with the money he'd hustled down south and used to sell music downloads from a shack in the middle of Lawra town. He didn't make much, maybe GH¢10 (just over

£3) on a busy day, on other days, nothing.

'Today, is OK, I made GH¢5. I will buy sen sen for my child.'

'What about other stuff. Nappies or medicine?'

'I think he won't need nappies today.' Nasir sighed, not even entertaining the prospect he might need them tomorrow, when the same dilemma would still apply. He tore a strip of Sellotape with his capable hands and resumed his story.

I was fascinated to learn he'd grown up as part of Lawra's elite and was a member of the Chief's clan. However, his childhood had been far from idyllic and whilst he lived in the Chief's Palace and had a little education, nothing, absolutely nothing, was secure. I could see that every day was a battle, an effort to scrape a few cedis at his stall, and I was shocked. That it wasn't just village children in rags who were struggling, that it was also the smart-looking people, people who could be in my house or at one of my parties or chatting with me, making communication fans.

It was very companionable, sitting there, laminating with this interesting, diligent, hardworking man. And he wasn't downtrodden. His childhood, his economic fragility, the whole *small boy* thing, none of it had destroyed his quiet self-esteem.

'Nasir, would you be up for helping at the workshop?' I held up the defecation card with its incorrect wording. 'We obviously need you.' He nodded, doubtless assuming no-one would come.

I deliberately made too much rice that night, handing Nasir a bag of leftovers and wondering how he felt about taking them. Of course, he was more fortunate than someone like Celina, who could go days without food. But for Nasir, a man from the Chief's family, to rely on handouts and leftovers, to hold a five cedi note in his hand and have to choose between food or nappies and never a beer (which he would have loved), for that man poverty was about more than hunger or shelter, it was about being powerless.

'Thank you, Sarah,' he murmured, and took his rice.

A couple of days later, as I bounced my way home from the Post Office (vacuum packed olives, plastic bottle of balsamic vinegar, can of Diet Coke, bless you, Karen) I was greeted by fifty overexcited children, all shouting at once.

'Sister Sarah, Sister Sarah! Snake in the house! Snake in the house!'

Celina grabbed my hand and led me to one of the windows, where the corner of the mosquito screen had come away. Unsurprising, given the number of tiny fingers pulling at it recently.

'These children,' she pointed to a couple of boys, 'saw a snake go here.'

'Snake.' One of the boys poked his finger through the gap. 'Danger.'

I knew exactly the kind of snake he was talking about. The thin, foot-long, earth-coloured deadly kind they'd warned us of during In-Country Training. The kind that are impossible to find in a property filled with years' worth of unused teaching aids. The poisonous kind.

Suddenly, there were children all over the house, hunting for the snake. Teenage boys shifted the furniture, the rest poked about inside cupboards and under cushions, relishing, I'm sure, their opportunity to nose around. I decided it was a worthwhile exercise for me, too, learning to trust them. Then again, what choice did I have?

'Can you come straight over?' Nasir was the first and only

person I considered calling. 'There's a snake in the house.'

It was pandemonium when he got there and carried out what I thought was a rather cursory search.

'Please, Sarah, I will use your Yamaha. I go to the juju man.'

As soon as the children heard the juju man was involved, everything became a lot less urgent, Judith took command of the freezer – handing out pure water bags to her friends – and a sort of party broke out.

Nasir returned brandishing what he mysteriously referred to as *special powder*, which he sprinkled enthusiastically, leaving flourishes in the corners of the rooms. This wasn't insecticide or poison, you understand, it wasn't designed to kill the snake. It was intended to magic it away.

Once he'd distributed the powder, everyone left, convinced the snake was gone and the emergency over. And there I was, with a snake and some powder. On the other hand, I never did find the snake.

I have no idea what was in that special powder, but after the incident of the snake in the house, something magical happened to my life in Lawra. Planning the disability workshop with Makum gave me purpose, hanging out with Jeremiah, Judith and Celina gave me pleasure and things gradually made sense. But it was seeing more and more of Nasir – and knowing he was there if I needed him – that was the clincher. Somehow, in the space of what felt like a lifetime and was in fact a few weeks, I'd gone from being out of my depth, gravely ill, isolated, terrified and totally lost, to having companionship, security and someone to be a team with. It was all I had ever wanted and now my wish had come true.

SEVEN

FAN

When the chance came to get my own snake deterrent, I grabbed her.

May 24, 2012

Last week, I got a puppy in exchange for a chicken (I didn't actually have a chicken, so I gave about £3, enough to buy a chicken from the market). She spent the entire first night crying and urinated in my bed, twice, but now seems quite happy and even occasionally goes to the toilet outside! I'm sure she'll grow up to be a fearless snake-killer and guard dog, she's already the healthiest/fattest/most spoilt dog in Lawra. My friend Nasir wants to eat her, Angola (dog meat) is a delicacy here ...

I named her Shilea, hand-fed her tuna from a can and carried her when she was tired. Everyone thought I was absolutely barking. People do have dogs in Lawra, loyal dogs that follow them round and growl at snakes and strangers. They don't, however, treat them as pets (and definitely not as babies). The children didn't get it – this pampered dog living in a building they weren't allowed in – and occasionally threatened her with sticks until I shouted at them, the only time I ever did. I was, of course, aware of the irony, the unfairness, the extra expenditure, none of which I could justify other than I needed her, and not purely for snakes.

Surprisingly, Nasir developed his own soft spot for the

puppy. We'd stroll through Lawra, stopping to buy a cold drink or a boiled egg from the nice lady by the roundabout, Shilea at our feet, Nasir showing me his town.

'Before Independence, the colonial master lived here,' he told me one afternoon as we passed a derelict mansion. Now tumbledown and overgrown, it must once have been luxury.

'What's that?' I asked, glimpsing a sunken concrete area.

Nasir laughed. 'That was his swimming pool.'

Further along the road, we came to a falling-down sign, emblazoned *Women's Empowerment Project*.

'I think, perhaps,' said Nasir, 'in sixty years, not much has changed.'

'What do you mean?

'People still come to Lawra and say they want to help. They don't work with the community, they don't learn and then ...' he gave the sign a defiant kick, 'they leave us with nothing.'

I thought of the broken desks in the Bagri classrooms, all stamped *US AID*. And the dusty, underused Teachers' Resource Centre. And my own place, bursting with supplies.

We counted thirteen billboards, each proclaiming important work long since abandoned. I expect the people who erected them came with the best intentions, little knowing those signs and that mansion and those desks and the TRC would become awful monuments to 'we know best'.

I watched Shilea chase a chicken round the *Women's Empowerment Project* sign, grateful Nasir had any faith in me and Makum and our communication fans, and pushed away the niggling feeling we could very easily repeat history.

The following week, we held the disability workshop. We didn't know what hit us.

At least I was using the Teachers' Resource Centre, and arrived with Makum and Nasir to scrape off the top layer of dust, open the louvres, put the fans on and lay mats.

A woman appeared with a heavy metal pot on her head containing sixty bags of watery, sugary koko (porridge) and I hoped someone would show up to drink them. Makum had arranged for fliers to be distributed through churches and schools and I'd handed them out in classrooms. But it was a big ask. *Come to a meeting*, bring the disabled child you've hidden from society for the last however many years, get that child to the TRC – hungry and probably against the wishes of your husband – carry that child on your back if need be, carry them even if they're fifteen and incontinent and haven't seen the light of day since they were born. *Come to a meeting!* It was a big ask.

I brushed dust off my blue Ghanaian dress. 'Nasir, do you think we'll get many people?'

'Sarah, we are not giving money for transportation, you must be prepared for no-one to come.'

Then, miraculously, there she was.

The lady who sold boiled eggs at the roundabout. Someone I'd passed whenever I'd been in town, someone selling snacks. Now, as she cycled towards the TRC, she wasn't simply the boiled egg lady, she was Patience, mother of four-year-old Michelle, who had cerebral palsy.

Patience had everything to lose by outing herself as the parent of a disabled child. Would people say she was cursed, would customers buy her eggs, would she be able to feed Michelle and the baby she had strapped to her back? Would she even be able to feed them tonight, having lost half a day's egg money? For Patience, walking into the TRC, Michelle limping beside her, was an act of extraordinary bravery. And all we had was communication fans.

'Angsoma,' said Nasir. And we were off.

People came, twenty mothers, a couple of dads and their children. Some were physically disabled, with twisted or missing limbs, many had learning difficulties, many seemed distressed. There wasn't much talking as the adults cautiously checked each other out, registering anyone they recognised, silently acknowledging, for the first time, *I am not alone.*

Soon, there was a chaotic crowd on the mats, parents helping children suck noisily on packets of koko, attempting to keep them upright whilst being screamed at and dribbled on and clunked round the head by a wayward arm. A few shared a portion with their child and slipped another into their bag to take home for later. Others ate quickly, in case someone took it away.

After breakfast, Nasir stepped to the front. The parents stopped talking and turned towards him, nervous, apprehensive, no-one – not them and certainly not me – knowing what the day would bring.

'Makum, will you lead the prayer?'

The parents clambered to their feet, some with children still in their arms, pressed their hands together and bowed their heads as Nasir translated. We prayed, for the success of the day, for the health of the children and to thank God, who, Makum assured them, loved their children. It was possibly the nicest thing anyone had ever said about them and the parents were visibly moved.

Meanwhile, I was struggling. Because it's one thing to work with disabled pupils in the speech and language unit of The Winchcombe School, it's quite another to be confronted with twenty profoundly disabled children in filthy clothes, shouting, whacking their mothers, peeing on the floor. In my three months in Lawra, I'd never come across that level of poverty, disability or bodily fluid and I was horrified. By what I saw, and by my own reaction to it, of which I was not proud.

'Amen,' said Makum.

'Amen,' said the parents.

'Amen,' said Patience. She caught my eye and smiled.

We handed out the fans to a more or less silent crowd. The woman sat with them in their hands, wondering, no doubt, how our bodged-up craft project could possibly be the answer to their prayers. After hours of drawing and laminating (without ever asking one of those women what *they* might find useful) they were a symbol of my naivety, my presumption, yet another example of 'knowing best'. Then Patience said something in Dagaare – something funny, because everyone laughed – and began flicking through a fan with Michelle. Soon, others followed her lead.

Of course, the fans were *not* what they needed, and I could see even the non-verbal children already used sign language or grunts to get their message across. But, with a smile here and giggle there, something else was happening. Parents and children were talking, playing, connecting.

We made the fans into a game – *let's pretend you're thirsty* – and I've got photos of children holding a sachet of water and the card with a tap, which was pretty bloody amazing since many of them had never seen a tap before. I suppose we were all on a learning curve.

'Sarah, you have a few words?' Nasir was translating as I led the session.

'Yes, thank you. What I want to say is that everything you're doing today will benefit your child and your whole family.' I looked across at Patience, her head close to Michelle's as she gripped her laminated fan, and felt inspired. 'It's important to communicate with your child, even if it feels hard, even if they are not able to communicate with you the way other children do. Your children are people and they are worthy of love.'

'Thank you, Sarah,' said Nasir, who must have turned it into something less patronising because he had the whole room hanging on his every word. He was, it turned out, really good at this. I hugged the toddler sitting on my knee, sensed something warm and wet seeping into my new dress and thought, *I'm covered in urine and still having one of my best work days ever.* Then a boy came over gripping a bag of jollof rice and a communication fan, open at the page saying *Happy.*

And that was the whole message, the more attention and affection the children got, the better they would respond. Yes, they needed medicine and wheelchairs and clothes and food, and we wanted to get to that. And, of course, one session couldn't reverse years of parents being told their child was *not human,* of being urged not to interact, of the impact of this isolation on the children's mental and physical development. But it was a start. A messy, promising start.

I'm not going to whitewash it though, some of it was brutal.

'Sarah, please.' Patience took my hand. 'I want you to meet this girl, Elvisa.'

Elvisa stood there, looking frightened and ill, as Patience explained she was thirteen, 'retarded' (as they say in Ghana), living on the streets and pregnant by a middle-aged man who'd paid GH¢5 (less than £2) for sex. Now, other men did the same.

My heart went out to her, even if I had no idea what to do. Less even than I realised – that evening, updating my blog, I wrote she was *making enough money to buy food by allowing various men to have sex with her.* As if that vulnerable, abused child was in a position to *allow* anything. How dare I?

'Attention.' Nasir took charge. 'It is time to finish.'

We closed with a reflection session (evidently, I had *plenty* to think about) and Nasir was wonderful with the women, encouraging them to say what they thought of the day and what they needed in the future.

They spoke quietly, confidently and with one voice. Yes, they appreciated the laminated fans, the food and the bar of soap we gave them, but mostly they appreciated being together and wanted to do it on a regular basis. Could we help make that happen? We all agreed to meet monthly, set up a committee, arrange medical insurance and vaccinations for the children and access whatever support was available.

Maybe this was how those thirteen defunct charities and organisations, with their busted signs and broken promises, had once been. I remembered Nasir's words – *they don't work with the community, they don't learn* – and knew how easy it would be to do the same. Watching Nasir, though, so inspiring and engaged, and Patience, with her quiet strength and a light in her eyes, I felt a spark of excitement. Maybe, I thought, we were doing things differently. Maybe, this time, it could work.

We ran the workshop again the next day for another group

– we welcomed thirty-nine children and their parents across both sessions – and they also loved it and wanted it to be the start of a new thing in their lives. And while me and Makum did our bit, Nasir was the ultimate catalyst for everything that was beautiful and hopeful, not least because he too was wrestling his own culturally embedded attitudes. I noticed he never quite brought himself to touch the children, yet no-one could dispute his commitment to their cause.

'You were brilliant,' I told him over a celebratory drink at a spot. Tipping my Club in his direction, we clinked.

'Thank you, Sarah.'

If it was a revelation to me, it was not, I suspect, to him. I think he'd always believed he was something, he'd just never had the opportunity to show it before. And when he'd stepped in front of the parents at the workshops, he came alive. Those women needed a hero, and he was it.

They weren't the only ones. I was a fan.

EIGHT

YOURA

My life in Lawra drifted into a modest routine. Morning jog with Shilea, shuffling papers in the empty TRC, stopping by Nasir's music stall to see if he wanted lunch. I loved that cramped wooden shack by the roundabout, music blaring from the three-foot speaker, shelves packed with DVDs of Nigerian films – *The Girl and the Snake*, *The Girl and the Snake 2*, *The Girl and The Snake Returns* – and Nasir downloading songs onto memory cards for ten pesewas (about three pence), a hand-written edict scrawled on the wall, *NO MONEY, NO MUSIC.*

Often, we'd get boiled eggs and hot pepe sauce from Patience at her stall on the other side of the roundabout, Nasir would find me a blue chair and some shade, and we'd watch the world go by. Or we might dine at one of the roadside food huts, eating kenkey (fermented corn dumpling with hot pepper stew) in companionable silence.

One lunchtime, as we sat outside the police station with Felix, Nasir nipped off and returned with his son, Bie, all grins and wriggly limbs, not even a year old. Bie sat on the table, playing with Felix's keys, and as I fell for him on the spot, Nasir supported him with one hand and ate sen sen with the other.

Since the incident with the snake, Nasir had become my support too, mending mosquito nets, catching spiders, accompanying me to market and I was glad to reciprocate by getting the beers in on our occasional trips to the spot. It was the perfect way to end the day, Nasir teaching me Dagaare with some flashcards he'd found in the house, before dropping me home on the Yamaha. He'd then vanish into the dusk, to whatever he did in the evening, and I'd play my recorder or examine that map of the world. Or read a book, I wasn't a complete hopeless case. We'd got into the habit of him borrowing the bike and ferrying me around – an ideal arrangement because he bloody loved riding it and I bloody hated it – so he'd call by next morning for my commute to the TRC and we began again.

It wasn't exactly *an adventure*, yet after the grinding loneliness of my first few weeks, those moments with Nasir made it tolerable. And what girl doesn't get a thrill when a man turns up at her house on an enormous bike?

I was cooking for eight every day – me, the puppy, the children and enough for Nasir to take for his family. I knew he was struggling because one evening he quietly asked me to pay for Bie's health insurance, which I willingly did.

A couple of days later came another soft-spoken request.

'Sarah, it is my son's birthday. You have money for a party, for drinks and snacks.' It was how people asked me for stuff, a statement not a question. *Sister Sarah, I will drink the water.*

I don't recollect how much he wanted, only that it felt a lot at the time. What with the extra rice, the insurance, the kenkey, the beers, a new school uniform for Celina, textbooks for Judith and getting Jeremiah's bike mended, I just about had enough cash til payday.

'Sorry Nasir, I don't have it.'

I hated saying no, and he seemed pretty pissed off with me, unable to comprehend why someone with apparently ready cash wouldn't oblige. I was pissed off too, and embarrassed and confused, uncertain how to navigate these cultural and financial differences, wanting our friendship to be more equal than that.

I spent the entire weekend guiltily tracking down the ingredients to bake some biscuits for Bie, searching VSO boxes for a gift bag and red ribbon and ceremoniously presenting them to Nasir, who scarcely acknowledged the gesture. Obviously, he'd have preferred the cash and his own choice of snacks. And though I never added it up, I had an uncomfortable suspicion the ingredients cost more than if I'd given him the money in the first place.

I wasn't invited to the birthday party and Nasir never mentioned it again. I hoped, at the very least, that Bie liked the biscuits.

I couldn't be annoyed with Nasir for long, and anyway, I was soon on the move. I had malaria again and this time VSO flew me to Accra for treatment. One minute I was sobbing *I wish you could come with me* on Nasir's shoulder and he was reassuring me, *you will be home soon, Youra,* and the next I was on a small plane flying out of Tamale, guzzling my own snacks in the form of a complimentary Coke and mini packet of Pringles.

It was a taste of luxury to be repeated in Accra. After a week of excellent medical attention in a private clinic where needles were sharp and drugs came in pill packets and not loose in a bag, I felt stronger than I had for months. With spending money from Mum, I hit the town.

A reminder of normality

Accra, Ghana

Jun 3, 2012

Despite feeling a bit tired and malaria-ish, I have been seriously enjoying my weekend. Highlights so far have included –

- *Pizza*
- *A pedicure (I thought the girl was going to cry when she saw my feet, I was there over 2 hours and most of her time was spent scraping 4 months of dust from my heels)*
- *Wireless internet (I've downloaded series 5 and 6 of One Tree Hill)*
- *Diet Coke*
- *Air conditioning*
- *Conditioner (I ran out 3 weeks ago.)*

Tomorrow, I have a massage and then I'll go to the supermarket and buy as much cheese as I can afford/fit in my bag. My optimistic plan is to journey north Monday night, if my blood tests are clear ...

I can't tell you how invigorating it was to jump in taxis, receive international-quality pampering and eat international food. In February, I'd experienced Accra as vibrant in a 'developing' sort of way. Now, I was looking at its skyscrapers, dual carriageways and throngs of people through my Lawra eyes and it seemed rich and as different to my new home as Ramsbury was. In a city of contrasts, people with the latest iPhone dodged open sanitation in their Converse trainers, beggars stumbled past swanky apartment blocks and children hawked salty groundnuts to drivers outside the Total garage that sold Kit Kats. It was lively, energising and exactly what the doctor ordered.

Showered, blow-dried, toe nails freshly shellacked, I wafted to the bar at Byblos Hotel and ordered a glass of generic 'white wine'. As I relaxed into a wicker chair, nibbled tapas and began to feel my old self, my phone pinged. It was Nasir, messaging me that my dog was OK (he'd moved in to babysit her) and that eighty-four parents and children had attended the first of the official monthly disability meetings they'd asked for. And there, in the buzzing metropolis of Accra, all I could think of was what I was missing in Lawra. Singing at the workshop, beer at the spot, boiled eggs at the roundabout, Shilea, Makum and, of course, Nasir.

'Welcome home, Youra.'

Nasir and Shilea met me at the bus station.

'Hi Nasir. Shilea!'

I was happy to be back, and soon we were at a spot, drinking in early evening sunshine and large Clubs.

'Why do you keep calling me Youra?'

Nasir laughed. 'It's your Dagaare name. Everyone in Lawra should have a Dagaare name. It is often given by the Chief and has a special meaning, but this one I have given you.'

'And what does it mean?

'Youra is *Roamer*. Because you are always going somewhere.'

We sat for a while. It was another of the things Nasir had taught me about his world, the ability to simply *be*. Then, I had a momentary flashback to the excitement, the social vibe, of Accra.

'Nasir, would you like to bring your family for dinner sometime?'

He was surprised. They don't do dinner parties in Lawra – at least, no-one had invited me to one. To Nasir, it was probably another English eccentricity, akin to sleeping with your puppy or wearing a motorbike helmet. Though I expect he was also flattered, pleased I would pay him that compliment, that I valued him enough to make a fuss of his family.

'OK, Youra. I think that will be fine.'

On the day of the dinner, I heard the distinctive sound of the Yamaha turning off the main road and ran to the veranda to watch him drive (too fast) across the field towards me, the cool man riding round town on my motorbike.

He was soon chopping onions and boiling rice – there was *no way* either us thought I should cook the meal – and I popped a carton of red wine in the fridge and lit a few candles. It was a far cry from my Ramsbury dinner parties, where I'd be chilling Prosecco and filling bowls with posh crisps.

'Sarah, I will get my family now.'

I was curious. Nasir never discussed his partner Kendey, keeping her separate from work and social life, which I gathered was typical for a Ghanaian man. But he was my best friend in Lawra so, of course, I wanted to meet his other half. Perhaps we could even become friends.

I'd just slipped on a fresh dress (loose now, after the malaria) when I heard the bike. Bie was sitting up front, Nasir's hand over his boy's face to protect him from flies, proud to be a man with a son and a motorbike.

Kendey was behind, side-saddle, in multicoloured kaba and slit (traditional top and tight fishtail skirt), a scarf over her hair. She was about twenty, nervous-looking and the spit of

Bie, with kind, calm eyes and a sweet smile. Climbing carefully off the bike, she followed Nasir and Bie up the steps, possibly wondering what the hell she was doing there.

After we'd shaken hands, Kendey headed straight to the kitchen, scurrying around, assisting Nasir. Bereft of my usual dinner party props, I wasn't sure what to do so I played with Bie, which was infinitely more fun than a glass of Prosecco. That lasted three minutes. Abruptly, food was served and we were eating. In silence. Ghanaians, I'd noticed, tended not to chat over meals.

'So, Kendey,' I said, when I could bear it no longer, 'how do you find living in Lawra?' I knew she'd moved up from Kumasi to be with Nasir.

'I am becoming used to it, thank you.'

More silence, broken by the odd giggle from Bie, perched on the table picking food from his parents' bowls. I wondered what was going through Kendey's mind as she politely ate her jollof rice. What did she make of me, this white woman, this *roamer* with her strange ideas about dinner parties?

It was over quickly, and twenty minutes later they were gone. I grabbed the last of my cheese from Accra, poured a cold glass of red and sat on the veranda feeling quite alone. Maybe the cultural divide was too vast and the economic divide too deep. Maybe a meal was never just a meal in Lawra, because someone was always paying and someone else would always owe. Maybe my attempt to introduce a taste of Accra – a taste of Ramsbury even – was always doomed, because I was trying to *have it all* and, let's face it, even in Ramsbury I didn't *have it all* and it was ridiculous to try.

I took a swig of wine and a bite of sweaty cheese. It had not, I noted, travelled well, and I realised it might be some time before Youra threw another dinner party.

NINE

THE SNAKE IS IN THE GRASS

I cherished my morning jog with Shilea. The sunrises in Lawra were stunning, especially after the rain when the light was diffuse and shimmery and it felt like only good things could happen. We'd go at the crack of dawn, five-ish, to avoid a pack of children jogging behind, all finding it completely hilarious, the nasalpog – the white woman – out running. Shilea would zip around, chasing pigs and guinea fowl, stopping to bark at the now-growing grass whenever she thought she saw a snake.

It was one of those radiant mornings when I set off on the bicycle to Karbo Primary for the long-awaited, malaria-blighted phonics class. *Maybe this time*, I thought, a mere three months after I'd arrived in Lawra, *maybe this time I've started.*

Then I spotted Jeremiah prodding his cows away from the family's tidy mud-walled compound and Celina, new uniform nowhere to be seen, fetching water from the borehole. My heart sank. Clearly, they weren't going to school, a taunting reminder that whatever miracle of phonics I was about to perform, it wouldn't solve the complex problems those children faced, not by a long chalk.

Phonics, though, was all I had. At Karbo, head teacher Mary led me into a packed classroom to face seventy-eight perplexed pupils and twelve sceptical staff with the aim of engaging them in this interactive teaching style. They were a tough crowd.

'*The snake is in the grass, the snake is in the grass,*' I sang, to the tune of *A Hunting We Will Go*. *'Sss, sss, sss, the snake is in the grass.'*

Phonics is an excellent way to learn, bringing every sound to life with an action or song, and it went down well with my Winchcombe pupils. At Karbo, they stared blankly, baffled by the strange woman prancing about like she had a scorpion in her knickers. To them, singing and dancing were for the kindergarten or church, teachers were to be respected and feared, lessons were serious and repetitive and the best students sat still, shut up and tried to concentrate through the gnaw of hunger.

'Now let's use *sss* in a word,' I announced brightly and handed out flashcards I'd made in the TRC, each one representing a letter and a sound.

'Who has *sss*, a hissing *sss*? Can you hold it up?'

The children didn't move, their cards passively in their laps, not wanting to do it wrong, not wanting to do it at all, eyes silently screaming *don't pick me, don't pick on me*. Torn, because this type of behaviour would usually result in a beating, afraid if they didn't comply I would beat them anyway.

'It's OK, I promise.' I stuck my hands in the air. 'Let's see an *S*.'

Although caning was illegal in Ghana, it went on. A senior GES official had told me it was permitted for one teacher per school to be assigned to beat the pupils, *as long as it doesn't leave a mark*. No wonder those children kept a low profile.

Their passivity was a huge obstacle. When I asked them to talk to each other, they were mute, when I asked them to role play, they were rooted to the spot and when I asked them to hold up S, A and T, to do something as elementary as spell SAT, that's what they did, they sat there. Across the room, Mary gave me an encouraging look, acknowledging the uphill struggle it would be for even the smallest progress.

And working with the children was the easy bit. My real challenge was the teachers. They'd witnessed my performance with what felt like a combination of horror, fascination and contempt, and when I suggested they did the lesson with their own classes, they were (with the exception of my friend Olivia) totally not up for it. Maybe they were wary of abandoning *chalk and talk*, believing it gave them status and control. Maybe they just couldn't get their heads round this unfamiliar approach. Either way, I decided that phonics – which really needs to be embedded during training – was too ambitious and I downgraded my plan to one simple aspiration. Fun.

'Do you prefer dancing or reading?'

One afternoon, a couple of weeks later, I stood in front of the same teachers, aware most of them couldn't care less who preferred dancing to reading. I clicked my laptop and as a hit from the Ghanaian charts blasted across the classroom, I began to sway.

'Listen to the music for a minute,' I said, shimmying to the blackboard to write the words *Personality Quiz*. Behind me, I heard a soft laugh and when I turned around Olivia and the Year 4 teacher were throwing azonto shapes and a few others began to sing.

'Now, write down if you were a) singing or humming, b) dancing or c) watching the others.'

More laughter as they scribbled their answers.

'Half of you,' I revealed at the end, 'respond best to words, diagrams and lectures.' They nodded approvingly. To them what I had just described was 'teaching'.

'The other half learn in an entirely different way.' I swayed again. 'You favour moving, doing, touching. Now, what do you think that means for your children?'

It was a game-changer. They'd never heard of kinaesthetic learning, yet once I'd made it personal and showed them the evidence, they became open to trying something new. Soon, I was working in several schools, training teachers and running my own phonics classes. I wouldn't say it was an unqualified success, but to see children learning, and doing it with smiles on their faces, put a smile on mine too.

Of course, it didn't change the fundamentals. If anything, now we were in June, with last year's food stores long gone and this year's harvest months away – it was worse than ever. Everybody was hungry. The only things growing were mangoes and boys would climb trees to grab at the hard, unripe fruits, which they'd boil, desperate for whatever nutrients and pleasure they could suck from them. One break time at Bagri Junction, I noticed a few pupils pool coins to buy a miniscule cellophane bag of cracked, salty groundnuts from a woman who'd come to sell her wares. With no breakfast club or school lunch – and not much at home either – chances are, that handful of nuts was all they'd eaten that day.

I was teaching one afternoon, doing the *c* sound with half a dozen gaunt children, when one girl limply, quietly, no drama, slumped forward onto her desk, sick with hunger or sick from something she couldn't fight because of hunger. I ran to get the head teacher, who gently picked her up and took her off to hospital, not the first time he'd made that trip with a hungry child. And all I could do was turn to my depleted class and sing about a crocodile, telling myself I was making progress and that the sound of music and occasional laughter might drown out the hiss of hunger, even though I knew it couldn't. What these children needed was one decent meal a day. And you can't eat phonics.

I took one look at the queue and sighed.

Nasir and I were outside the regional office of the NHIS (National Health Insurance Scheme) and there must have been fifty people ahead of us, mostly women and children, inserting themselves into slithers of shade round the edge of the modern yellow brick building.

'How long do you think it'll take?' I glanced at one woman who'd been there so long she'd fallen asleep on the ground (or was she just so sick she'd collapsed?). But Nasir was already heading past the masses to the front of the line, shaking the hand of the official at the door and signalling towards me.

I can't say I felt great about jumping the queue, even though we were there to organise health insurance for one hundred disabled children (paid for by friends from The Winchcombe School and Makum). It was our first time out in the world, advocating for those families and, preferential treatment aside, I did feel pretty great about that.

Once in, we were whisked off to meet the top man in his air-conditioned office, where Nasir reverentially requested that staff from NHIS attend our next disability meeting to sign up the children. This was a new Nasir, self-assured as he sipped his chilled water and confirmed to these senior staff that we had the money. More shaking of hands.

On our way out, we passed through the main office, where rows of jobs-for-life clerks were either laboriously inputting data or else brazenly watching films on their computers, no sense of urgency whatsoever. I peeped out of the window at the queue, snaking itself around the building.

I'd missed one meeting of the disability group – now officially named SNAP (Special Needs Awareness Programme) – and already so much had changed. The atmosphere was upbeat. The children appeared better cared for, happier, cleaner, in their best clothes. The women were more relaxed and trustful of each other – and of us – with a burgeoning confidence in their abilities as parents and a desire, a need, to share their traumatic experiences.

'When I am at my stall,' said Patience, 'I put Michelle on a mat beside me. But it creates a scene. People glare and say she is not human, a demon. One day, someone showed me a particular bush. They instruct me, *leave her there for seven days. This will give her the cure.*' Patience looked over to where Michelle was cheerfully playing. 'But she doesn't need a cure. I didn't leave her, I came to SNAP.'

Nasir, translating, gave Patience a warm smile. He understood quite how exceptional she was, for taking her child outside the home, for bringing her to work, for challenging the stigma.

'If you have one of these children, the pressure is very heavy. You can lose your business, you can be harmed. Your child can be harmed. One of my friends had the pressure. She could not fight it. In the end, she poisoned her child.'

Almost every woman there had experienced something similar.

I have been chased from my husband's house by his brother because of my child.

When my daughter is alone, the children at my late husband's compound mistreat her. They put her head under water, they cut her leg from the hip to the knee, she has scars.

Even my grandmother asked me to throw the child away. I was told not to send him to hospital anytime he was sick, so he will die early.

Children dying of treatable illnesses. Children dropping out of school because of brutal bullying. Women who feared if they went out to get water, their housebound child might be raped. And four out of five parents 'advised' to kill their children. At a time when people were emailing me and telling *me* I was brave, I was in the company of women who were truly courageous.

And this was now *their* project. I didn't even think about my own reactions, like I'd done for so much of that first meeting. They drove it, those women, with strong, clear voices, sharing feelings they'd never expressed before, being heard when before no-one would listen.

We talked, we played, we prayed, we sang – the women loved to sing and dance and the meeting was a rare chance to let their hair down – and the NHIS sat at a desk in the corner and signed people up for the vital health insurance that could be the difference between life and death.

At the end of an emotional and productive meeting, as Patience and I swept up the mess of rice and plastic bags, a woman – a girl really, about eighteen – walked nervously up the steps and straight towards me, a dirty, raggy bundle in her arms. Distraught, speaking in hysterical Dagaare, she attempted to hand me the bundle, sobbing, insisting, begging me to take it.

Inside the bundle of cloth was a baby.

Can you imagine? The desperation. The sheer desperation, to give your baby to a stranger you assume can care for it better than you? *You must take this baby. I can't look after this baby. I can't feed this baby. Take my baby.*

As Nasir gently led her away, my positivity departed too and

I was suddenly overwhelmed by my own emotions again. I was furious. With the people of Lawra for not supporting her, with the entire world for allowing such inequality and unfairness, with the father of the child, even with her a little, for giving up and not fighting, for not being Patience.

Nasir wasn't furious, he was kind, recognising her cry for help could be over something as universal as a bout of mastitis or postnatal depression or maybe the result of a domestic argument that might need more serious intervention. And although Nasir hated meddling in family matters, he offered his assistance and agreed to accompany her to the social welfare office to ask about benefits.

Once he'd calmed her down, given her a bag of rice and a five cedi note he couldn't afford, he tried to calm *me* down.

'Just when you feel you're getting somewhere …'

'Sarah, we have done a good job today. And the girl will be OK.' He picked up a thick pile of NHIS receipts. 'Next week, we collect the cards and these children will have health care. It has been a good day.'

He was my rock. It wasn't the last time he'd have to keep me strong, hold me straight, reassure me that although we couldn't do everything, the things we could do were worth doing. What united me and Nasir, from the very start, was our sense of injustice. But whereas I was on a constant rollercoaster of optimism and disillusion, he was pragmatic, presumed the worse and kept going anyway. I was always the girl from Ramsbury, where we can run barefoot through grass and never get bitten by snakes, and he was the boy from Lawra, where snakes are a fact of life and the best you can hope for is that, today, one doesn't kill you.

TEN

SHELTER

I'd seen rain before. Not just Ramsbury rain but Ghana rain,
early rainy season rain that came and went in minutes bringing,
almost immediately, the first new shoots of grass in the scrub.
Yet that rain was nothing – *nothing* – compared to what came
in July.

It was like the world was ending. First, wind whipping up
twists of dust and sending a plastic chair or an old NGO sign
blowing down the road. Next, swirls of dark clouds menacing
across the sky and, finally, rain, in Biblical volumes that soaked
you to the skin in a second if you were outside or made your
ears bleed with the rattle on a corrugated roof if you were
inside. The rain was so absolute, as if it would never stop. And,
in a moment, it was over, they'd be a rush of delicious cool air
and then it would be boiling again. As with everything in Lawra,
extreme.

Instantly, life was transformed. The view from my veranda
was now a landscape of activity, of women in luminous African
prints bent at the hip, weeding and planting seeds, of men with
six packs wielding machetes, of gangs of children setting off to
work. There was a beauty in it, the growth, the toil, less sitting
under mango trees, more eating mangoes on their way to a field.

And there was so much at stake. The average family in Lawra
could only expect to grow enough food for a meagre nine
months, and that's in a good year. In a bad one – when the rain
doesn't come, or comes and then goes again – it drops to seven

months. That's virtually half the year when there's not enough food. For a family with one bag of groundnuts saved from the previous harvest, the decision about when to plant them is critical. The risk of planting early – for an earlier harvest – is if there's no rain, there's no crop, nothing. Nothing.

So, the rain brought no guarantees, but immense promise. And, on a purely personal level, with the temperature now an optimal 28 degrees, my life was transformed too. I was delighted to be using my pac-a-mac, hair dryer and cardigan and pulling a sheet over me in bed to feel cosy. If anything, I could have done with an extra jumper and more socks.

And then there were the insects. Millions of them, everywhere. At night, if I was on the motorbike, I'd get whacked in the face with battalions of bugs and see them whirling round the streetlights. At the spot, mosquitos were rife and I coated myself in harsh DEET, sometimes spray, sometimes the gooey roll-on that made my trousers stick to my legs. Inevitably, the odd one got through and I'd struggle not to scratch, knowing wounds take longer to heal in humidity. Of course, it was just foreigners using DEET, though I'd taken to spraying it over Nasir's hair as we sat and had a beer, to combat the cloud of mozzies hovering two inches above his head.

And mosquitos weren't my only problem.

Termite Trauma

Jul 1, 2012

On the night of the first extremely heavy rain, the termites arrived. They swarmed to my outside lights in their thousands, covering the veranda and making a colossal racket hitting themselves against my screen windows. The whole place was alive with them, like a revolting blizzard.

It makes me itch even thinking about it. I woke up to discover hordes of inch-long termites, wings now hanging off, had crawled under my door and into the house. Evidently, they'd headed to the one property in the area with a light on and I was completely invaded. I tried to sweep them out – hampered by Shilea attacking the broom rather than the termites – but when I attempted to open the front door, I couldn't. The termites were piled up outside, two foot high.

I was deciding what to do and if it was urgent enough to call Nasir when I heard a wallop on the roof. Thud.

Shilea stopped barking. 'What the hell was that?'

Another thud. I looked out of the louvres, as I did when hiding from the children. Thud. Thud. Terrifying thud. And then I saw them. Twenty, at least. Swooping onto my veranda.

Vultures.

I rang Nasir.

'Termites! Vultures! I'm trapped in my house! I need you! They're coming to get me!'

He thought I was mad.

'Sarah, what you must do is go outside and collect the termites. We will eat them for dinner.'

I *think* he was joking. He did know I was a vegetarian. Anyway, the vultures beat him to it and spent the next hour devouring the termites which was, admittedly, a lot more efficient than my sweeping. While this sick buffet continued outside, Shilea and I remained trapped inside. It was something we were becoming used to.

Recently, as lean season tightened its grip, things had got rather intense again. I would wake to see children looking in through my bedroom shutters while I laid in bed and there was a permanent crowd on the veranda, waiting for me to emerge. It was what I'd been cautioned about. The more relationships I'd built, the more people wanted from me. And it was endless, an unfulfillable need for stuff the entire time, important, life-sustaining stuff – food, health insurance, bicycles, textbooks – stuff no-one had enough of and I couldn't provide for everybody.

I did my best, but it was stressful not being able to meet that need. And when some of the older teenage boys knocked on my door late one night all my old vulnerabilities came flooding back, though I'm sure they meant no harm. I felt cornered, wishing I could help everyone, wanting to protect myself, knowing if I gave everything, there'd be nothing left. So, sometimes, I did still hide to avoid people. And I know it sounds awful, but being trapped by the vultures was a variation on that theme.

I also got trapped by the rain, often for days at a time, feeling unable to do anything in the face of the downpour and my increasingly low spirits. Occasionally, though, I was reminded by VSO that my job wasn't to sit in a concrete house with my dog, and they would summon me to a meeting.

It took a whole day to get to Bolgatanga on waterlogged roads even more craterous than before, for a workshop about some new organisational model VSO was introducing that didn't seem relevant at all to life in Lawra. Once there, I doodled, gazed out the window and looked in awe at fellow volunteer Leela, who shone with insight and understanding and was achieving much more on her placement than prancing round a classroom.

On the morning of my return I got up at 3 am to secure my bus ticket and hung round the terminal until we set off at 7.30. The roads were treacherous, the bus swerving to avoid the massive rain-filled holes pockmarking the terrain. I was hardly surprised when, shortly before lunchtime, the vehicle lurched to a halt.

'Everybody off.'

The driver pulled up in front of what I'd have to describe as a river, gushing across the road. Despite there being a bridge a hundred yards away, he urged the passengers to wade through two-foot deep water before driving, with total conviction, straight into the hole. We were sixty miles from Wa, and I was up a creek without a paddle, phone signal, water or food.

After an hour of watching men fail to push the bus out of the river and other passengers, one by one, pick up lifts to their destinations, I wandered along the road, unsure what to do. In the end, someone took me under their wing and got me on a watermelon truck heading towards Lawra, and I sat on top of the melons, clinging on for dear life. The fruit had travelled from goodness knows where and the journey had not agreed with them because they were rotting beneath my bottom, exploding with every bump in the road. Scalded by the sun and soaked in melon juice, I told myself it was all material for a funny blog, even as my eyes stung with tears behind my sunglasses.

Four hot hours later I arrived in Lawra, sunburnt, sticky, bruised but safe and when I climbed down from the truck, Patience ran over with a comforting *sorry, sorry, sorry* and a welcome pure water sachet. It was a relief to be home, I thought, as it began to rain.

Next day, I pushed my bicycle down the slope and headed off, Shilea running behind. I'd struggled to get out to schools in rainy season, but Karbo Primary was nearby so I had no excuse for missing the teacher training I'd arranged. Although I usually loved phonics, I was slightly dreading the session, having once seen the teacher I was due to work with wave a stick at Celina. However, with term ending in three weeks, I didn't want to lose the shred of momentum I had managed to build.

Maize was growing around my house and as I cycled through it I could see children working the land, others heading for distant plots with heavy hoes and sacks of nuts to plant. Every few seconds now-ripe mangoes would drop from trees, the children burying their faces in the sweet, orange flesh. A pleasant scene, if only it hadn't been a school day and those children weren't meant to be in class.

Karbo Primary was quiet. I walked along the veranda to Gifty's classroom, but no-one was there was. No Gifty, no children. In fact, few children anywhere. I then spotted Olivia and spent a gratifying couple of minutes watching her teach phonics to half a dozen pupils.

'Are you looking for Gifty?' She indicated through the window to a field beyond, where I could just make out dots of activity.

Shilea and I got there a few minutes later to find her sitting comfortably – proudly – on a wooden chair, overseeing fifty children in school uniform as they pulled weeds from her land. I knew parents often withdrew their children from school during the busy rainy season. But the teacher …?

'I thought we had a phonics lesson booked.'

'Not today, the children are busy. There was much rain last night so they must farm. Maybe next term?'

Child labour, and she wasn't even embarrassed.

'Would you mind if I took a picture?'

She gleefully arranged herself in a pose, dress all pretty and clean, wrists all bangled. Behind her, children in orange and brown uniforms, worked on. It may have been socially acceptable, but I hated it. I also understood why she did it. Because without a bountiful season in the fields, everybody would be hungry again.

We got back as the heavens opened, and I thought about those children working Gifty's land, probably still out there in the rain though I suspected she'd be sheltering. I considered writing my blog and couldn't quite muster the enthusiasm. They usually took a whole day to upload with the dongle and often the connection would give out halfway through, especially in bad weather. As I listened to the rain drumming the iron roof, I just couldn't be bothered. Couldn't be bothered to try and make everything sound positive, didn't have the energy to spin how well I was doing, and how much impact I was having and how hilarious the watermelon truck escapade had been.

My phone rang. It was the regional VSO rep with harrowing news. Two international volunteers had been violently attacked in Wa, someone had come at them with a knife and, although the volunteers were safe, horrifically, the assailant was dead. I was to keep away until further notice. It had happened the day before, just as I'd hitched my lift through Wa, and all of a sudden Ghana felt threatening and dangerous, which it never had before.

There was a tiny knock on the door. One of the children braving the deluge, wanting something. I couldn't face it today. And as I hid behind the louvres hoping Shilea wouldn't bark, I questioned how far I'd really come since February, how much I was kidding myself, whether I was making any difference in Lawra and how I ever could, what with my own shortcomings and the poverty and the culture and the seasons.

Outside, through the din of the rain, I could hear whoever had been knocking walk away.

ELEVEN

END OF TERMITES

'Sarah. You are too fast. Walk slower.'

Wa market was throbbing, bristling with people yelling their wares, *dish cloths! pawpaw! xylophones!* and Nasir was jittery. 'Sarah, I don't like this. Slow down.'

I hadn't been able to stay locked up for long. An enthusiast at heart, I'd forced myself to forget about termites and vultures and shameless teachers and violent assailants, made my peace with the rain and got out of the house. Now, I had a new hindrance.

'Sarah,' snapped Nasir, as I browsed ripe mangoes, 'you are too slow, walk faster.'

It was my first trip to Wa since VSO had given the all-clear and Nasir had insisted on accompanying me.

'Let's buy some fruit.' I reached for my purse.

'Sarah, don't take your money out in the street.' He grabbed my bag. 'Or do you want to die?'

He wasn't the calmest of bodyguards, though I rather liked the urgency of his attention and the feel of his firm hand on my wrist. 'Sarah, we will go this way.'

He tapped the pocket where he'd stashed my penknife (a kind gift from a Winchcombe parent, mostly used to open bottles), his eyes darting round, partly checking for marauders, partly looking for a particular T-shirt stall. My parents had sent some spending money and I'd offered to buy him something, assuming he'd get a mega pack of nappies or a sack of rice. But it was these specific T-shirts he wanted and that's what we were searching for.

'Why don't you get this for Bie?' I picked up a basketball strip and when he declined I made him wait, twitchy and anxious, while I bought it anyway.

We trekked round that bloody market for hours until we found the T-shirts, nasty Chinese-made things in that stretchy polyester that smells of BO from the first time you wear it. Nasir chose one in salmon pink, embossed with studs, and an electric blue one with a flashy symbol on the front.

'A poor man,' he explained over lunch in a roadside shack, 'does not want to look poor.' He ate with one hand and clasped my purchases tightly in the other. 'That is my priority, not looking poor. Then people will respect me.'

It was the first time, I think, that I understood the aspirations, the pride, that motivated Nasir. It wasn't just about providing for his family, though that was part of it, it was about standing, status, how people saw him. About not being *small boy*.

As soon as we got to Lawra, he jumped on my motorbike and rode round town, the studs on his blingy new T-shirt glinting in the fading sun.

'Sarah, we are honoured to give you this fish.'

I did my own victory lap a few days later, driving home from the final teacher training of the school year with a huge, bloody fish strapped to the Yamaha. The staff had ceremoniously presented the gift after a particularly animated session and whilst I wasn't sure what I'd do with it, I was touched. Six months into my placement, that bleeding fish was a symbol of how much – and how little – I'd achieved.

I held an end of term party, and Leela and the crew from Bolga came, along with neighbourhood children and my Lawra friends, and one of my guests cooked the big fish. We danced azonto until 3 am and then I let my unwashed hair down (I'd run out of shampoo) and murdered a few Andrew Lloyd Webber classics on the recorder. It was a carefree night, but when I woke the next morning, it hit me. Ahead lay two months of school-free summer, two months with no lessons or training, two months before I headed off for a family holiday I was already desperate for, two months of ... nothing.

'Fancy buying condoms?'

I was in Wa with a Peace Corps friend and she was stocking up for a sexual health workshop aimed at people with HIV. 'Come to the session,' she suggested and I eagerly agreed, relieved to have something to do.

A few days later, with several dozen boxes of condoms, a wooden penis and a renewed sense of worth, I marched past a wall emblazoned *LOVE LIFE, STOP AIDS*, ready to give the HIV community of Lawra the benefit of my 'wide sexual experience' (and I cannot emphasise enough how ironic I mean that phrase to be!).

Place the condom on the tip of the fully erect penis.

I mean, the first thing is, why had some volunteer painted that slogan on a building hosting what was meant to be a confidential meeting? HIV was a terrible stigma in Lawra (despite the district then having one of the highest rates in Ghana) and I suspect very few of those thirty women and couple of men would have made the walk of shame if attendance hadn't been required to access antiretroviral (ART) drugs and a monthly allowance.

Pinch the air out of the tip of the condom.

Secondly, what did I imagine that me sliding a condom onto a wooden penis would accomplish? These were not young independent people enjoying casual sex at the weekends (me neither), they were women who lacked the power to tell any man what to put on his penis.

The man must hold the condom in place as he pulls out.

Thirdly, these people already had HIV. A few were obviously very sick and I was shocked to see the reality of it in close-up, the sores, the pus, the blindness, the evident pain. In some ways, though, I was more shocked to discover the majority (thanks to ART) were in reasonable health. And what I came to realise – what they politely yet plainly made me understand – was the last thing any of them needed was a lecture on safe sex from a well-meaning white saviour at a loose end. I put down the wooden penis.

'Any questions?'

After a long silence, a woman spoke. 'May I tell you about my life?' She was from a small village and wore a traditional outfit of shimmering fabric. 'I am a weaver. I have skills, then I became ill, I was on my bed and couldn't work. I sold my loom to buy health insurance and food. Now I have the drugs, I am feeling strong. But I have four children and no business and there's nothing left to sell. Please, don't give me more condoms. What I need is my business.'

She wasn't alone.

My husband has left and I have children's mouths to feed. I am a seamstress but I cannot afford a sewing machine.

Life is not easy and I have been too ill to make my baskets. All I want is to earn my daily bread, but where do I find the money to buy raffia?

I am a farmer, but everything was lost when I was sick. Give me equipment and seeds and I will make things grow.

Weavers, seamstresses, basket-makers, farmers, all with skills, all striving to provide for themselves in a place where there were no business grants or bank loans to give them a kick start.

I began to think. I'd already raised over £200 for the SNAP workshops without even trying. What if I could find the money to get their businesses going?

'How much, roughly, would you need?'

The weaver leant back, doing the sums in her head. 'To buy a new loom, to buy the threads, I think GH¢600.'

Two hundred pounds. I could manage that. Even if I financed, say, ten of them – two grand – I could do it. My mind was racing. If I could show how a small donation, wisely used, could change somebody's life, I reckoned I could raise funds from family and friends in Ramsbury. After all, I might as well use my privilege to do something someone actually wanted, something they'd actually asked for. Something that might actually make their lives better.

'Anyone else? How much money to open your businesses?'

Madame Madi, an esteemed community activist I recognised from SNAP meetings, raised her hand.

'Sarah, give me a piece of paper. I will write it down.' Everyone laughed, and we were off.

I suggested people split into groups so they could support each other during illness or other emergencies and soon there was a gang of weavers, a group of farmers, some women selling drugs, medical supplies and eggs, and Madame Madi, who planned to make baskets with her daughter.

As they came up with ideas, I thought of the skills my family could offer. My Dad was a management consultant who would relish playing Alan Sugar, my Mum, a psychotherapist and former social worker, was caring, organised and thorough, and my sister Karen had a wealth of business experience. Exactly the team I'd need for this to succeed. Meanwhile, Nasir and Madame Madi could co-ordinate things in Lawra.

It was an exhilarating meeting and when they filed out past *LOVE LIFE, STOP AIDS* there was a sense of excitement in the air. Word got round beyond the HIV group that an English woman might fund a few businesses, and Nasir and I spent a couple of days visiting people in their villages, pulling together shopping lists, *threads, seeds, refurbished bike.*

I put the lists in my notebook and hoped I'd not promised something I couldn't deliver, like so many others before.

There were still weeks to go before my family holiday in Majorca and in the absence of anything else to do, I decided to count my blessings.

A positive blog

Lawra, Ghana

Aug 13, 2012

These are some of my favourite things about living in Lawra ...

- *__The weather.__ Although hot season was boiling, it's worth it to live in a country where the sun always shines. I've always liked sunglasses and can now wear them every single day. My skin is never pale, I have plenty of vitamin D and never have to worry about wearing anything more than a dress. Bliss.*

- **The slow pace of life.** *Taking a nap at 2 pm is totally acceptable, no matter where you are. Sleeping in the office/market/school is normal and having 2 days off work to 'rest' after a long bus journey is encouraged. If I am tired, I go to sleep. Today I sat on a plastic chair in the middle of town, reading a book, for nearly 3 hours. I have an excellent work/life balance and wake up bright and early every morning with no need to set an alarm.*

- **My motorbike.** *It still gives me a buzz every single time I kick start my bike. There is nothing like riding through tiny African villages in the blazing sunshine, with a trail of dust behind you.*

- **The sense of community.** *Everybody in town knows who I am (my skin colour makes this very easy) and I hear the chant 'Nasalpog! How are you? I'm fine. Thank you.' from at least 100 children a day. I have long, daily chats with the post office man, the fruit woman, the bread woman, the egg woman, my favourite market woman and the man who smokes on the corner. It's refreshing to have the time to get to know the people whose lives exist around my own, to stop to hold their babies, enquire about their health and ask how they slept. This is my replacement for a social life.*

- **Shilea (my dog).** *Despite eating my shoes, urinating in my bed, howling all night and generally being a nuisance, she is pretty great company and very cute.*

- **Packages.** *It is utterly joyful to find a slip of paper in my P.O. Box. The fact that somebody bothers to buy, package, post and pay for mint Aeros/Skittles/shampoo/cans of Diet Coke/sachets of honey/ hot chocolate/G&T/plastic egg boxes/candles etc is staggering.*

- **Going natural.** *It's taken time, but I am now nearly completely without artificial improvement. My skin feels great, it clearly likes not wearing make-up. My hair is thicker and glossier, despite the lack of shampoo. It takes me roughly five minutes to get ready in the morning – three* *to brush my teeth, one to wash my face and one to brush my hair (admittedly I sometimes skip this step and wear a head scarf). I'm turning into a cliché of a volunteer – barefaced and wearing way too much African fabric. I may even come home with dreadlocks.*

- **My personal journey.** *Although it doesn't always feel like a plus, the biggest bonus of being here, in this house, in the middle of a field, all alone, with no colleagues and very few friends, has been getting to know myself. Living here is like living with a mirror pushed up against my soul. I see myself more and more clearly each day. I'm being magnified and forced to examine myself. I pray that I will be able to hold on to my learning when I return to 'normality', taking with me the new-found knowledge I have about who I am, and who I want to be.*

xxx

Blessings aside, time dragged that summer, the one highlight being when Nasir and his family moved in with me, to take a break from the Chief's Palace. Nasir cooked, Kendey did a lot of sweeping and I loved having Bie scampering around in his new basketball kit. After supper, Nasir would go out on my bike (in one of his new T-shirts) and I'd take Bie for a splash in the bath and watch movies with Kendey, appreciating her quiet, intelligent company. They stayed a fortnight and then, at last, it was time for my holiday.

My holiday. I fantasised about that holiday, and I feared it. On the one hand I yearned, physically yearned, for my family who I'd not seen in months, and for cocktails and air con and long hot showers. On the other, I was so knackered and battered by my experience in Ghana, there was a part of me that was scared of leaving Lawra, of losing my resolve, afraid that once I'd gone I might never come back.

TWELVE

FLIP-FLOPS

All it took was three little words.

'Feta cheese salad?'

I was in business class on the night flight from Accra, three glasses of Taittinger champagne to the good, and promptly burst into tears. Whether it was the booze, or that I'd not seen cheese for months, or the stress of worrying I was about to get bumped from the flight when I was in fact being upgraded or just the joyful prospect of being with my family, but there I was sobbing into a salad on the most comfortable seat I'd sat on for ages.

I glanced round the cabin, momentarily thrown by the sea of white faces. It was a different world, with its soft-murmured *may I top you ups*, complimentary eye masks and continental cheese, yet another world I didn't fit into. With my blue harem pants and dust-encrusted flip-flops, I half expected someone to move me to my real seat at the rear of the plane.

Opposite me was a woman, my age, who'd also been doing development work and had also been upgraded. Unlike me, she didn't look as if she'd been living in the bush – or dragged through one – and when she told me about the NGO she'd launched, I thought, *wow, you're so cool.*

And in a flash, I was back with Leela and Izzy and the others, out of my depth. Something, however, *had* changed since February. I'd learnt *one* thing, and not from VSO.

You know that proverb, *give a man a fish and he eats for a day, teach a man to fish and he eats forever*? The proverb everyone regards as so clever and profound? The proverb that sent me to Africa believing, more or less, that I was there to teach someone to do something I knew nothing about? Sorry, it's bullshit.

That's what I learnt from the people of Lawra. They had no need for a fishing lesson from a twenty-eight-year-old teacher from Ramsbury, but if I *did* want to be useful, they could do with a hand replacing their broken rod. In plain language – investment in the skills they demonstrably had, not some random volunteer who thought she knew best.

I couldn't wait to talk it through with my family. First things first, though. While everyone around me slept, I sipped another glass of Taittinger, ate all the food, watched two movies and fully exploited my upgrade.

I was nervous as I went down in the hotel lift. Looking at my reflection in its mirrors – six months without a mirror then twenty come at once – I scarcely recognised the barefaced gaunt, brown stranger staring back.

Even the few days before I'd left Ghana had been full of emotion. On the way to Accra, I'd stopped off with Makum, Nasir and a few others for a mini break at the idyllic Lake Bosumtwi, near Kumasi. Nasir had never been anywhere like that before, and picnics, pedalos, cocktails were new experiences to share with him. That evening, I sat with Makum, gazing at the spectacular view and feeling grounded and close to her. I had made true friends in Lawra and I carried that beautiful thought with me all the way to Majorca and into the mirror-lined lift.

And there they were. I threw myself at Mum, Dad and Karen, relieved to be with the people who loved me the most. We headed to the bar and I drank a massive glass of Sauvignon Blanc.

'Must you do that?'

Mum stared at me eating fish with my fingers in a charming beachside restaurant. 'Can't you use your knife and fork?'

I think a bit of me was, *look, I'm so Ghanaian, I can eat with my hands.* Secretly, though, I was struggling. When I crawled between clean sheets that night I panicked about mosquitos and when I awoke next morning, I automatically checked for prying eyes, panicked again – this time about whether the water had gone off – and ending up sweeping the balcony until I remembered I was on holiday, that I wanted for nothing and no-one wanted anything from me.

Mentally and physically, I was in a pretty weird place – unsurprising after two bouts of malaria, ongoing anaemia and a crushing sense of failure. Traumatised is taking it too far, but it needed a couple of glorious days by the pool with Karen, a few days of running water and no insects and no-one banging on my door, before I could quite trust the safety and comfort of it. Eventually, after sleeping and eating and drinking myself better, I told my family about Lawra, about some of the things I'd witnessed and how little I'd done.

'It's like I'm being abusive, being there, getting paid and achieving nothing. And I feel VSO has abused me, sending me there with an impossible goal.'

Karen put her arm around me, still upset I'd been so ill. 'Why don't you just come home?'

Why didn't I? Then Dad paid the bill, £100 – not a fortune for a family meal, not a fortune for my parents – and all I could think was *mend a loom, buy a plough, set up a sustainable business that would give a family in Lawra an income for (hopefully) ever.* I already felt guilty and if I didn't return I would have been bailing on everyone, the seamstresses and weavers, the SNAP families, the children. More shame, more guilt.

'Actually, I have an idea.'

I'm not sure what I was hoping for when I told them about hungry pupils and disabled children and seamstresses with HIV. Advice, perhaps a few hundred pounds, probably a nudge towards the people in Ramsbury who might give a few hundred more. I definitely didn't see myself in the same league as that NGO woman on the plane, I had no grander ambitions than to buy a couple of sewing machines and salvage something from my disappointing year. For me, that would have been a very good result.

As we studied the shopping lists it began to rain and it didn't stop for the rest of the week. Instead of hiding indoors, fretting about the electricity, deafened by the downpour on an iron roof, we had long lunches and talked and talked and talked.

'If we're doing this,' said Dad, 'it's futile to hand over a grant and walk away. We have to be different to what's come before.'

'What about training in bookkeeping and marketing?' suggested Karen. 'After all, small businesses in the UK get that stuff.'

'Yes, and it's more than that,' said Mum. 'It's getting their children fed and into school. It's giving your SNAP mums a chance to have their own businesses. It's all connected. Here ...'

She grabbed a paper napkin and a pen and scribbled a triangle, with a word at each point.

ENTERPRISE. EDUCATION. DISABILITY.

'That's it, isn't it?'

I read those three words, words that would form the cornerstones of what came next.

'That's it.'

It was all go after that. Once we decided to do things properly, to not throw money around and then withdraw, we made a commitment, the four of us. We agreed to set up a charity, focusing on what the people of Lawra had told me they wanted. Backing for a business. School lunches so children could learn on a full stomach. Help for disabled families.

My parents offered to make a donation to kick things off, and I was thrilled we had a project to do together, for Mum, Dad and Karen to put their trust in me, for us to take our skills and money and apply them to the skills and motivation already in Lawra.

There was so much to do. Dad was going to create an application process for businesses, Mum would set up the charity and Karen took on branding and the website. Meanwhile, I would talk to the people who could make things happen in Lawra, Mary Karbo, Madam Madi, Patience and, of course, Nasir.

At the end of the week, Mum and Dad left and my friends arrived for a few days. Despite having fun and feeling excited about the charity, I was still all over the place.

'I'll literally pay you not to go back,' said Laura after she found me early one morning on the balcony, weeping into the broom. 'You don't have to go back.'

It was what I needed. Permission to give up made it easier to keep going. Though, when we said goodbye at Majorca Airport, my friends disappearing on the travellator, I thought my heart would break in two. I missed them immediately, regretted immediately my decision, doubted everything. Just as I had feared the leaving of Lawra, now I feared the re-entry.

Once I got through security, on the way to my own flight, that all changed. My mind filled with the new challenge, the people to see, the things to do, and in that moment, I did one more flip-flop and couldn't wait to be in Ghana again.

THIRTEEN

TO-DO LIST

I was fizzier than a Club, bubbling over with excitement. Nasir and I were at Las Palmas, our favourite spot, and he was swirling beer round my glass to rinse out the dust. Ordinarily, I liked this ritual, but tonight I wanted him to stop fussing so I could share my news. He discarded beer froth onto the ground and it sparkled, fleetingly, in the red sand.

I'd been in Lawra a few hours, enough time to hug Patience at the roundabout, have an ecstatic reunion with Shilea and make a pot of rice for the children. Then I'd gone in search of Nasir, desperate to tell him my plans. Now, they came spilling out.

'We can really do something, Nasir, feed the children at Karbo Primary, open SNAP groups in the villages, encourage businesses. We can build on what's already here, work with the people of Lawra, really *with* them, make something sustainable, for the future. Maybe I'll give up teaching, maybe *this* is what I'll do. It's exciting.'

He burst out laughing.

'Sarah, you can't plan that far ahead.'

'Of course we can.' Relentless positivity, always my greatest strength.

Nasir, though, was suddenly subdued. 'I don't know. But I wish someone had fed me when I was at school. I think I would have advanced.' Decisively, he put his phone on the table and sat back in his plastic chair. 'OK, Sarah. Talk.'

I ran through my to-do list, *open bank account, recruit small businesses, see Mary Karbo at the school …*

'The bank account,' he interrupted, 'that will be difficult. The road to Wa is bad and the bike needs an oil change and we must choose the right day because the queues can take many hours.'

'Well, we don't need the bank account straightaway …'

'But Sarah, until we have the bank account, we cannot do anything.'

There was a lot of that. Me, racing ahead to the promised land, him focusing on the bumps in the road. And it wasn't personality differences, not all of it. Partly, it was cultural, a divide between someone who expected life to sparkle and someone whose experience told him dreams would turn to dust.

'This could be very beneficial for my community. But the thing is, you don't know what will happen until you get there.'

'Nothing will *ever* happen unless we try.'

In the end, we drank to that, toasting our new adventure. The truth was, neither of us had a clue what lay ahead, but, for better or worse, we were both committed to the journey.

Nasir waved a clear ziplock bag of human faeces round the Teachers' Resource Centre.

'That is the worrying problem. Free range shitting spreads disease.'

It was the monthly SNAP meeting and despite looking at excrement, it felt good. SNAP was the most successful thing I'd been involved with in Lawra, and it was uplifting to walk into the TRC alongside fifty participants, wave at Patience and lovely Michelle, see the mums gossip and the children play, interacting in a way that was unimaginable a few months earlier.

'The main danger is not in the villages, it is in Lawra town, where people defecate near food and water and dwellings.'

I smirked. Nasir often retired to the bush with a roll of my loo paper, though he was more than welcome to use the facilities. Old habits, I suppose. Anyway, he got his message across and soon the women were joining forces to dig more long drop toilets, a constructive example of what can be done when you work with the community.

I chose not to ask Nasir where he acquired the bag of poo. There are some things it's best not to know.

Next day, we headed east out of Lawra for the fifteen-minute motorbike ride to the village of Zambo, where we were greeted by a crowd of weavers, traders and farmers interested in building businesses.

'Please, when do we repay the money?' asked a weaver.

'The money is not a loan,' said Nasir. 'If you spend it on what we've agreed, you do not pay it back.'

A few jaws dropped and a couple of weavers applauded. We'd all heard of people taking loans from NGOs and becoming trapped in a crippling cycle of debt. Getting a non-repayable grant was critical for them – and for me. I had no desire to be anyone's bank manager.

'We want you to grow your business,' I explained. 'We want you to buy stock and equipment, and get health insurance so you don't miss work. The grant is there to make your life better.'

'This is not easy money, though,' warned Nasir. 'You must sign a contract. You must work five days every week unless you are sick. If you need help, please ask.'

We went round each group, helping them complete the

application form Dad had drawn up. In the process a few dropped out and we ended up with a dozen viable businesses, including Madame Madi's basket weavers, a collective from Kuoli (groundnut farmer, petty trader, tomato seller) and a group of weavers from Zambo with one broken loom between them.

With Nasir by my side – who am I kidding, with Nasir front and centre – we'd made progress with two prongs of Mum's triangle, *disability* and *enterprise*. For the third prong, *education*, I was on my own.

A couple of days later I sat opposite Mary Karbo in her office at Karbo Primary and made her an offer.

'I can get the money to feed your children. Let's open a kitchen.'

It was what she'd told me she wanted back in March, but I'd seen wheels turn so slowly in the Ghanaian education system I expected her to drown me in bureaucracy. Or laugh. Instead, she made a note in her diary.

'Sarah, I will arrange a PTA meeting for you to talk to the parents. Can you come on Friday?'

I spent the rest of the week showing my face at the Teachers' Resource Centre and hoping nobody noticed I'd largely stopped VSO work and was now setting up my own charity. I needn't have worried. No-one at GES had the foggiest what I was meant to be doing and no-one at VSO seemed to care.

Friday morning, I put on my smartest T-shirt, squeezed into skinny jeans and cycled through the leafy maize to the school. Based on past experience of meetings that never happened, I braced myself for an hour under the mango tree with no-one but Shilea for company. Maybe, if I was lucky, three or four parents would turn up.

Not for the first time, I couldn't have been more wrong.

The courtyard was packed. There were hundreds of people and more still coming, farmers on cycles with tools lashed to the back, women carrying sacks. I even spotted Judith's mother perched on the gnarly root of the mango tree, shelling groundnuts. Whatever the magnificent Mary Karbo had told the parents (*the white lady has an idea*, I found out later), it had worked.

I joined Mary on the steps leading up to the classrooms. Behind us, children hung out of windows to see what was going on, next to us teachers assembled. Jeremiah's mum waved from the crowd.

'Go ahead,' said Mary.

'Me?' I gazed out at four hundred faces. 'I can't speak to all these people.'

'Go on.' She pushed me forward. 'I'll translate.'

Unaccustomed as I was to public speaking, I was terrified. In England, I'd once feigned sickness to avoid addressing a Winchcombe staff meeting and in Lawra, well, so far, Nasir had done the talking. Yet, here at Karbo, it felt right for me to take the lead alongside Mary, one of the few professional connections I'd made through VSO and someone who seemed to respect me. With her steady hand on my shoulder, we did it together. In the end, blind enthusiasm got me through.

'I will do whatever it takes to open a kitchen. I want your children to come to school, to be strong and healthy and able to learn. I guarantee I'll find a year's money for food and cooks. I give you that promise. And you must make a promise. The children must be in school to study. They can't eat and then go to work your land. This is a not a food programme, it's an education programme. Then your children can fulfil their potential.'

It *felt* like it went down well – who knows, working through an interpreter – and I'm sure Mary covered for my nerves and gave it a polish. After me, she introduced an elderly gentleman, who looked a lot more at ease than I had.

'Dabuo is the chair of the PTA,' she whispered to me. 'He was at school in colonial times, he knows the importance of education.'

Though I didn't understand him, I could feel his authority and passion as he held the parents' total attention. When he finished, there was stunned silence. Then …

Jubilation. Everyone leapt to their feet, applauding and doing the distinctive whooping I've only ever heard in Ghana. Dabuo turned to me and shook my hand.

'We agree. We will build the kitchen. Let's do this for our children.'

From that moment, we were in it together. He organised the parents into work groups and announced a contribution of two cedis (about 75p) from each pupil to pay for materials. It was a fortune for those families (especially ones with several children) and made me even more determined to uphold my end of the bargain, not that I doubted I would.

'Sarah, this way.' Mary pulled me into the throng.

Parents surrounded us and we posed for a photograph to commemorate the occasion and the promises we'd made, as the high-pitched sound of women singing filled the courtyard.

I cycled with their voices fading into the distance and Shilea running alongside me, and was so pumped I rang Mum from the bike.

'They've already set a date for the build, it's moving fast.'

'Hang on a sec.' Three thousand miles away she fumbled for a calculator. 'Let's work out what you've committed to.'

The longer she tapped, the more panicky I got, numbers crashing round my head. Four hundred pupils. Two thousand meals a week.

How on earth were we going to pay for two thousand meals *every week?*

'I've got the figures. It's £30,000 for the year.'

And for the second time that day, I was freaking terrified. I'd stood in front of those parents and made promises I now had to keep. And school lunches were just the start. What about the business grants? And resources for SNAP families? I was up to forty grand and counting.

By the time I got home, I knew that relentless positivity and a generous contribution from my parents weren't going to cut it, and suddenly my promises felt like me abusing my power and privilege again. More panic. And yet, deep inside, the uncrushable bit of me was thinking *surely this will be easy? Won't my mates give a tenner a month? Who doesn't want to feed a hungry child?*

As I crashed between naive optimism and paralysing fear, one thing was undeniable. I had to get serious. To raise money – not just from friends and family – I needed to learn stuff, about fundraising, about international development, about running a charity. As a plan formed, I briefly wondered if I was now the interesting, irresistible person I'd wanted to be when I came to Ghana to impress a man.

I rifled through the cupboards, found some Post-it notes and began to write. A few minutes later, among the family photos and holiday snaps, I stuck a Post-it on the wall. It read:

TO-DO LIST
RAISE £30,000
DO MASTER'S DEGREE
GET BACK WITH BOYFRIEND

FOURTEEN

SACKFUL

Groundnuts grow beautifully in Lawra. Tiny green bushes carpet the land, and by the end of September they were ready to harvest. My teacher friend Olivia had some farmland and I offered my labour.

'You pull this way.' She tugged a plant at its base to reveal monkey nuts hanging like bunches of grapes. 'It is a good harvest.'

She handed me one and I picked off the shell and ate the brown nut inside. 'Delicious.'

'Yes. And now, we work.'

Women, as far as I could see, usually did all the work. Whenever I visited family compounds I'd been struck by how often the man would be snoozing under a mango tree while his wife tended a field or went to market with a mattress on her head. Life was challenging in the Upper West and women, apparently, bore the brunt. So it was, that day, picking Olivia's groundnuts alongside her grandmother and daughters.

As we laboured (Olivia bent at the hip, me, like a nob, sat on the floor), she talked about her life. *It's complicated*, she'd once said and crouching among the groundnuts, she told me why.

'I am the second wife and there is a first wife. She was unable to have children, and so we are two.'

I tried not to be shocked. Yet, even though I knew the practice of taking multiple wives was common in the Upper West, to hear about it from Olivia, a professional woman, a fellow teacher, was disturbing.

'It is not what I wanted for my life, but it is the way it is. This week I live at the family home with my two children and my husband's family. Then, every six days, on market day, I go to my husband's home on the other side of town. The first wife, she goes the other way, to the family home, to care for my children. In the middle of town, we pass.'

'Do you speak?'

She shook her head. 'The only time the agenda changes is if one of us is bleeding. The husband cannot do without.'

'That's awful. Can you divorce him?'

She laughed. 'My family would have to repay the dowry. And also ...' She looked at her children, pulling groundnuts, 'I would lose them. For our people, children are the property of the man. The saddest thing for me is I am not permitted to take Communion.' She was a devout Catholic. 'That is my saddest thing.'

She patted the sack, now bulging with nuts.

'Yes, it is a good harvest.'

Harvest Time

Oct 4, 2012

This weekend is the annual Kobine Festival in Lawra. This is a celebration of harvest, giving thanks to God for the rain and successful crops. It's a huge deal, the highlight of the year. I plan on enjoying the fun, dancing and perhaps even staying out after dark.

Town is full of people, noise, colour and fun – it's pretty chaotic, and terrifying trying to negotiate the traffic. Lawra has come to life in a way I didn't think possible.

Maybe it was the piles of yams and sacks of millet everywhere. Or the sight of slightly less hungry children returning to school, having absented themselves for the harvest. Or maybe it was the food shacks and music stands and multi-hued tents set up all over town. Whatever it was, Lawra seemed different, less on the edge of the world.

Anyway, that's how it seemed, until the three horrible things.

The Festival kicked off splendidly, with a parade of tribal chiefs in flouncy ceremonial smocks, canopied by regal-red umbrellas and led by a man waving dried elephant ears and another with antelope antlers who performed the *dance of the hunters.* Then followed a volley of gunfire, speeches, traditional dancing by bare-chested men in beads and skirts, xylophone-playing, drumming, dance competitions and plentiful pito, the local beery fermented drink.

The atmosphere was electric as we cheered the Lawra football team to victory in the prestigious inter-community gala. The players then lined up to receive the champions' cup from the chief, impressive in his tribal outfit, swathed with woven fabric and slung with a large, lethal-looking knife.

It was only when I heard a yelp and saw a mini version of Shilea being held aloft that it dawned on me the knife was more than ceremonial. The custom, it turned out, was for the losing team to present the winners with a dog, the resulting meat to be shared in a celebratory feast. Open-minded and accepting as I wanted to be, this ritual had found my limit. I ran home and gave Shilea a heartfelt hug and a tin of tuna.

The next morning, still shuddering, I climbed on my motorbike for the 10 km trip to Eremon to collect my Peace Corps friend Leahy, who was coming to stay. I was petrified riding the Yamaha at the best of times and driving with her, her luggage and her five-week old puppy was pretty tricky, as I tried to swerve the worst of the bumps and one random cow.

'Give us your money!'

I emergency stopped, almost unseating the poor puppy, as four large men jumped into the road, brandishing machetes.

'Give us your money,' they shouted – it was in Dagaare, but it felt like *give us your money* – and they waved their machetes again.

Then I clocked the harvested maize along the side of the road. These men with machetes weren't murderers, they were enterprising farmers hoping to extract a spontaneous road tax from a couple of nasalpog.

'No,' I cried and sped off in disgust. The farmers, I guess, sheepishly resumed their day job, but I shook all the way to Lawra. There, I attempted to report it to the police, which, if nothing else, gave the officers a laugh.

In some ways, the third incident was the worst. After two days of puppy sacrifice and machete marauders, I had a much-needed Friday night at Las Palmas with Leahy, Makum and Nasir until the beer took its toll and I headed to the urinal.

Nearly midnight, I shoved my Nokia in my mouth so I could pee by the light of the torch, and promptly dropped it. With my trousers round my knees and in the pitch dark, I groped around and encountered something squashy. I had put my left thumb in a human poo.

I put the three horrible things out of my mind and focused on the several marvellous ones. That's me, a sack half full kind of girl.

'This is incredible.'

I was at Karbo Primary with Nasir, two weeks after the PTA meeting. 'This is flipping incredible.'

What had been a derelict outhouse on some scrubby ground behind the school was now a building site buzzing with activity. Women carried weighty pans of stones on their heads, men laid foundations and there was a sense of purpose, of men *and* women pulling together for the common cause.

Despite renovating an existing structure, there was lots to do. Bushes grew out of crumbling walls, there was no roof, no chimney, no fireplace to cook on. Lots to do and they were doing it, those mothers and fathers, bringing a kitchen to life. One man took a break from plastering to lean out of a half-finished window, his eager Dagaare telling me all I needed to know.

'He is very happy,' translated Nasir.

'It's brilliant.' I turned to the man. 'I'm very happy too.'

Nasir left me chatting with the workers while he nipped off on the bike and when I ran out of Dagaare and sign language I just watched in awe as they laboured in the heat. Mary Karbo wandered over from the school.

'My PTA are building a beautiful kitchen, Sarah. And then it will be over to you.'

Nasir came back with jerry cans of pito and handed it out in a calabash (half a large seedpod) as a thank you and for sustenance. A few of the men gathered round, and from their gestures I could see they were pointing out the kitchen's layout, where the fire would go, where the children would queue. Nasir asked a question and there was much nodding in response.

Until then, I suspect, Nasir had been there to assist me, to indulge *me* in an endeavour that would probably never come off. Now, there in the sunshine, with the clatter of stones and slurp of pito and voices of enthusiastic parents ringing out, somewhere in his mind's eye, he saw children with bowls of food and classrooms with attentive pupils. And I knew, in that moment, Nasir had started to believe.

'I like to see the community working together.' We were cooking spicy spaghetti back in my kitchen. 'It is coming from the people and I think it will succeed.'

He spooned tomato paste into the pasta, half lost in thought. 'What I am saying is … what I am thinking is … what I think is … unless the children learn, they will always be hand-to-mouth. Praying for rain. A few groundnuts from hunger.' He hesitated, searching for his words. 'They cannot learn if they are weak. An empty sack cannot stand.'

It wasn't the last time I heard him say it – *an empty sack cannot stand* – but it was the first. The first time he took ownership of the project, the first time he tested his own wisdom and conveyed the simplicity of what we were doing with his own exquisite words.

An empty sack cannot stand. No-one has ever said it better.

FIFTEEN

TA-DA!

The moment I opened my laptop, I heard a familiar cry from outside.

An Announcement

Nov 1, 2012

As I write this, Richmond is shouting "Sister Sarah, I am TIRED" at the top of his voice as he repeatedly walks around my house. What he means is he's hungry. Of course, I will feed him, how could I not? Though how on earth can I feed them all??? I try, but it's expensive and completely not sustainable.

Luckily, I have a long-term solution. I'm going to open a school kitchen, employ cooks and pay for food. My amazing family and I are setting up Action Through Enterprise, a charity which will focus on school feeding as one of its primary objectives. Website coming soon ...

Richmond's lament – a month after harvest, with groundnuts packed away and mangoes no longer dropping from trees – was a timely reminder of why the charity was needed. At least now I had a plan, to feed not just Richmond, but all the Richmonds.

With rice bubbling, I fiddled with the dongle, uploaded my blog and checked – as I'd already done a hundred times that day – whether the website was live. My heart stopped when I saw it. I gave Richmond his food, grabbed the laptop and cycled into town to show Nasir.

NDC! NDC!

I turned onto the main road and was almost knocked over by a swarm of young men who whizzed past on motorbikes, banners flapping behind them, flush with campaign fever for the upcoming General Election.

I'd first spotted election activity out in Bagri, a hand-painted sign proclaiming *No Light, No Vote* and then a work crew smoothing out the worst craters in the road – a literal last-ditch attempt by the incumbent party to fulfil at least one pledge made four years earlier.

Soon after, on the outskirts of Lawra town, a massive billboard was erected, with a beaming face pasted across it promising one of the big words, *HOPE/ VISION/ CHANGE.* And that wasn't all they were offering. Activists from one of the parties had been doling out T-shirts and sachets of industrial strength gin to anyone who might vote for them.

Support NDC! Support the President!

Now, cycling headlong into what felt like a million cheering, singing, dancing people, I vaguely recalled VSO's advice to keep a low profile during the campaign in case things got edgy. Ghana had the reputation of being one of the strongest democracies in Africa and it certainly felt pretty vivid that afternoon. Regardless, there was no way I was hiding behind my louvres any more, not for anyone.

NDC! The President is coming! The President is coming to Lawra!

In the distance, I could make out the National Democratic Congress Presidential cavalcade, all open-top black jeeps, sidelights flashing as MPs cars always did, and then the crowd surged, carrying me with it.

'Excuse me … sorry … could I just …'

NDC! NDC!

I was bounced towards a drinks' stand made from an old container, somewhere I often stopped for guava juice, and I abandoned the bike, squeezed myself onto a bench in the corner and was sighing with relief when I got an angry finger in my face.

'You are not part of our democracy,' yelled the woman on the end of the finger. 'Go home. You don't have a vote, you are not welcome today.'

I was shocked. It was the first time anyone in Lawra had been hostile to me and no-one – not even those roadside machete bandits – had felt so threatening. I reached for my phone.

Within minutes, Nasir had whisked me away.

'Sarah, you must be careful,' he told me once we were safely home. 'There are high emotions. It's a dangerous time.'

'I know.' I inserted my dongle. 'But I wanted you to see this. Ta-da!'

The website was magnificent. Our name, *action, enterprise*, purposeful and bursting with momentum. The inspiring logo, the red A incorporating the shape of Africa, the green T and golden E, the colours of the Ghanaian flag. The vibrant photographs of children at our SNAP group and the building at Karbo Primary, now almost a kitchen. It was official. Action Through Enterprise – ATE – had arrived.

While I was admiring the website, Nasir watched Shilea, who was parading around with her tail in the air.

'We must keep the dog indoors. With our eye on her.'

'Because of the election?'

'Not the election. That dog is looking for trouble.'

Nov 2, 2012

Shilea is in season. It's ridiculous given she is 7 months old. Aside from flirting with two male dogs next door, she is moody, aggressive and agitated. It's like living with a teenager. Last week, she followed me to town, sat down in the shade and refused to walk. I had to carry her, in blistering sunshine. This caused quite a commotion, as I shouted 'Baa biere' at the gathering crowds, which means something like 'dog sick'. White people carrying dogs and screaming in inaccurate Dagaare is apparently very funny.

I'm so not ready to be a grandmother.

It wasn't long before we spotted Shilea's swollen nipples and expanding belly. I panicked.

'I can't look after a litter of puppies,' I said to Nasir. 'How could I protect them? They'll end up as angola!'

'Sarah, I will give you the one hundred per cent efficient way to make the dog miscarry. Every day, you must feed her rice and beans. Every day.'

I didn't see how it could work, but dutifully initiated Shilea's new diet and crossed everything, not really believing either would bring the desired result.

Still very much pregnant – and extremely grumpy – Shilea plonked herself under my chair at the front of the Teachers' Resource Centre for the inaugural meeting of BizATE, the charity's business programme.

Nasir stepped forward to address the twenty aspiring entrepreneurs who'd made it this far. 'Setting up a business is not for one month to collapse. You are setting up your life and today we will help you achieve that.'

This was a critical moment for us, the first test of our plan to fund sustainable businesses. Dad and I had drawn up a questionnaire, Nasir had roped in his distant cousin, the impressive Gabriel, who worked in development, and I'd spent ages culling a Peace Corps training manual and googling *business for beginners*. For a primary school teacher from Ramsbury, I felt reasonably well-prepared.

'Question number one,' began Nasir, 'what makes a successful enterprise?'

Silence.

'Anybody?'

Eventually, one of the Zambo weavers spoke.

'I will work hard.'

'That is good, very good. Can anyone tell us what skills they have to bring success?'

An egg seller raised her hand. 'I have the skill of working hard.'

Nasir and I exchanged glances, his face saying, *I think this is going to take a while.*

I'd scheduled half an hour for that session and three hours later, as the lady with the lunch rice set up in the corner, we were still going.

'Can you explain how you will make a profit?' Gabriel asked a groundnut farmer, who replied with a bewildered shake of the head. Then followed a long and frustrating exchange.

'He says he will make a profit,' Gabriel translated, 'because he will work hard.'

And that was how it went all day. What were distinctly separate questions to us sounded like the same question to them. It wasn't that Dagaare didn't have the business terminology, it was that everyone's understanding of commerce was on totally different pages. Even Nasir with his empathy and Gabriel with his expertise were unable to find the right language, especially with such a large group and so many different types of businesses. I looked at the questionnaire I'd laboured over and realised quite how wrong we'd got it.

'Sarah, I suggest we call them back tomorrow,' said Nasir.

'You think?' Under my chair, Shilea growled.

The next day was much better. We went through everything methodically, one-to-one, agreeing on individual mentoring as the way forward. By the end of the session, I had a pile of business plans to type up for Dad.

'Fancy a beer?' I asked Nasir as we packed up.

'Thank you, Sarah. I would like that.'

But instead of steering the bike towards Las Palmas, Nasir pulled up in a clearing where an election rally was taking place. The next thing I knew, he was up on stage with fifty people, shouting, chanting slogans, waving his fist in the air. It was a whole new side to him, a public side, and I was surprised.

'I didn't know you were involved with politics,' I said later, at the spot.

'I am not so involved, but a friend invited me. Sarah, are you satisfied with how it went today?'

'We got there. In the end.'

'We are learning how much we will need to learn.' And with those wise words, Nasir clinked for more beer.

We both found our feet during those frantic, fledgling weeks, as we raced around putting things in place for the launch of ATE, making mistakes, learning from them, loving it. I watched as Nasir emerged from the shadows into the spotlight, his confidence growing, as mine did too. Undaunted by election crowds or workshop setbacks or how much we *didn't* know, the charity's momentum became our momentum, and once we were off, it felt as if we could do anything.

'Miss Sarah, are you ready?' A policeman shouted across the roundabout. 'I have been holding these cars for more than one hour.'

When I arrived in Ghana I'd been afraid of everything, including the traffic. Now, I was stopping it. Me, and two hundred and fifty teenagers in red T-shirts proclaiming *LOVE LIFE, STOP AIDS.*

We'd just marched through town to the beat of a twenty-man drumming band for a flash mob to raise awareness on World AIDS Day. Me and Leahy had spent weeks working up a routine, creating a Ghanaian/Western megamix, rehearsing with youth clubs and schools and negotiating with the authorities for our traffic-stopping performance.

'We're ready.'

I waved to Nasir, who cranked his speaker up to eleven. Celine Dion's *My Heart Will Go On* boomed across the roundabout and we went into our moves, in unison, full of smiles. Frustrated drivers began honking their support, hundreds of stunned onlookers clapped along and Patience bopped round her egg stall. I was in my element. We finished with Shakira's *Waka Waka (This Time For Africa)*, throwing our arms in the air and shouting *GET TESTED!*

'Don't have sex! Use a condom!' Nasir bellowed through a megaphone, before leading us to the Community Centre where he and I set an example and were the first to take HIV tests.

When four news websites covered the event, I was thrilled to be quoted. Even more thrilled that Nasir was too.

Nasir, a community educator from Lawra said: 'On Saturday plenty of residents were given a free HIV test. To reduce infection, we must encourage more people to get tested and know their HIV status'.

Community educator. I liked that.

A few days after the flash mob, the rice and beans kicked in. Poor Shilea. After I wiped up the mess, I gave her a hug and we settled down for a much-needed quiet weekend.

Voting is on Friday, so I'm grounded by VSO for three whole days. I'm planning a Harry Potter movie marathon.

Love xxx

SIXTEEN

MERRY

We had a trying day at the bank.

Nasir and I went first thing, past the mirrored exterior, past the two armed guards and into a different world, where a TV in one corner blasted Ghanaian news, a unit in another blasted cold air and the staff behind the counter wore suits.

'Shall I do it?' I asked after a fractious half hour.

We were there to collect the money Mum had sent over for the business grants and Nasir, as the Ghana resident receiving the transfer, had insisted on doing the paperwork.

'Sarah, I am handling it.' He checked and rechecked his phone for Mum's details, carefully inserting his own address at the Chief's Palace, writing everything in those little boxes with a pen chained to the counter. 'I need your passport,' he barked, and I handed it to him for the third time. Such a palaver.

Form finally completed, we sat on plastic chairs in a zigzag line, Shilea sliding under each seat in turn as we progressed up the queue. Thank goodness for air conditioning, it was lunchtime before we were called.

'Please, I have a transfer to withdraw GH¢5000.' Words I doubt Nasir ever dreamed he'd say and there was no mistaking his pride, that he was a man withdrawing so much money and I trusted him to be that man.

The teller painstakingly verified the form and counted out a wodge of cash, which we recounted. And looking at the money in Nasir's strong hands, it all felt very real.

'Sign here, please.'

Over the next few days, Nasir, Gabriel and I rode round Lawra district disbursing grants to nineteen businesses, starting with the Zambo weavers.

We gave them the pep talk, *this money is to build your enterprise, you must invest your profits, buy health insurance for your children.*

We gave them the warning, *it is not a gift, do not spend it on food, do not give it to anyone else. Break these rules and we will reclaim everything.*

Then we gave them a pen.

'Sign here,' said Nasir. 'A cross is OK.'

The three women looked bemused. One, her baby in one hand, fumbled the pen in the other. Signing a contract – even with a squiggle – takes forever if you're not use to holding a pen.

Gabriel held up his thumb. 'Next time, we bring an inkpad.'

Signatures aside, it was a productive day. They showed us the broken loom they planned to get fixed and demonstrated a complex contraption used to organise their colourful threads. The Zambo weavers were raring to go.

Nasir gave a few last words, the women nodding solemnly in response.

'What did you say?'

'I tell them, be open, be honest. Tell us the good, tell us the bad. You are human, you can make a mistake and you have to be forgiven and we move on.'

'Well, let's hope they don't make *too* many mistakes.'

'Sarah,' he said, touching my arm, 'everyone makes mistakes.'

I thought of the ink pad we needed to purchase and took his point.

'And now, we present the money.'

I dug into my bag and retrieved the GH¢600 allocated to the Zambo team. Less than £200 and for those women, life-changing.

'Smile, everyone,' called Gabriel, taking photos for the website. I fanned out the cedis and posed with the weavers like they were lottery winners, which they sort of were.

One afternoon, on the way back from dispensing grants in Eremon, Nasir drove past the Karbo kitchen, now finished and ready to open in January. I could practically smell groundnut stew in the air.

We headed to Las Palmas for a celebratory drink.

'A Club, a Striker and a Fanta,' Nasir told the gangly youth who took our order.

In the end, we made a night of it, Nasir eating angola, me drinking Striker (a *really* strong gin) to forget it was dog meat. Nasir waved for the bill and the gangly youth assessed bottles, sachets, plates and meat bones, instantly calculating the bill in his head.

'Is that right?' I was amazed at his speed.

Nasir laughed. 'Kanyiri is a genius.'

Once Kanyiri redid his addition – quite unnecessarily as it turned out – I handed over the money and the most generous tip I could manage. 'Impressive. How old are you?'

'I am fourteen. I like mental arithmetic.' He put the tip in his pocket. 'Thank you so much.'

'That boy is very determined,' Nasir told me as we climbed on the bike. 'Very diligent, clever. When his father died, the family dwelling was lost and the mother went to Kumasi with a baby brother, to find money. Now Kanyiri works, attends

school and cares for another brother. They live over there ...'
He pointed to a one room structure behind Las Palmas. 'I wish
someone would believe in him. In Lawra, it is a problem until
someone has belief in you. I know that too.'

It was a sobering thought, all those impressive people
who needed a leg up and a vote of confidence. Not totally
sobering though, what with the gin. Maybe one day we could
do something for Kanyiri, but that night, what I remember is
driving home from Las Palmas, hands on Nasir's waist, leaning
back on the motorbike, feeling free.

A few days later, Nasir and I did a follow up with the small
businesses. The Zambo women had already got the loom fixed,
their toes pushed through metal rings operating the pedals,
weaving like there was no tomorrow. Madam Madi was also
busy, her compound piled with shiny raffia.

But in Lawra town, where we'd organised a few traders into
a loose support network, the group had fallen out.

'Stupid man, stupid man.' Lady, a rice seller, was spitting
feathers.

'What happened?'

'Gilbert ran away, stupid man. To Burkina Faso, to bring
goats and sheep over the river, all illegal. Here ...' She put her
hand in her pocket. 'Three hundred cedis. We chased him
down and he is no longer in our group.'

More lessons learnt, and the first of what would be many
dramas. Yet the sound of the Zambo women happily sharing
their one working loom and the sight of Madame Madi hawking
her baskets to market made me feel we were on the right track.

Riding from Zambo to Kuoli to Eremon, delivering cheer in the form of non-recoupable business grants, wasn't my usual build-up to Christmas, but I loved it.

Of course, I *really* loved Christmas in Ramsbury, my greetings card English village. It was magical, the decorating of the tree in front of The Bell, the candle-lit carols, the Nativity play at The Winchcombe School, the festive jumpers.

Christmas in Lawra was *not* magical. Or maybe it was, somewhere, but I couldn't see it, so I'd decided to make my own festive fun and hold a Nativity at the Catholic Church. For weeks, me and fifty children from Karbo Primary rehearsed carols and a Nativity play, not easy since they'd never heard the songs before and my Dagaare didn't run to *lowly cattle shed*.

On Christmas Eve, we assembled at the church, excited children in white T-shirts, Nasir with his speaker, two hundred parents.

The carols were uplifting if imperfect. My abiding memory is of Celina singing her heart out, radiant in white, relishing all eyes on her, especially her mum's. For many parents, it was the first time they'd seen their children twinkling in the spotlight.

I twinkled too, conducting the choir and prancing about in reindeer antlers, which I *may* have found in the VSO house though it's not impossible I'd brought them with me, I don't quite recall.

'And Mary and Joseph got on a donkey,' proclaimed Judith, and a surge of pride washed over me. I wasn't under the tree outside The Bell and I had no mulled wine, yet with children carolling and the community gathered, there was nowhere I'd rather be.

After the concert, I held a party to celebrate Nasir's *something* birthday – as with many in the Upper West, there seemed to be some confusion about exactly what year he was born – and I was pleased to put a smile on his face. He'd recently told me that Kendey and Bie had moved back to Kendey's family home in Kumasi and I knew he missed his boy desperately. It was the time of the year for family, and those of us apart from ours had to stick together. I gathered friends around me, put twigs in a box as a makeshift tree and along with my cards from England and home-made streamers, it was beginning to feel a lot like Christmas.

On Christmas morning, I woke to the chime of goats bleating outside my bedroom window. At the bottom of the bed was Shilea, a stocking from Leahy (who was staying over) and a small pile of gifts from England. Memories of idyllic Christmases came flooding back, of my parents as brilliant hosts with a fridgeful of wine, another of food, a cupboard erupting with nibbles and mountains of presents, which we'd unwrap and celebrate one by one.

In Lawra, I sat in bed and opened my parcels with Shilea, then hung out in the kitchen with Leahy and Nasir, preparing jollof rice, sen sen and a roasted guinea fowl. Leahy and I had spent hours – and a fortune – buying potatoes in Wa and we topped them with precious butter and popped them in the oven for a treat that was really more for us than our guests, Celina, Judith and Jeremiah.

'Sister Sarah, Sister Sarah.' Celina's mother had popped in, smiling with those same high cheekbones as her daughter. She presented me with a rare packet of chocolate biscuits. 'For you.'

It wasn't the chattiest of lunches, but I think people enjoyed themselves. The Ghanaians left once the meal was over, Nasir on to the next thing as he so often was. Leahy and I retired to the veranda with a carton of cold red wine and the chocolate biscuits and watched Shilea chase the passing goats as the sun went down.

On Boxing Day in Lawra, as custom would have it, everyone gets drunk. Keen to embrace the local culture, I headed with Gabriel and Nasir to Las Palmas, where Kanyiri administered beer and gin until we'd properly upheld the tradition.

'You know what we should do?' Gabriel swigged his bottle. 'We should accompany you to Accra, myself and Nasir.' I was travelling south the next day for a family holiday before bringing Mum and Dad to Lawra for the opening of the Karbo kitchen.

'That is the right thing,' said Nasir. 'We will come with you on the bus.'

How could I refuse? 'I can't afford your tickets though.'

'That's OK,' said Gabriel, who was relatively well-paid. 'I will get them.'

We clinked bottles and arranged to meet at the trotro station the following morning. I was too merry to think about it at the time, but my two worlds were about to collide.

SEVENTEEN

BUMP

IF I SEE YOU AGAIN, I WILL KILL YOU!!!!

A Nigerian soap blared from the coach's speakers, as it would all the way to Accra, reassuring me, if nothing else, that the driver might not fall asleep at the wheel. Up front sat a security guard with a gun and, if I glanced to the rear, there was my own security, Nasir and Gabriel in the only seats they could get, Nasir – T-shirt, faux leather jacket – rocking the bodyguard chic. Though, as ever, he took his role as minder a little too seriously, fuming when we got to Accra bus station because, apparently, it wasn't OK for me to go alone to the loo at four in the morning.

'There she is! Karen!'

We'd headed to the airport to meet my sister (who'd flown out a couple of days before Mum and Dad) and – despite coming off a night flight – she oozed freshness and glamour. After fourteen hours on the bus, goodness knows what I oozed, or what Karen made of the two men I had in tow, both looking rather out of place, one twitching with anxiety.

'Sarah, Karen, this way.' Nasir led us through the throng of touting taxi drivers, negotiated a deal in urgent Twi and soon we were in a cab on the way to the coast.

Big Milly's was a popular volunteer hang-out with a low key tropical vibe, an hour from Accra and it felt like paradise. Dotted around the grounds were thatched one-bedroom chalets, and I dived under my shower, looking up to see there was no roof, just a banana tree for shade.

Suitably restored, Karen and I ate fresh fruit and fried eggs in the sea view restaurant and watched fishermen bring in the nets aided by a shoal of children. I'd offered to buy breakfast for Nasir and Gabriel but they preferred the familiar flavour of banku (another dumpling) and spicy pepe, and were down on the beach, fingers red from sauce. As I poured my third coffee, they edged nervously into the restaurant.

'Sarah, we have come to say goodbye,' said Nasir.

'At least have a coffee.'

'I think we must leave now. Karen, it was a pleasure to meet you.'

We had an awkward, bumpy hug, and he was gone. Next day he texted to say he was home and Shilea was OK, and it felt good to know they were both waiting for me back in Lawra.

'You do realise,' said Karen, 'that you smile when he texts.'

'Don't be silly.' I focused on the menu in Big Milly's shady bar. 'Now, what are we having?

Karen and I had two fantastic days, chilling with Leela and some other VSO volunteers. On the third morning, a taxi swept into the sandy forecourt and Mum and Dad got out. And there we were, the whole Gardner clan, in Ghana.

We took the taxi along the coastal road, where everyone drove a hundred miles an hour and lorries veered wildly to avoid potholes. At one point, I got the driver to stop for me to spend a perilous penny by the side of the road.

'It's OK.' My family looked horrified. 'Everyone does it.' Then I noticed a trader weaving fearlessly through speeding traffic and bought pure water sachets, showing my folks how to bite off the corner and suck.

We did New Year at the exotic Elmina Bay Resort, where we ran into fellow volunteer James and his family. When they expressed an interest in supporting ATE, I retreated to my balcony and composed a persuasive email, attaching a photo of some Karbo children. It was my first attempt at fundraising from people I didn't know well and by the time we were back in Lawra they'd taken out a standing order. It was milestone.

Karen flew home and my parents hired a private car for our journey north so we arrived in style, via Kintampo Waterfalls, a night in Tamale and an outing to Mole (Ghana's biggest national park) for the elephants. Nasir and Shilea were waiting.

'This is where I live. And there's Nasir.'

While I busied myself with Shilea, Nasir, self-assured on home turf, enthusiastically shook my parents' hands.

'Mum and Dad,' he said, which I thought was maybe *a bit much*, though he later told me it was a mark of respect. 'Welcome to Lawra.'

That first night Nasir made sen sen (now my favourite) and we shared a convivial meal – my parents with forks, me and Nasir, fingers – knowing we had a momentous week to come. Opening Karbo kitchen, inspecting new businesses, me showing off my Lawra life.

'Sister Sarah! Sister Sarah!'

It was the unmistakeable call of Celina, Judith and Jeremiah, turning up for their dinner. I ran to greet them.

Reality has a way of striking when you least expect it. Actually, this was *two* realities. In front of me, children I loved, with threadbare clothes and hungry faces, skinny again now we were into dry season. Behind me, the chatter of my parents, the chink of cutlery, the memory of a glorious holiday. And let's be clear,

I thought my parents were amazing for even *being* in Lawra, but so far their trip consisted of a posh hotel, a comfortable car, delicious food, cold beers and a warm reception from Nasir, with the odd urinal Mum had gamely taken in her stride. One look at Celina's sunken cheeks and I decided this might be more reality than they were ready for.

'Stay there.' I grabbed some bananas and rice to take away. 'Sorry, we've had a long journey.' They didn't mind, Jeremiah contentedly unpeeling a banana as they sloped off into the dark.

Of course, I couldn't shield my parents forever but, for one night only, they slept at peace, not quite knowing how tough life was for the people asleep around them.

Next morning, that peace was shattered. I'd told the children to spread the word about three huge suitcases of clothes Mum and Dad had brought with them, donations from school assemblies in Ramsbury and Marlborough. As Dad finished his stand-up bath and Mum sipped her coffee, I opened the front door to discover word had indeed been spread. When Mum joined me, a hundred barefoot children in rags stared back.

It took two days to distribute the clothes. I managed the flow, inviting the boys and girls inside, two by two, while Mum and Dad measured them and found outfits among the piles. Nasir translated and guided the children, so gentle as they pulled tops over swollen stomachs and trousers over spindly legs. There was a pretty dress for Celina, a blue shirt for Jeremiah, a skirt and top for Judith. One boy loved his fluorescent green trainers. Another girl shyly twirled a flowery skirt. Children who'd walked in dirty and afraid, walked out looking gorgeous.

It was overwhelming for my parents, and in the moments

when Mum became visibly shaken, Nasir was gentle with her too. We kept back some clothes for the SNAP families, taking photos at Patience's stall as she joyfully received the blue dress I'd saved for Michelle. Then we bought eggs and pepe and nibbled them on our way to the spot for a never-more-needed beer.

Nasir did the ordering, very much in charge – as he was throughout that week – and I felt such admiration and gratitude for everything he was doing. Then, randomly, don't know why, I was staring at his hands. And I couldn't take my eyes off them, those hands that had greeted my parents and helped children try on clothes and cooked for us and clinked for beer, and I thought, *God, I fancy those hands.*

It wasn't much, and I quickly forgot about it. But it wasn't nothing.

After a heart-lifting SNAP meeting, we embarked on visits to small business owners – SBOs, in our charity lingo. Dad went with Nasir on a borrowed bike and Mum gripped on for dear life behind me on the Yamaha, until we juddered up a steep slope to Kuoli and she slipped right off the back. Fortunately, I'd been going *really* slowly and she wasn't hurt.

A few more bumps down the road, we arrived at a mud compound.

'Welcome, welcome,' said farmer Francis, four children darting round his feet. Beside him, his wife Betty, a petty trader, was cradling twins. Industrious and driven – as evidenced by neat piles of tools, groundnuts and bulk-bought products – they were the only couple who'd got two ATE grants, one for each of their businesses.

'Let me show you how I've used the money.' Francis led us to the field by the side of the property. 'I used to have one acre for groundnuts and if the harvest was poor, it was not enough for my family to survive. With the grant, I've purchased another acre, and my children will live a good life.'

'Excellent,' said Dad. 'Now let's look at the books.'

We sat in the fierce sunlight of their central courtyard, reviewing the figures for the farm before moving on to Betty's trading of salt, sugar and Maggi stock cubes.

An hour later, we were still there.

'Dad won't let this go,' said Mum, moving to a wooden bench in the slivered shade at the edge of the courtyard. 'You'll have to let him finish.'

After another two hours, Dad was done.

'Unbelievable. She was selling at a bloody loss.'

'What?'

'Literally breaking up the packet of stock cubes and selling individual cubes at a loss.'

'This is the problem,' said Nasir. 'If someone gives them money, to them, they are earning. They don't realise it is not the same as profit. I think she realises now.'

And suddenly, I understood our struggle at the workshop, and why so many enterprises fail. And that without Dad's tenacity, Nasir's understanding and ATE's ongoing mentoring, Betty's would have done too. She raised her prices and people kept buying. Those three hours saved her business.

We bounced between failure and glory all week. When we visited the Zambo weavers, they had a full order book and a pile of exquisite woven material. In town, we were received by Madame Madi brandishing colourful baskets and a shrewd price list. She definitely understood the concept of profit.

And it was with great expectations that we called on Emilia, who I'd first met at the HIV meeting. Unusually for a young woman in Lawra, she'd been to vocational school and was a skilled seamstress, making her an ideal candidate for ATE. We'd awarded her £150 (our largest individual grant) believing if she applied herself – and medication kept her illness under control – there was every chance she would make something of her life. That day, however, she stumbled painfully across the family compound to greet us.

After introductions, Dad got down to business.

'Emilia, have you bought your sewing machine? Can I see it?'

There was a short exchange between Emilia and Nasir.

'She says the man is delivering it tomorrow. There is nothing to see today.'

Nasir arranged another visit and we probably would have left it at that had not Emilia's father ushered us, with great show, into a storeroom and dragged a sack of rice to one side. Behind it was a dusty, clapped-out sewing machine that had obviously been there for years.

'He is now saying *this* is the machine she has bought,' said Nasir. 'There is no other machine coming and the grant is gone.'

Dad sighed. 'I think they need to get their stories straight.'

It was awful, standing in their compound, Emilia flagging, her father trying to explain away the disappearance of hundreds of cedis. Calmly, quietly, Nasir got to the truth.

'As you can see, her sickness has become very bad and the father says it is an investment, so she is strong for work ...'

'What's an investment?' said Mum. 'I'm sorry Nasir, what's going on?'

'She gave her money to the juju man. This man is a healer, a traditional healer. She paid him to make the disease go away.'

'And how does he do that?'

'He has sacrificed a sheep.'

I was furious. Furious and dumbfounded and desperately sad, that anyone could squander such a golden opportunity. Maybe because he understood the culture – maybe because a bit of him thought the juju man might indeed cure her – Nasir was less angry, more accepting. For my parents, it was a brutal reality check. And for Emilia, it was the end of her chance, at least with us.

One afternoon, with Mum and Dad napping after an exhausting trek to Eremon, Nasir drove up to my house with a smile on his face and little Bie in front of him on the bike. I was elated.

'What a lovely surprise.'

'I wanted him to meet Mum and Dad.'

We had a cheerful evening at the spot, Bie in my arms, Mum playing with him, Nasir and Dad deep in conversation. Of course, I didn't think about the one person who wasn't there – Kendey, who had made the ten-hour bus journey from Kumasi with a toddler because Nasir had asked her to.

The following morning, escorted by Nasir and Gabriel, we drove to Karbo for the climax of Mum and Dad's trip, the launch of the school kitchen. After months of building, fundraising, recruiting cooks, buying equipment and sourcing food, we were finally ready to feed some children.

Smoke poured out of the repurposed building and inside three cooks stirred steaming cauldrons of rice and beans with a long stick. Standing over them, hands on hips, was Mary Karbo.

'Smells good, yes?'

One of the cooks emerged through the billows with armfuls of bowls, which she piled on the steps.

'The children will queue here, starting with the youngest,' said Mary. 'They have been told to bring bowls, but we have a few if anyone forgets.'

Soon, parents began arriving, and just before eleven Dabuo from the PTA climbed the steps of the kitchen to address a crowd of two hundred.

'We are here today thanks to the generosity of Sarah and Charles Gardner and the wife, Philippa. They have faith in your children, and now your children will grow and be strong and will learn.'

Next, Mary stepped forward to speak, pulling the three of us with her and clasping Dad's hand, which she held throughout. 'These people from England have brought a dream to life, the dream that Karbo Primary would be a feeding school. This family has made that dream come true.'

And then the lunch bell rang. It had never sounded sweeter.

Beginning with the kindergarten, the pupils followed their teachers out of the main building, hundreds of bedraggled children, some with shiny new trainers, queuing for their first school lunch. And they seemed terrified. Terrified, sad and underfed, like every pity-messaging emergency appeal you've ever seen. Then I noticed something else.

Almost none of them had brought a bowl.

'Mary?' She'd spotted it too and was already shouting instructions. A few dozen children ran off, some cycled on rickety bikes, towards the houses on the main road.

'The ones who live nearby, I've sent them to bring bowls.'

Within minutes, the first of the children were back, then more, a cavalry armed with aged Pyrex, calabashes, tomato tins and pan lids, four or five apiece.

'Why they didn't they bring them in the first place?'

Mary patted my arm. 'Because when a stranger promises food, I am sorry to tell you that they don't believe them.'

One by one, Pyrex and pan lids were filled and with each spoonful, a little of their distrust faded. All around, children ate. Some in groups, others on their own, still, perhaps, not quite believing no-one would take it away. We fed three hundred and fifty children that lunchtime, and when Mary put her arms round Mum, Dad and me and gave her heartfelt thanks, I had to fight back the tears. And yes, I did think we'd done well, but other than the money, we hadn't done anything. They had done it, the community, the parents, the cooks, Mary and Dabuo, they had fed their children.

One of the cooks came over with rice and beans and (though tasty) it was a bowl of food Dad instantly regretted. He prised himself from the clasps of Mary Karbo and got Gabriel to drive him home, just in time.

Mum and I stayed, watching the children lick their bowls clean before rinsing them in a bucket and going for lessons, bellies full, minds ready to learn.

Once everyone had recovered their emotions (and their stomach), Nasir took us to Lawra Methodist School, where his father was head teacher.

'You have come, that is wonderful.' Karlley was exuberant, engaging and immediately I could see where Nasir got his magnetism. The man had charm, chatting easily with Mum and Dad, showing off his school. Then it came.

'I hear you've been spending time with my Small Boy son.'

Quick as a flash, Mum responded. 'We don't think he's a small boy. We think Nasir's rather impressive.'

I thought my Mum was rather impressive. Both my parents were, actually, and not just for defending Nasir. The trip had been a rollercoaster, gruelling and fulfilling and shocking every single day, and probably a lot more than they thought they'd signed up for. On their last night, we threw a spontaneous party. They deserved some fun, for Mum to have a dance and for us to witness with amazement my Dad's attempt at azonto.

I was proud of Nasir too, who'd been brilliant all week, guiding, hosting, connecting with my folks, and of course, his immeasurable role in everything we'd achieved. Seeing him handle those sensitive situations with businesses and children, and now dancing merrily with my parents, I could scarcely recognise the nervous man from Big Milly's who'd given me that clumsy hug.

'This is the Charles Gardner shuffle,' laughed Nasir as Dad randomly punched the air, and we all laughed and punched the air, partly to tease my Dad, mostly because punching the air felt right. We had done it. Five months after deciding to set up a charity, fifteen small businesses were trading, thirty families with disabled children were supported and hundreds of school pupils were nourished and learning.

'This is how he dances.' And Nasir made a fist with his lovely big hands and punched the air.

EIGHTEEN

SAFELY HOME

I travelled to Accra with my parents, savouring every last minute of their company, not to mention a night in a hotel, a nice glass of wine and a large pizza. Saying goodbye was horrible, but I knew I'd soon be flying home, into the arms of endless wine and pizza and (yes, I was still vaguely hoping) the boyfriend.

First, there was work to be done, and I had a hideous time in Accra trying to officially register the charity, queuing for hours in various government corridors and struggling with countless forms, returning the next day and the day after for more queues and forms until I finally met an official who said he could help. That's when things went a bit strange and I ended up at his house, hanging curtains, which, given my track record, was not the worst possible outcome. Predictably, he wanted a bribe, and I remember eventually opening my wallet and shouting *I have no money*.

It made me wish Nasir was there, and I wished it again at the bus station when I discovered there were no tickets for a whole week because schools were going back and the place was overrun with students. My only option was a jolty trotro, where I had a rolled-up carpet jammed into my neck, chickens pecking around my feet and I tried not to drink any water because we never stopped for a loo break and I wasn't bold enough to ask for one. If Nasir had been there, he would have made the driver stop.

After a night in a grotty hotel halfway up Ghana, I got a second trotro to Wa and then another to Lawra, where I arrived at the bus station in the dark. Nasir was waiting.

He drove us to my place, fed me rice, put his arm round me and we watched a movie together on my laptop, each with a headphone in one ear. I was home.

I woke up in agony. Two days of bladder abuse had caused the most excruciating infection and I could barely stand. Nasir gently delivered me to hospital – where I endured an invasive procedure with a dusty speculum – and then delivered me back again. I crawled into bed with Shilea and didn't move for a week, while Nasir fetched juice and bananas and kept the fridge stocked with water.

As I laid under the mosquito net, I had time to think. In six weeks, I was due to leave, to resume my old life and my old job, and the challenge of how to juggle teaching *and* fundraising and not mess both of them up threw me into utter panic. After a year as a useless volunteer, what if I failed at this too? The prospect was more unbearable than the pain in my bladder, and once I was well enough I emailed the head teacher at The Winchcombe School, thanked him for his support, told him I'd be available for supply teaching and quit my job.

Oh, the freedom, the privilege, to make that decision, to be twenty-nine and walk away from a career knowing I had parents who would support me. I'm not sure, then, if I registered how lucky I was, but I see it now. Leaps into the unknown are a lot easier with a safety net like that.

I dreaded leaving Lawra, if I'm honest. Especially leaving Nasir. We'd become so close and worked so intimately, I couldn't bear the thought of not always being around him, riding out to the villages together, talking about ATE.

One thing I was pleased about was the decision we'd made to pay him (advocated very strongly by the charity's other trustee, the experienced Peter Maple). Nasir had done so much – an incomprehensible, indispensable amount – out of both loyalty to me and a commitment to the work, and we'd reached the point where he needed financial recognition, particularly now, with me going. We couldn't afford a lot, but that first time he cashed his MoneyGram was an important moment for ATE and for Nasir.

During those last few weeks, I raced around visiting businesses, attended an emotional SNAP meeting – horrendous saying goodbye to Patience and the others – and cycled over to Karbo, pretending to inspect the kitchen but really just watching the children tuck into banku and okra soup, getting stronger every day. Already, school attendance was up and Olivia told me she could see the difference in her pupils and their work. I took lots of empowering photos, organising them on my laptop as I played sad music and tried not to think about more *goodbyes*.

VSO wasn't replacing me, the right decision, I thought, given its unrealistic idea of what a volunteer could do in Lawra, and I was instructed to close down the property. I redistributed anything not on the inventory – furniture, water filters, even the map of the world – and children carried away mattresses, chairs and cooking equipment on their heads, plus a bag of my colonial linens, a throwback to those first sweaty out-of-my-depth days.

And then, I was packing my own stuff, my dusty jeans, my Ghanaian dresses – along with a pile of Madame Madi's baskets and rolls of Zambo fabric to display in Ramsbury – and as I packed I began to mentally prepare, for the night bus to Accra, for the night flight to Heathrow, for being back home.

I had a wild leaving party, my women neighbours doing azonto, Nasir, of course, providing the music with his big speaker. How I loved that big speaker, and those women, and the children, and the sachets of Striker and my special hummus, and as we danced the night away I loved everything about Lawra.

Then I saw Judith retreat to my bedroom and found her lying next to my suitcases, in tears. I sat with her, on the concrete floor, hugged her, comforted her, promised her I'd be back. But the truth was, I didn't know. And whatever happened, I would never live in the VSO house again or cook their rice every night or be so available to her and Celina and Jeremiah. That part of our lives was over.

Goodbyes on the morning I left were awful, the sight of the three children and my dog as I climbed into the nyaaba, the sense of loss, the deepest hopes they'd be OK.

Nasir and Gabriel accompanied me to Accra, Nasir wanting to protect me after my last ordeal. On the coach, as red scrub and women balancing pans and boys and girls carrying water flashed past, he started to get anxious about being in the capital. And I became excited, excited about a couple of nights in a big city, excited about the next chapter of my adventure. My mind must have already been in England, because I jumped off the bus for a night time wee without dousing myself in mozzie spray and got totally bitten.

In Accra, I suggested we *go to a fancy hotel* for a meal, but Nasir wanted takeaway fried rice in one of the bedrooms, scared I'd be mugged, nervous, maybe, to walk into *a fancy hotel*. And the more excited I became about England, the more withdrawn he was, with the unfortunate Gabriel caught in the middle. Then, while we were eating rice and watching a Nigerian film on the fuzzy TV, Nasir got a phone call that made him go silent.

'What's happened?'

'That lady, Emilia, the seamstress. She has died.'

Poor Emilia. She wasted her money on the juju man but in the end he couldn't save her, and neither could we. The three of us sat there, on the bed, devastated, and the film played on.

I met up with Leela and we spent several frustrating hours getting some paperwork sorted. But it was good to be with her, ending our tour of duty together, full circle. She'd had an outstanding placement and all of a sudden I was embarrassed by my small achievement in setting up ATE, like a consolation prize I'd presented to myself.

That evening, when our taxi came for the airport, Leela's boyfriend loaded our luggage. And instead of helping, Nasir walked off.

'Nasir, what are you doing? Aren't you coming to the airport?'

'I will miss my bus.'

'You've got time ...' But I knew he wouldn't come. We had another of our bumpy hugs and he left, back to the coach station, back to Lawra. In the taxi to the airport, with Leela enveloped in her boyfriend's arms, I felt so alone.

We sat in Departures, reminiscing about our year in Ghana, the people we'd met, the people we'd miss. Then I got a text from the once-boyfriend, *can't wait to see you*, asking for my flight number and when I pictured him at Heathrow emotion flooded over me. I didn't get an upgrade that trip and I didn't care. I didn't need feta cheese.

We got in at six the following morning, Mum standing with Leela's dad at Arrivals. Despite my hopes, there was no further reception committee. I checked my phone all the way to Ramsbury but the only message was from Nasir, making sure I'd got safely home.

NINETEEN

MISSING

Was it really a year since I'd stood in the stark Lawra bedroom, drowned in linen and out of my depth? Now, I was in my parents' spare bedroom, admiring myself in an actual mirror, slim, sun-blonde hair, sun-tanned skin, exotic, travelled, every inch the woman who'd ventured to a distant land and set up her own charity. The kind of woman who wouldn't get stood up at the airport. What a total fool I was.

Still, it was wonderful to be home. To hand my suitcases to Mum, who put everything straight in the wash (even stuff I thought was clean), to step under the power shower and let a year of dust drain away, to slip on my pink hoodie, warm from the tumble drier, to sit in the conservatory on a soft sofa, drinking filter coffee and eating toast slathered in good butter.

That evening, Dad made my favourite meal and I surrendered to a sea of Sauvignon Blanc and pasta pesto and an almond Magnum. Later, I slipped between crisp, clean sheets in a wine-pasta haze and tried to forget about the missing pieces of my life and focus on the challenge ahead.

We booked the Memorial Hall in Ramsbury and I made a poster on my laptop – *From VSO to ATE: The Journey of a Volunteer* – a *talk on my year in Ghana*. I used a picture of me with Patience's children, Michelle and Rainy, which I can see with hindsight could be categorised as *a bit white savioury*, so I'll say in my defence that I was genuinely close to those children, they weren't a prop for a photo opportunity, their mum was my friend.

We stalked the village with a hammer, pinning fliers on lampposts and getting permission to stick them in windows at the Post Office, the local shop and The Bell, where we stopped in on our way home.

Sarah, you're so brown.

Was it a life-changing experience?

I bet you learnt a lot.

It was the old crowd, welcoming me, buying drinks I couldn't afford to reciprocate. Yet, lovely as it was to see everyone, I didn't know what to say. I mean, how could I convey in a pub conversation everything I'd been through? Where to begin? That I hid behind my louvres from hungry children, that I failed at my job, that I had malaria and shit in the bed? How can you tell someone who's just bought you a large white wine that you saw your neighbours struggle for food every single day? How do you also explain that this place in remote Ghana is teeming with industrious, skilled people and is so much more than the stereotype of poverty and illness and death? In the end, it came out in a jumble of broken desks and weavers and school meals and singing, and realising none of it made any sense I gave everyone a flier.

Making sense of things was a crucial part of what I did that first week. In Ghana, I was so immersed in whatever problem was in front of me, there was no time (or maybe there was time, but no head space) to reflect on the experience. At last, sitting in my parents' conservatory, a blank document entitled *Speech* on my laptop, I fully confronted what I'd witnessed and wrestled with how to tell my story. I knew that in Lawra, people were relying on me.

I threw a welcome-myself-back dinner party on the Saturday and invited some friends over for Mum's spinach and ricotta lasagne and a preview of my talk.

'You look great,' said Laura, arriving with a bottle of champagne.

'Missed you,' said Owen, handing over a fistful of pens 'borrowed' from work. I popped open the champagne and put the contraband in the charity cupboard, already brimming with baskets, donation boxes and stuff for my Master's in Poverty Reduction, that I'd just begun.

It was bliss to be together – Laura, Owen, Nicola, Karen and a few others – though perhaps less of a gang than we'd once been, because even in one year, with a new job here, a new relationship there, everyone had moved on.

'So, this is what I've been doing,' I announced after drinks and nibbles. 'Can I get feedback at the end?' I positioned myself behind my recorder stand, which I'd draped in a Ghanaian flag, and Dad fired up the second-hand projector we'd bought off eBay.

I clicked on the first picture – me in my pink hoodie at Heathrow. 'It all began a year ago, when I set off for my adventure as a VSO volunteer in Ghana ...'

'Can I have a pen and paper?' asked my friend Becca. 'I've got notes.'

'Any sign of the lasagne?' A guest (who shall remain Nameless) scraped the last crisp crumbs from a bowl.

Mum and I had scheduled thirty minutes, but an hour later I was still speaking, repeating myself, indulging myself – there was *a lot* about how much I'd messed up – processing my experiences even as I was recounting them. My friends were getting rowdy.

'Are these the same weavers you've already told us about?' Becca was onto her third sheet of A4.

'Yes, they are.' I picked up some shimmery material and handed it to Laura. 'And this is what they've made on their new loom, the one they used the grant for, to fix it because it was broken, well one of them had a broken loom, so they share it. The fixed one, that is.'

Laura passed the material to Nameless.

'And some grants have gone to people with HIV?' asked Becca.

'A few, yes.'

'Urghh!' Nameless dropped the material, as if toxic.

'For God's sake,' said Laura, stroking the fabric. 'I think it's beautiful.'

Over dinner they ripped me to shreds. Long-winded, that was a popular opinion. Self-obsessed was another. And there was a lot of nit-picking about spelling mistakes on the slides.

'School lunches are a nice idea.' Nameless chewed on his third piece of garlic bread. 'But surely poverty is more complicated than that?'

'Poverty may be complicated, but feeding a hungry child is not.'

'I love that.' Nicola consulted her notes. 'The rest is a bit *woe-is-me.*'

'Yes, you need to change the rest,' said Karen, as only a sister could. 'Otherwise you'll bore everyone to death.'

They were right. In Lawra, I'd met so many impressive and brave people – especially the women – and I was determined their voices were heard, their experiences recognised, their skills celebrated. I rewrote the speech, knowing if ATE was to mean anything, then it couldn't all be about the blonde white girl.

'Oh, my God, half your hair's fallen out.'

Despite imagining I looked fabulous, actually I was in quite a state, and it wasn't only my hairdresser who thought so – my GP took one look and immediately referred me to the Hospital for Tropical Diseases. Even the journey to London was too much and when Karen and I became separated on the Tube, I stood there, rabbit in the headlights, everything happening too fast, life happening too fast.

'I'm knackered, I want to sleep *all* the time,' I told the consultant as I scratched one of my bites. 'I had malaria, twice. And salmonella. And anaemia.'

'It could be recurrent malaria. Let's run some tests.'

It wasn't malaria, though I was severely anaemic. Karen steered me home and I was grateful to crawl onto the sofa and let my family care for me. That evening I worked my way through half a loaf of bread and a block of cheese, definitely the food I'd missed most. After a year off dairy, my stomach rebelled and I went to bed in pain, feeling sorry for myself, realising the return to my old life was going to be harder than I'd expected.

It wasn't just about cheese. There were so many things I assumed I'd slot into, yet when it came to it, I simply didn't fit. I attempted supply teaching – trying to be the sunny, positive teacher I once was – but the glaring inequalities between Wiltshire and Lawra did my head in. Seeing disabled pupils with state-of-the-art electric wheelchairs, specially adapted iPads and one support worker per child reminded me of my SNAP children sitting in the dirt with absolutely nothing, and the world felt a horribly unfair place. The same when a pupil moaned about their school lunch, it made me cross, a little with them, but mostly with the system.

If anything, supply teaching motivated me even more to promote the fundraiser, sending emails, posting on social media and forcing Laura to watch me practice the speech a thousand times. I squeezed my Master's in where I could, struggling with remote learning and finding the online student chat room intimidating, a flashback to my training in Ghana. On the upside, the module on *Understanding Rural Poverty* validated much of ATE's thinking around business grants, gratifying since we'd made a lot of it up as we'd gone along.

Nasir and I hadn't spoken since our weird non-goodbye in Accra, although we'd texted and he told me he'd been to Emilia's funeral and that school feeding was going well. One night, lying in bed, I tried to picture being at the spot with him, sipping Clubs, playing with Shilea. Yet there, in Ramsbury, I couldn't quite conjure the image and despite spending most of my time talking about Lawra, it somehow felt a million miles and another world away. I reached for my phone.

It took me two goes to get through, the line was bad and all we did was discuss the next SNAP meeting and the amount of rice to order, but it was comforting to hear the news and to hear his voice, even it was a little unnerving to realise quite how much I missed him.

TWENTY

IN MEMORIAL

The day of the speech arrived and I was pooing myself. Not in a malaria way, more an unaccustomed-as-I-am-to-public-speaking way, and a sleepless night didn't help. What if everyone thought I was talking nonsense? Or saw me as a failure for my VSO work? Or would rather donate to an established charity with a track record? Or imagined they'd catch HIV from a piece a cloth?

What if no-one turned up?

I loaded Dad's car and headed to the Memorial Hall, where I fiddled with my projector and laid out long tables with leaflets, collection tins and Lawra produce labelled *made by Madame Madi*, *made by Zambo weavers*, alongside photos bringing their stories to life.

I tested the sound system with music from my laptop and when Mum and Dad appeared I was belting out songs from *The Little Mermaid* and dragging round chairs.

'How many? Thirty?'

'Be positive,' said Dad. 'Do them all.'

A hundred chairs. I could count on family and close friends, but did I seriously expect another ninety people to come to a village hall on a Friday evening in March? At least we had booze – Ian Smith (a Ramsbury legend who often provided refreshments for community events) had kindly agreed to run a bar and donate the profits.

He'd just handed me a glass of wine when people began drifting in. At first, an older crowd, Mum's friends, Dad's tennis buddies, and soon dozens of neighbours, families with children, faces from the pub, my mates.

'These baskets are gorgeous.' It was a lady I recognised from The Bell. 'How much are they?'

'Sorry, they're not for sale. I'll bring more next time.'

What had I been worried about? Everyone was so supportive. Then I noticed a glass of red wine casually left on the Zambo material, a delicate piece woven in gold and duck egg blue, and it stopped me in tracks. And that incongruous moment – the careless glass set against the glorious cloth, the wine that cost the same as the Zambo women could live on for a week – made me vow to fight for them even harder.

It was an evening of unforgettable moments. Walking to the flag-swathed recorder stand, turning to the audience and seeing Mum, Karen and Laura in the front row, Owen and Nicola behind. Getting a thumbs-up from a teacher friend. Dad introducing me and people applauding.

'Hello everyone, thanks for coming.' On the screen behind me was the ATE logo, luminous in red-green-gold. 'My name is Sarah and in February 2012 I left my job as a primary school teacher at The Winchcombe School for a year as a VSO volunteer …'

Yes, a lot of it was still about me.

'After training in Accra, I arrived, exhausted, emotional, hungry and hot, to this house …'

Click. My concrete house.

'Lots of adventures followed including snakes in the kitchen and candles melting in forty-five-degree heat.'

Click. Me with a limp candle in a wine bottle.

Fine, a lot of it *was* about me, but those hundred people in the Memorial Hall knew me and more importantly, they knew my life and my upbringing because it was the same as theirs, and I thought if they understood why *I* cared, *they* might care too.

Click. Boys and girls, scavenging for food. There was an audible gasp.

'In this picture, the children that lived near me are eating my rubbish. They were desperate.'

Click. Click. Click. Children foraging in the scrub, children pumping water, children in raggedy clothes. I paused. This was the moment I'd been most dreading.

'I was told not to engage with the children. Not to feed them. Not to make friends with them, to maintain boundaries. One night, that all changed.'

Click.

'A little boy was brought to my house and his sister told me he was sick and asked me to take him to hospital. Although my motorbike was outside, I was afraid of riding in the dark and said I could not take him. I closed the door and went to bed.

'Next day, I heard the terrible news that he had died. It was something I felt very responsible for and very guilty about, and still do. That little boy was called Kojo.'

It was a beautiful picture of him, close up, smiling. Taken when he'd been hanging around with his friend, hoping for bananas. It might have been the first photo ever taken of him. It was probably the last.

I scanned those faces in the crowd and wondered if they were judging me. Talking about Kojo had been a difficult decision, his was such a tragic story and I didn't come out of it well. But I needed people to understand my motivation, otherwise, how could I motivate them? I wanted them to see that if you're talking about life and death, you can't assume someone else will take up the slack.

'From that day, my boundaries disintegrated and I swung the opposite way. Soon, I had the children in my kitchen, on my sofa and embedded in my heart.'

I spoke about how my family started ATE, about the kitchen at Karbo Primary, about the Zambo weavers and their newly fixed loom, about Patience and Michelle and the singing at SNAP.

Click, before and after pictures at Karbo. Click, Francis and Betty at their groundnut farm. Click, the day we handed out the clothes and shoes donated locally.

'Oh!' A boy in the audience pointed at the screen where, crouching in the red dust, was a boy of similar age wearing fluorescent green trainers. 'Those used to be mine.' It was a tangible link between Ramsbury and Lawra, a connection with the power to change, encapsulated in a pair of trainers.

'Unless I can raise more money, our work will end in three months. I am determined not to let that happen. Poverty is complicated, but feeding hungry children is not. Please help me keep my promise to the people of Lawra, because together we can make a difference.'

Click. A photo taken a few days before I left. Half a dozen children from Karbo Primary holding a hand-made sign.

Thank you

A final click and a montage of photos floated across the screen as the Akon song *Freedom* filled the hall, along with rapturous applause. I know she wasn't the only one, yet all I could see was Karen, in the front row, crying.

There were some tricky questions. The people of Ramsbury were no soft touch and wanted to be sure their money would be used for long-term, sustainable development. Someone challenged why we were giving grants not loans, and I was thankful for my Master's and satisfied with my answer. A few questions didn't go quite so well, and I realised I needed to learn more and have more faith in myself. Then someone said *we're so proud of you* and everyone clapped.

They threw money at us. We got dozens of standing orders, people invited me to events, told me they ran charitable trusts, asked me *what do you need, what can we do?* That night, my community in Ramsbury heard the message from Lawra and were their magnificent, magnanimous best, raising a life-saving seven thousand pounds.

Afterwards, we went to the pub. I presume someone put the chairs away but I was all, *I've got to network, pass me my wine.* Yes, there was relief I had the money and the charity work would go on, but there was also adrenalin, being the centre of attention, the thrill of believing in myself.

That Sunday, I rang Nasir. We'd been having weekly calls and it felt good to tell him we had our funding and get the news from Lawra, to update my parents, the sun very much shining on Nasir whenever we talked about ATE, because he was doing such an excellent job.

And we talked about ATE constantly. In the end, we put up a wallchart in the kitchen with our faces on it and squares labelled *happy to talk about ATE* and *not happy to talk about ATE,* and if you didn't want to talk you moved your face into that square. Because it was incessant, infused in every breath we took and everything I did. And, now, I had two lots of responsibility, to the people of Lawra *and* to the donors of Ramsbury. If I'd doubted whether I'd ever return to Ghana, if I'd secretly wondered if I might slink back to my old job at the Winchcombe, I wondered no more. ATE was real and I was in it.

After the Memorial Hall, it went nuts. People were literally knocking on the door, *come to the scout group, come to the school, come to my knitting circle*, and I was zipping to local meetings in Dad's BMW and up to London on the train. I'd be at a Rotary Club on Monday, a networking thing on Tuesday, a race night on Saturday. I thanked every donor personally, sure that if I made one contact from each event and they invited me to something else, the money would roll in. It was such a blur, I was busy, busy, busy, rushing around, loving it.

But also, I was lost. Because, in the gaps between the busyness, I realised other things didn't add up and that my efforts to sustain the charity made my own life unsustainable. My folks couldn't support me forever. I couldn't live in their spare bedroom forever. Dad needed his car back.

And there'd be moments, random moments, in a shop – a well-stocked shop – or looking across at well-dressed people at a fundraising dinner, and suddenly I'd be thinking, *how can you all be OK, with so many hungry children in the world?* I was pulled in all directions, unsure who I was, nostalgic for the simplicity of both my time as a teacher and my time as a volunteer, though, in truth, neither one of those added up either.

I didn't tell anyone how I felt, no-one would have understood. And in those moments, I knew. I had to find a new way of living, one that embraced everything, Rotary dinners and Karbo lunches, The Bell and Las Palmas, Ramsbury and Lawra.

I booked a flight for June. With a colossal thirty thousand pounds burning a hole in the ATE bank account, piles of donated clothes and a wheelchair destined for a SNAP family, I yearned to be out there. And when Nasir offered to meet me at the airport I knew he would be waiting for me and he would not let me down.

TWENTY-ONE

MAMA SARAH

I wasn't quite sure how it had happened, but Nasir and I were together. Well, not exactly together, but giving it a go. Well, not exactly giving it a go, but not *not* together. I'd had seven hours in neutral air space to think about it, yet when I got to Accra I still had no idea what we were doing, which is what I'd told my parents before I left.

'Truth is, I've found it extremely tough the last couple of months and I've missed Nasir deeply. We've become partners in so many ways that we've decided to see if there's more. I'm not certain what it is …' I had a fleeting image of his hands and felt a little flutter. 'But it's something.'

'We want you to be happy,' said Mum. 'And we like Nasir and admire the work he's doing. But it's complicated.'

Dad nodded. 'It's fine now, but what if there was a dispute within the charity? There could be a conflict of interest.'

'But it's Nasir …'

Of course, they were right. So we agreed to discuss it with the other trustee, Peter Maple, and monitor the situation. I couldn't envisage a problem and was just dying to be with Nasir, and everyone, again.

Yes, there was a flicker of doubt at the airport, manoeuvring two trolleys with broken brakes down the slope to the exit, catching sight of him waiting – as he promised he would – and, for a few seconds, seeing him as perhaps others did, uneasy in the big city, a touch out of his depth. Then he spotted me, and instantly he was strong, capable Nasir, the man I recognised from Lawra, giving me a distinctly less bumpy hug, sorting out the taxi and lugging suitcases and a wheelchair into the Joska Lodge hotel.

Downstairs in the bar, it was lovely to have him order me a Club, and drinking that Club with him, along with Gabriel and Gabriel's heavily pregnant wife Adeline, and seeing Adeline's bump where we knew she had twins, and knowing I was to be the godmother of those twins. And with the taste of beer in my mouth and the occasional touch of Nasir's hand on my arm, the stress of balancing two different lives receded, because in Ghana there was one life and I was throwing myself into it one hundred per cent.

Next morning, we got a Metro Mass bus to Kumasi, a city in the centre of Ghana, where we were picking up Bie. Nasir was a devoted dad and desperately missed his son, so when he'd suggested he spend the summer with us in Lawra I happily agreed to do my bit, delighted because I adored Bie too.

We got to Kumasi late afternoon, dropped our stuff at a cheap hotel and travelled by trotro to Kendey's family house. City trotros were terrifying, so packed, so fast, whipping in and out of relentless, seemingly unregulated traffic. We had to change twice, squeezing ourselves through sardined bodies, Nasir, as usual, angsty with me and it was all rather tense. And also, exciting. We were on an adventure.

'Sarah, this one.'

We got off at an overpass slung across a main road in a poor district on the edge of town. Pungent sewage wafted from open drains, music blared from windows and groups of men gathered on street corners. Nasir grabbed my hand, not exactly romantically, more because he didn't want me to get assaulted or get lost or fall down a hole.

As soon as we saw Bie, sitting with his mother on a bench outside their compound, Nasir's face broke into a broad smile. He scooped up his son, showering him in kisses.

At the hotel, Nasir went out for nappies, leaving me with strict instructions not to open the door. I'm not sure who was more nervous, me or Bie, stuck in a hotel room with a relative stranger. Then I remembered the fun we'd had the previous summer.

'Bie,' I said, picking him up. 'Let's have a bath.'

When Nasir returned, Bie was playing in a bucket of water, and half an hour later we were all in bed, asleep, with Bie in the middle. And that was that, it was the three of us.

We woke before dawn to get a Metro Mass north. At Kumasi bus station, Nasir flapped about, bribing the driver to take my unwieldy luggage as I sat in the wheelchair snuggling Bie, sharing that woozy four-in-the-morning moment until it was time to board. The moment was not to last. Bie had a horrible stomach bug and was ill the whole journey. I held him close and, despite the diarrhoea and vomit, I loved him even more.

Then, halfway home, we got a message from Gabriel saying the twins had been born. Somewhere between Monday and Thursday, somewhere between Accra and Lawra, somewhere between choice and fortunate coincidence, Nasir and I had gone from being friends and colleagues to being parents, and I had become a godmother.

'Food is here,' announced Nasir, as he walked into the master bedroom of our newly rented house. The four of us had slept on the super king-size bed, Shilea at the end and Bie in the middle again. Apparently, it was normal for children to sleep with their parents until they were older, and I wasn't complaining because I liked having him there.

Nasir makes the best fried eggs, and Bie and I ate ours in bed as I looked around what would be my bedroom for the next two months. It was well-proportioned, with its own en suite bathroom – maybe a bit too en suite, the walls not reaching the ceiling, and I swore never to use the toilet for a number two.

Bie toddled into the spacious living area, where his dad watched TV from a battered sofa. The charity had rented the property so we had somewhere to hold workshops and accommodate UK guests, and I was delighted to find two spare bedrooms and a dignity-preserving extra bathroom. There was a compact kitchen with a two-ring gas hob, and a small fridge bought by Nasir, who'd recently acquired a well-paid second job. Fridge aside, we'd pooled our finances, me handing over £200 worth of personal cash so he could take care of everything. It just worked better like that in Lawra.

Nasir clicked the remote control. 'I think I will go to eat.'

In the end, we all went and Bie and I watched as Nasir had banku and groundnut stew outside a food shack on the roundabout in town.

'Sarah!' It was Patience, calling across from her egg stall, baby Rainy bound to her back in colourful fabric. 'Where have you been? I haven't seen you this week.'

Returning to Lawra

Jun 15, 2013

Arriving in Lawra was special. People ask 'Did you travel?' as if I've stepped out of town for a few days. I feel the warmth of the Dagaara people, it makes the last 3 months of exhausting, manic fundraising worthwhile.

After a weekend of rest and acclimatisation, I started work on Monday. Visiting Karbo was magical and the whole school sang a song called 'We love you Mama Sarah' which moved me to tears. The children are visibly healthier, looking fitter and fatter. I haven't done any analysis yet but I'm told attendance, attainment and motivation are all significantly improved. The head teacher, Mary, said the feeding programme has changed the children's lives.

If I say so myself, Karbo Primary's *We Love You Mama Sarah* is a banger. There's nothing like it, thinking, *oh, I might do a charity* and six months later having a charity, and people saying you're wonderful and four hundred children singing you're wonderful, and having a bankful of money to spend on what they need.

Nasir and I went shopping. We bought 100 yards of cloth and recruited tailors to make uniforms so that sixty new pupils could go to school. We bought an eight-foot water tank in Wa, strapping it to a trotro for the precarious ride to Karbo, where it was connected to the mains to provide clean water for cooking, drinking and handwashing. We held a health insurance sign-up day and paid for 437 pupils to access basic health care. These activities, made possible by Ramsbury generosity, were key to our mission of getting those children into education and keeping them there. A spending spree had never felt so good.

'Who wants presents?'

Judith, Celina and Jeremiah had trekked to the new house (on the other side of town to Tuori) and I was reassured to hear they'd been attending school, no-one had a septic thumb, no-one was pregnant.

I had gifts coming out of my ears, spending what I could afford on toiletries and clothes from Tesco and Primark, knowing even the most untrendy logo was prized in Lawra. For the Tuori children, there were also school provisions and it was a pleasure to watch them, a bit more flesh on their cheeks and in new clothes with the labels still attached, choosing pencil cases and playing with calculators.

They'd often hang out at the house, playing with Bie, company for me whenever Nasir zoomed off on his bike. Bie was a dream, a sunny, loving two-year-old and that first week I fell for him over and over again.

Which made things complicated.

As a VSO volunteer, I'd been strangely independent – yes, useless at my job, vulnerable and lonely, but concerned only with myself, irrelevant basically to everyone else. Now, with a child who spoke a different language and a man I was committed to without having a clue where it was going, plus two godchildren and hundreds of pupils relying on me for food, I was both dependent and depended on. It was very different from before, joyful and productive and purposeful, yet scarier, more nuanced, more at stake.

I felt a warm-wet lick on my hand. Shilea was my one constant and there was nothing nuanced about our relationship. She stood patiently as I examined a tiny wound on her ear and then the children descended on her, becoming a mess of little hands and wagging tail and laughter.

Hope

Jun 22, 2013

Sunday evening brought the naming ceremony of Leah and Leala, my Godchildren. After the service, we drank alcohol-free blue 'champagne' and I was offered part of the sacrificed goat. Then we danced in the dust until late. 8.30 pm.

It was our first official public outing as a couple, as a family really, and I felt proud as we entered Gabriel's compound, Nasir in traditional smock, Bie in a new shirt, me, in tight-fitting local dress. I had no idea what Nasir had told his family about 'us', but we were living together, with Bie and a fridge, and that was good enough.

'This is Sarah, the wife.' Nasir's father, Karlley, introduced me to a cousin.

'Actually ...' It didn't matter. To them, I was Nasir's pog. His woman.

Actually ... it felt great. Great to be welcomed into the family, to dance with Nasir and Bie and kiss the twins and pray they would grow to be healthy and happy and successful, great to be called godmother and pog and Mama Sarah, great to drink blue champagne with Bie's arms wrapped round my neck, until the three of us climbed on our bike and headed home.

By late June, it was still an oppressive forty degrees and hadn't rained for weeks. All around, the first shoots of growth shrivelled under harsh sun and farmers feared their crops were dying. Even the weekly market was cancelled, which I gathered was the Chief issuing an ultimatum to the gods, *there will be no market until it rains.* That, or there was no food left to sell.

One hot day our eighteen small business owners met under the spinning ceiling fans of the Teachers' Resource Centre for a workshop entitled *Evaluating Success.*

'I now have respect,' said one of the Zambo weavers. 'I can provide for my family, I am seen as a contributor. My husband is having a different relationship with me. Things are peaceful.'

'The same for me,' said Nana, a drug seller. 'I have pride in my work, and so does he. Life is better.'

'Hear, hear,' cried Madame Madi and everyone laughed.

We'd learnt a lot with these entrepreneurs and the shortlisting for the second batch was more rigorous, a selection process rather than accepting whoever showed up. Nasir had found some excellent candidates, including my friend Patience and John Gandaa (the sole SNAP dad). The induction we hosted at the ATE house was far slicker than that first chaotic workshop in December and as Nasir, Gabriel and I ran through everything, it was clear this determined bunch had potential.

But we took nothing for granted. Remembering poor Emilia, hearing the awful news that one of our precious SNAP children had died, noticing Youribaa (a petty trader) limp from the workshop with a clearly serious injury, we *never* took anything for granted.

As soon as we could, we visited Youribaa. Her leg was so severely broken I could see the crack through her skin.

'When did it happen?'

'She's not sure.' Nasir spoke to her quietly. 'It is several weeks.'

I was horrified. Ghanaian health insurance didn't cover broken limbs, and she couldn't afford to travel to a hospital which had an X-ray machine (which Lawra Hospital didn't), never mind pay for treatment. Despite her suffering, though, she'd still dragged a table and her bags of salt and sugar to the front of her compound, looking for passing trade. I can't imagine the agony she'd endured walking the 3 km to the workshop, that effort alone putting a whole new spin on the words *evaluating success.*

'I know this doesn't strictly qualify as sustainable development,' I whispered to Nasir, 'but …'

'I agree.' He gave her GH¢50 (about £17), enough for treatment at Nandom Hospital, 30 km away.

'Barka, barka.' Youribaa squeezed my hand. 'Barka.' It was one Dagaare word I definitely understood. *Thank you.*

I rang Dad and told him what we'd done, admitting Youribaa would struggle to ever make a profit on her barely trading business or to repay ATE the GH¢50.

'Sarah, are the others are doing well?'

'Really well.'

'Then let's make good decisions about individuals. It can't always be about profit.'

I was relieved, wanting to do the right thing in a place where it's often impossible to work out what that is. Anyway, the next evening, I was on the veranda with my Master's folders when Youribaa and her husband appeared. It was bad news from the hospital, where she'd been told her leg had set in the break and there was nothing they could do. The journey had cost six cedis and they returned the rest of the money. They insisted on it.

Three days later, they were back and, despite my protestations, they pushed the remaining six cedis into my hand. As Youribaa shuffled away, leaning on her husband, I had to admire their self-respect. I swallowed my tears and vowed to get her some crutches.

'Is Kanyiri around?' We'd not seen our young friend at Las Palmas for a while and were trying to track him down. One of the neighbours had news.

'I saw him walking to his family land with a machete.'

The next week, there was a knock on our door and it was Kanyiri and his eleven-year-old brother Kakpe, heads dipped, cheekbones jutting, clothes hanging off them.

We fed them jollof rice and they ate quickly, silently. Nasir waited until they'd finished.

'Why didn't you come to us sooner?'

'I have been farming. I haven't been at school.'

Nasir sighed. 'Kanyiri, you are bright, you work hard, you can study, be a professional, then you can be useful to your family and your community. The other way, even with a favourable harvest, the food will soon be gone. And that will be your life, every year. You must trust me, education is the way for you.'

In the end, we sent them off with rice, beans, onions and an ultimatum, *go to school or else.* In a culture where good boys usually did what their elders told them, we could only hope they followed our advice. Nasir put his hand on Kanyiri's shoulder. 'If you don't do it for yourself, do it for your brother.'

On the Monday, Kanyiri knocked on the door again. This time, he was wearing his school uniform.

The boys were part of a steady stream of people calling on us and the house was fast becoming a community hub, a vital resource that gave ATE standing and gave us standing too. People needed us, sometimes a little too much – they saw we had money and Nasir would have to reject the constant requests for handouts that were nothing to do with the work of the charity. It was a small price to pay, I thought, for me and Nasir becoming this Lawra power couple, immersed in our mission, a fantastic team, the heart of an extended and beautiful family. It was exhausting, intensely demanding and what I'd always wanted.

I love you, I told Nasir at some point that summer. He'd already said it to me on numerous occasions, though quite how we both meant it, I wasn't sure. But in that house, in those meetings, at that spot, with Bie and Shilea and the charity and everything, it was most definitely love.

And it had all begun a year before, when Nasir had found me and Makum laminating communication fans. A whole year, and now it was time to celebrate. Nasir bought some blue and pink material and had it made into a dress, a suit for Bie and a shirt for himself. In our matching outfits, we were ready to party.

Special Day

Jul 5, 2013

Wednesday was SNAP's first birthday! We had a wonderful celebration, over 200 people came, mainly our special-needs families, it was AMAZING! The best thing is the change in the parents. One woman said 'I used to sit on my bed and weep. I asked God why he had given me this child. Now I know I'm not alone, my child is special. I don't cry any more'.

We held the party at the Chief's Palace, a coup in itself since most people in Lawra didn't recognise disabled children even existed, let alone think they should be celebrated. The whole thing was an organisational triumph, with Nasir arranging nyaabas to transport the families, ordering food and water and co-ordinating the entertainment.

We did face-painting and games for the children and Makum led the prayers. There was xylophone music (Lawra's world famous for its xylophones, honestly, google it) and Nasir brought his speakers for the dancing. The spectacle of the mothers moving rhythmically to the music, some with their children, others swaying with each other, in the central square of the Chief's Palace, was more than heart-lifting, it was historic.

The Paramount Chief made a distinguished entrance in traditional robe and white hat, surrounded by eight sub chiefs carrying umbrellas. Then came the speeches, first me and Nasir, then the Chief himself. I watched the crowd, those families who a year ago had hidden their offspring and been shunned by society, as they stood proudly to hear their leader address them.

'Children with disabilities are human beings,' he said in a deep voice. 'They have a right to live. Thank you ATE, for bringing them into the light.'

And in one moment – well, one moment after twelve months of dedicated work – the perception of disability was upturned. Not quite changed, because these things are deeply embedded, but still, progress, huge progress.

As the retinue of umbrellas led the Chief away, he stopped

to shake our hands. 'This is what my community needs. I have instructed my sub chiefs to make an announcement to their people, to warn that nobody should intimidate a parent with a disabled child.'

'Thank you,' I said. 'That will mean so much.'

He leaned towards me. 'In my experience, NGOs come with big ideas and many vanish into air. I will be interested to see if you stay.'

It was fair enough, and I thought *I will rise to that challenge.*

It had been a phenomenal summer. Most SBOs were thriving, attendance and performance were improving at Karbo Primary and the SNAP party was the talk of the town. Kanyiri passed his exams with flying colours. Shilea was in season again and we broke out the rice and beans. And, finally, the rains came.

One evening towards the end of my trip, me, Bie, Makum and Shilea got stranded at Las Palmas as the heavens opened and sheets of rain blocked our path home. We sheltered with the owner until Nasir dramatically emerged through the mist, soaked to the skin, and I felt swept away by my very own Mr Darcy.

I'd left the UK a single woman on a promise. I returned a *who knows what.* And I'd spent eight weeks in the arms of someone I couldn't have loved more. Bie.

When I went back to Ghana in the November, Nasir and I picked up Bie and took him to Lawra with us, this time for good.

TWENTY-TWO

DOUBLE LIFE

It was the year of two autumns.

The autumn I went in a taxi to an outlying suburb of Kumasi and collected a two-year-old boy, travelled to Lawra with him and his father and set up home.

And the autumn I put on a just-short-enough red lacy dress and stepped onto the stage at a glamorous charity dinner with the prospect of raising tens of thousands of pounds.

Two autumns. Two very different worlds.

Sometimes it was hard to believe it was me in both of them.

As soon as I got back from Ghana, I jetted off to Spain with my friends for a week of lazy mornings, beach afternoons and dancing through the night.

Nasir hated the thought of me on that holiday, the cost, my swimwear (exposed stomachs were a no-no in Lawra), me in a villa with male friends, he just couldn't get his head around any of it, even though he said he wanted to. How could he? He didn't know what a water park was, or a karaoke bar, or Prosecco. In truth, he had no concept of my type of holiday at all.

I'd disappear onto the balcony for his calls, not wanting to be overheard – *no Nasir, he's just a friend, yes, Nasir, everyone's wearing a bikini* – worried they'd only see the controlling behaviour and wouldn't understand the cultural nuances that allowed me to excuse it. I dreaded those awkward balcony exchanges, wishing

I could tell him what a fantastic time I was having, wanting to get past what was bothering him and onto the Lawra news I longed to hear. Under the same autumn sun, very much apart.

Then, there was a drama. Nasir was sick. Or someone was sick. Or Nasir hadn't eaten, or someone hadn't eaten. I can't recall which because that stuff seemed to be happening more and more. And I was resentful. On a holiday I couldn't really afford, I was resentful of sending fifty quid I also couldn't afford for a convenient emergency I only half-believed.

'Everything OK?' asked Laura as I made a money transfer on my phone. I'd told her almost nothing about me and Nasir and if she'd been forced to describe our set up she might have tentatively called it a holiday romance, ironic since it wasn't a holiday and – rainstorm aside – there was precious little romance.

'Everything's fine.'

And it was like that the whole autumn, two realities bashing against each other, individually often brilliant but essentially a double life. In Lawra, I loved being Mama Sarah, loved even being Nasir's pog. Nasir, however, didn't know his pog also loved the water rapids and preferred the white wine that cost £3 more a glass. He'd never seen his pog dance on tables or do a Britney Spears routine with her sister, he didn't know the details of her life when she wasn't being his pog.

And in Ramsbury, did anyone know the Lawra me? The me who spent hours cooking rice on a two-ring hob or who held the hand of a mourning SNAP mother, the me who never answered a late-night knock at the door without trembling at what sickness or hunger or crisis lay on the other side. They just thought, *Sarah feeds poor children, isn't she marvellous?*

But I knew the truth. That it didn't always feel marvellous

and I was far from marvellous in it. That I couldn't help everyone and sometimes I did stuff to help myself. That within minutes of bidding farewell to Nasir at Accra Airport, I'd blown twenty-five quid on souvenirs and cheese croissants and beer, more money than I'd spent in the previous week. That in the first month of being home, what with the holiday and a spree at H&M and one too many Sauvignon Blancs in The Bell, I'd notched up more than a thousand pounds, enough to launch several Lawra businesses. Cognitive dissonance – holding two contradictory thoughts or values at the same time – is the fancy term. But I was just being the person I needed to be to survive.

And that, I think, is how I came to be on the overpass near Kendey's house in Kumasi, climbing into a taxi with Nasir and Bie. Nasir had decided his son should live with him on a permanent basis, there being a sort of unspoken acceptance that we could give Bie an education and opportunities, and an even less spoken one that tradition deemed Nasir to be his rightful guardian now he was no longer a baby.

I had no idea how Kendey felt, how a mother would feel as that taxi pulled away and we took her son with us. In another world, without tradition or gender roles or power imbalance, perhaps things would have been different. But in this one, she was a twenty-five-year old woman just doing what she was doing, doing what was happening. Though I never asked her what she really wanted. Maybe I should have.

I glanced out the rear window, blinking a tear as a blurry Kendey retrod her steps to the family compound and the rest of her life. Did it feel good to be leaving with another woman's child? Of course not. Yet, as I turned to see Bie sink into his dad's loving arms, Nasir whispering words of endearment I didn't understand, their heads buried in each other's, completely in the moment, I knew it wasn't that simple.

It wasn't my decision, but if it had been, I could have certainly justified it. Not that I tried. There was Nasir, there was Bie, there was Shilea, there was ATE. It all just *was*.

Wouldn't have wanted to explain it to the crowd at The Bell though.

The crowd at The Bell pulled out the stops that autumn. The whole of Ramsbury did, with quiz nights, race nights, sponsored this, sponsored that. One enterprising youngster sold home-grown figs from a wooden bowl in the High Street, another baked biscuits, which she traded from her garden. The Beavers, Cubs and Scouts donated £555 and my choir, Vibrant Voices, did a fundraising concert. One supporter, Stephen Hodgson, kindly donated a room in his Swindon office and the day Mum and I emptied the ATE cupboards at the house and moved us in felt symbolic, of us being a credible charity.

The most lucrative – and glamorous – event that autumn was the Gamma Ball Rally. My neighbour John Haw (whose son Charlie had donated his green trainers) rang to invite me to a swanky function held by his employer, Gamma, a telecoms company based in Newbury. The sales team was taking its clients on a three-day car rally through Europe, ending with a gala dinner and charity auction. Would I be interested in coming to Budapest (all expenses paid) and taking a half share of the auction pledges?

Would I? I was virtually packing my bag before we'd finished the call.

The whole thing was a whirlwind. I slipped into the aforementioned red lacy number and stood in front of over a hundred well-oiled executives, introducing them to the Karbo kitchen and the Zambo weavers and the SNAP group. I did the full twenty minutes, ending with *Freedom* and the photo montage. I'd never been in the corporate world, I didn't know they were only expecting three minutes, but the warmth of their response – led by John Haw and my friend Nicola in the front row – suggested I'd got through.

They were *very* generous. After the auction, I ran out of the ballroom and called Mum.

'Oh my God! Oh my God!'

'How much?'

'Twenty-seven thousand pounds.'

It was a transformational amount. What with the office and our growing network of supporters, the Gamma Ball Rally was the crowning moment for ATE, like a miracle that seemed to come from nowhere and meant nothing would ever be the same again. We were a proper charity, we could confidently make plans, we could realistically grow.

I texted Nasir and he replied straight away, *well done my wife*. Of course, by then I wasn't thinking about plans or growth. I was in a nightclub, champagne, shots, dancing, attention, feeling fabulous, feeling *I've nailed it, I'm saving the world, I'm having a ball.* I vaguely recollect being pushed back to my bedroom in a luggage trolley, laughing my head off, at six in the morning.

Later, waiting in reception for a taxi to the airport, I noticed one of the guests staring, and before I could get too big for my boots heard them mutter something to their companion.

'Oh yeah, that charity lady, she was wasted last night.'

I glowed, that autumn, in Lawra, on the trip when we collected Bie.

'Sarah, this is for you.' On the first morning back, Nasir handed me a black plastic bag. 'You can open it.'

Inside was a traditional smock, dark blue with white stripe detail and a white heart stitched over the left breast. Nasir had never given me a present and I was touched.

'Sarah, it is a love smock.'

It couldn't have been more different to my red Gamma dress, but I looked pretty smoking in it and felt incredibly loved up as we strolled to Las Palmas, Nasir proudly beside me, Bie and Shilea in tow, Kanyiri ready with the beers, me in my love smock.

Although it wasn't an official ATE visit (I'd paid for my own flight), work was pretty full on. But also, it was a time for family and fun. We hung out with Adeline, Gabriel and my goddaughters and I've got dozens of photos of me with a massive smile, hugging those gorgeous twins or Patience's children or Bie, and I'm shining with love for them all. And yes, amidst all that love, I did notice that Nasir was maybe a little less present than over the summer, often out on his bike in a shiny new T-shirt, often glued to his phone. And that I was doing a lot more sweeping and mopping and clothes-washing. So, despite paying for it myself, it was still no holiday and despite the love smock, there still wasn't much romance. Either way, it was a glorious three weeks.

I reached the UK in time for my thirtieth and a celebratory weekend at Center Parcs. On the morning of my birthday, my friends covered the bed with balloons and presented me with a pair of diamond earrings.

My phone rang. It was Nasir.

'Sarah, there is a problem.'

I went into another room, not wanting the others to realise Nasir had forgotten my birthday, not wanting Nasir to overhear them already merry on it.

'Bie is unwell. He must have medicine.'

I felt awful. Here I was, Prosecco in hand, ears studded with diamonds and about to hit the water rapids for the third time. Three thousand miles away, Nasir was a single dad of a sick child asking me to pay for medicine.

Of course, I sent the money and the next day Bie was fine. Nasir never did remember it was my birthday.

It was the year of two autumns. A red dress and a love smock. Partying in Budapest and Spain and Center Parcs. Partying and mopping in Lawra. It was the autumn I raised twenty-seven thousand pounds and the autumn me, Nasir and Bie became a family, a family I told virtually no-one about in Ramsbury. It was the year of two autumns and I was two different people in them.

TWENTY-THREE

'TBC'

Christmas came, with its flurry of Ramsbury fundraising, wintry weather and the usual fan-bloody-tastic festivities with my family. On Boxing Day, Mum drove me to the airport and I headed to Lawra, bags bulging with presents for Bie, something for Nasir's birthday and the dress I'd bought for New Year's Eve.

I flew out with my friend Dee Anderson (our first international volunteer!) and soon we were sitting at Las Palmas, Kanyiri serving drinks, Nasir swilling a glass, Bie on my knee, Shilea (and the flies that lived on her ever-gammy ear) under my chair. It was Dee and her husband who had run the Gambian teaching trips that sparked my interest in Africa and development work, so there was real sweetness in introducing her to my charity and my family and the life I was building in Lawra.

Happy New Year!

Jan 1, 2014

As I counted down to midnight, it was impossible not to feel emotional about the last 12 months. It's a bit of a cliché, but it truly has been the best year of my life.

'I'll babysit Bie,' suggested Dee on New Year's Eve. 'You two can have a night out.'

We only made it as far as Las Palmas, feeling liberated to be there without Bie, our first proper date as a couple, me in my new dress, Nasir in one of his T-shirts, hitting the Striker and Fanta, dancing the night away. Just after midnight, in the midst of a particularly grindy dance, Nasir came out with it.

'Why don't we get married?'

It wasn't the first time he'd said it, he'd been saying it a while and so far, I'd laughed it off. I mean, how could it ever work?

'Yes,' I agreed. 'Let's get married.'

He looked as surprised as I was. I blame the Striker.

I was still blaming the Striker the following morning as I nursed my hangover.

'Good morning, my wife.' It was Nasir with the eggs and bread.

A minute later, he was off on the motorbike to get banku. It was pretty typical, I gathered from my female friends, of how Ghanaian men did romance. *I love you, I want to marry you, I want to impregnate you.* A status update requiring little discussion. Maybe it sounds better in Dagaare.

I lazed in bed with Bie and Shilea. I did not, I noted, ring my parents with an ecstatic *I'm getting married!* And when Dee popped her head round the door – *good night? I heard you stumble in about two* – I did not, I also noted, mention it to her. Evidently it wasn't a big deal for me either, more a commitment to where we were in our relationship, less an actual commitment to get married. And even less of a commitment to actually *be* married, you know, forever, like my parents. Likewise, I doubt Nasir told anyone, not that it was a secret, more that, in the eyes of his family, we'd been married for months anyway. So, despite a drunken promise to reconvene on New Year's Eve 2014 for the wedding, nothing had really changed.

As ever, there was no time to dwell on that stuff anyway and I soon was caught up in the drama of what I came to think of That Bloody Container.

'TBC' was the brainchild of Sue Brady, a dynamic Marlborough businesswoman who had approached me with the idea of collecting donations – anything from clothes to mobility aids to furniture – and dispatching them to Lawra in a massive container. I could find takers for as many wheelchairs as she could lay her hands on and eagerly agreed.

Sue did everything, arranging local events, rallying businesses and linking with charities who wanted to send disability equipment overseas. She raised funds for the transport costs, stored donations in her catering unit and dealt with the onerous logistics of getting them across the sea to Accra and up to Lawra by low loader. One wet afternoon back in December, me, Sue and a group of volunteers had assembled in front of a forty-foot-long container to load the impressive array of donations:

Bicycles, fifty. Wheelchairs, eighty. Zimmer frames and crutches – including a pair for Youribaa – hundreds. Spiderman cars, two hundred. Pool table, one.

The pool table – along with a piano, dozens of chairs and desks and a whole climbing frame – came from a prep school that had closed down. Strange to think the next time I saw it all would be in Ghana.

Now, several weeks later, it was there, and from that moment it became a complete crapping nightmare.

'The container cannot be released from the dock in Accra,' the shipping agent rang to tell me. 'There is a fee to settle.'

'But everything's covered.' I knew Sue had paid five grand

for the entire journey, including the agent's hefty commission.

'It's a special fee.'

'A bribe?'

'For each day the fee is unpaid, the container will accumulate tax. You will pay?'

'I will not,' I told him, and when he rang the next day I was confident my bullish stance had prevailed. It hadn't.

'This is ridiculous,' I ranted to Nasir after refusing to pay for a second time. 'It's wheelchairs for disabled children, how can they do this?'

'It is how the system works.'

On the third morning of stalemate, I started to panic. What if the container was never released? Or – worse, possibly – it arrived after I'd gone back to England and without me to supervise, its contents simply disappeared into Lawra's black economy? Not that I didn't trust Nasir, I did, but it would definitely ramp up the already increasing pressure he was under from friends and family asking for their share of what they saw as his good fortune. It might have been *how the system works,* but I wanted to protect him and I wanted to protect our reputation.

In the end, one of the charities that had donated equipment paid the 'fee' and, at last, the stress of dealing with That Bloody Container was over. Now would come the fun bit.

So wrong. A couple of days later, the low loader carrying TBC arrived and Nasir instructed the driver to park outside the Chief's Palace, where it was secure on family land. It seemed somehow bigger in Lawra, and when the driver asked how long it would take to unload because he had to deliver the empty container to Accra the next day, Nasir looked at me in dismay.

'Surely he is meant to leave the container here? We cannot empty it on the spot, it is not safe.' He puffed up his chest. 'I will handle this.'

His *we're-all-in-it-together* camaraderie was quickly followed by much arm waving, angry phone calling and handing over of mobiles between himself and the poor old driver, followed by more camaraderie. Eventually, Nasir's charm, along with the unspoken influence of a growing crowd from the Chief's Palace, did the trick and the driver agreed to leave the container with us.

It was then our problems really began.

'Nasir? I'm not being stupid, but how are we meant to get it off the loader?'

'Sarah,' he replied, his phone pressed to his ear, 'I am dealing with that.'

He was on the phone, on and off, for another two hours, roping in his father for extra clout. They were working something, pulling strings, using the Chief's Palace connection, doing what they needed to do to *make the system work*. With the sun going down, excitement rippled through the assembled masses as two red fire engines cruised in, all the way from Wa.

It was, I'm told, the most enormous kerfuffle Lawra had ever seen. The crowd, now numbering a couple of hundred, watched with bated breath as chains were attached and multiple cranes triumphantly lifted TBC from the loader and onto the ground. When it landed in front of the Chief's Palace sign, everyone whooped.

'It is too late to unload,' said Nasir. 'The container is locked, it will be safe for tonight.'

'Whatever you say,' I agreed, as the crowd dispersed and the low loader drove into the darkness towards Accra.

Gabriel, John Gandaa, Shilea and I stood in the early morning sunshine as Nasir pulled open the container doors. Behind them was a tangle of Zimmer frames, floor to ceiling. I saw the expression on Nasir's face as the scale – of the job at hand *and* of the possibilities, the outcomes – dawned on him. Hundreds of people in his town would be able to get themselves around, in some measure due to him. He allowed himself a half-smile and began unloading.

We put everything onto nyaabas and sent them up to the house, the frames precariously balanced ten feet high, teetering towers of bicycles and boxes upon boxes of books, toys and clothes. After a couple of hours, having manhandled the piano onto a nyaaba and with the container still three quarters full, I begged Nasir to get help.

'Bad idea,' he said, unwilling to trust anyone else. So, we kept going, in the boiling sun and soon the container was half full, which was progress. Then my phone went. It was the company who had supplied the container, and they wanted it back.

And they weren't exactly asking. They were furious and demanded we transport it to Accra forthwith, at our own cost. Again, I was outraged, this international company trying to get cash from a tiny charity whose money was for school meals and weavers. I found the strength to refuse them by focusing on that, and then I found the strength to continue unloading by focusing on the Club beer I planned on drinking that night.

In the end, I went to bed with sunstroke, the bedroom crammed with boxes and bikes and Spiderman cars. Next morning, there was no eggs and bread. Nasir couldn't get to the hob because the kitchen was also full of boxes.

The house was organised chaos. Alongside the satisfying task of distributing donations to the community, we launched the selection process for the next tranche of small businesses. We'd be piling a nyaaba with bikes for school children in remote villages as a nervous trader knocked on the door to collect an application form. Peace Corps volunteers left with hundreds of books to set up libraries, seamstresses walked away with old-fashioned sewing machines in leather boxes and I personally went to Youribaa's compound, where she was sitting outside with her bags of salt and sugar, and presented her with the crutches she'd needed for months.

Once we'd shifted the bulk of stuff from the house and Nasir had located the hob and fortified us with eggs and bread, we drove into town to meet one of our SNAP mums who wanted to start a business.

'Sarah, welcome, welcome, please sit.' Peace fetched Blessing, her profoundly disabled and very smiley nineteen-year old daughter, and placed her on a mat under a dappling mango tree.

'Since we go to SNAP, I see many changes in her and now I feel able to work. I used to make a living in the market, selling special kenkey wrapped in maize leaves. Yet, whenever people heard about Blessing, no-one would buy and I could only trade from the house, small, small. Then my husband had a bad accident, our money went for treatment and the business collapsed. I must be the breadwinner and with your aid and God's, I believe I can make a good business again.'

Peace was a religious, uncomplaining woman whose years of caring for her husband, Blessing and three other children had clearly taken their toll. But she spoke so eloquently, in fluent

English, and was so supremely capable and conscientious that Nasir was able to give our decision on the spot.

'Peace, I am glad to say you will have the grant, the mentoring and our full support.'

On the way home, we stopped at the roundabout for a boiled egg and to check in with Dee, who was devoting her time to teaching a couple of our SNAP children. Next to the stall, she and Patience's daughter Michelle were poring over a book. For a child with severe cerebral palsy to be taught, in public, was a pretty big statement in Lawra and when Patience saw us she gave Michelle an encouraging nudge. The five-year-old smiled and tentatively began to speak.

'Bonyeni ... ayi ... ata ...' As Michelle recited what I recognised as *one, two, three*, a proud Patience grabbed Nasir's hand, a tumble of emotional Dagaare – and a few tears – spilling out.

'She remembers when the child was born,' translated Nasir, 'and she was told to abandon her in the bush because she was the devil. And today she is learning to count and everyone can see.'

With a strong sense that we were all were flipping awesome, Nasir and I headed home, collecting Bie from his new school on the way. He'd been so smart when we'd dropped him that morning, now he was filthy. Within minutes of getting back after a triumphant day, I was elbow deep in cold water, scrubbing his uniform with a bar of laundry soap, as Gabriel and Adeline rifled through boxes of donated clothes, Nasir issued various orders on the phone, Bie played with Shilea and organised chaos still reigned.

We took the afternoon off for Valentine's, me, Nasir and Bie riding round Lawra on the bike in matching red outfits, as per Ghanaian custom. Other than that, we never stopped. One afternoon was spent weighing and measuring children to assess the impact of twelve months of the feeding programme at Karbo Primary, where attendance was already up an encouraging fourteen per cent. The whole mood, attentiveness in class, the energy in the courtyard during break time, was so unlike the monotone soundtrack of 2012, I could literally hear the difference.

Everywhere we went, we passed someone walking with a Zimmer frame or a child riding a donated bike, the effects of our work all around. And we'd become a significant injector of cash into the Lawra economy, Nasir frequently handing money over to tailors and rice-sellers and nyaaba drivers. Updating my numerous spreadsheets was a never-ending job.

We were always on duty. Once, while I was being chastised by Bie's teacher for sending him to school with a dirty vest (my idea of white was apparently *not* Lawra white) another teacher wandered past with a profoundly disabled child strapped to her back and I interrupted my laundry lecture to invite them to the next SNAP meeting.

That meeting was one of our best. Dee ran a music session using instruments made from plastic bottles and dried groundnuts, with Blessing, Michelle and the others rattling their shakers, their parents clapping in delight. And, after her intensive tutoring, Michelle could now count, do basic greetings, recognise simple words and draw pictures, which was nothing short of a miracle.

At the end, we handed out disability equipment, giving children and mothers a degree of mobility, of freedom, they'd never dreamt possible. Watching as Peace put Blessing into her new wheelchair and push rather than carry her home made all the aggravation worthwhile.

TBC had become That Brilliant Container, the gift that kept on giving. Even the climbing frame was put to use, donated to a welding business as scrap metal because the walls in the local schools were too crumbly to attach it to. And we did keep a few things for ourselves. The piano went on the veranda where I occasionally gave it a tinkle and the pool table was left outside, a place for Nasir to chill with his mates. Though I doubted either artefact would survive the rainy season, they were nice while they lasted.

Perhaps the most cherished donation was a pair of orange swimming armbands. Despite being in sub-Saharan Africa and miles from the sea or a swimming pool, despite not even knowing what they were for, Bie wore them round the house all the time.

We were still distributing items when the container was quietly removed from outside the Chief's Palace and I subsequently received an email from the container company saying I was blacklisted. But with the contents of TBC being used in homes, schools, hospitals, libraries and businesses throughout the Upper West, I honestly couldn't have cared less.

We achieved so much in those two intense months and, crucially, discovered our voices on behalf of the people of Lawra.

And then we were in Accra before my flight home, the two of us, the unity suddenly under stress. We found a smart-ish restaurant that did Ghanaian food – a compromise that worked for us both – and after a congenial evening I suggested we go on somewhere.

'I don't want to.'

'Come on. It's my last night.'

Somehow, I coaxed him into a swanky wine bar in Osu, where I hit the G&Ts and he sulkily nursed a Club.

'So, Nasir ...' Fuelled by alcohol, I decided to find my voice not only for the charity but also for myself. 'Shall we talk about the wedding?'

It had been two months and we'd not discussed it since the moment on New Year's Eve when I'd said yes.

'We will discuss this when you are in Lawra.'

'But there's never any time in Lawra. And anyway, when will I *be* in Lawra? I'm getting on a plane and we haven't even talked about me coming back. We haven't talked about *anything*.'

I'm not sure who went ballistic first. I remember him shouting. I remember me storming off, and I'm not a stormer-offer. I remember him coming after me, because the thought of me, alone, in Osu, filled him with terror. And I remember trying for the rest of the night to fix things with this man, my fiancé, a person I'd promised to marry yet had no idea when I was next going to see.

It was not, all told, a very merry end to what had been a fantastic stay. As soon as I got back to Ramsbury I booked a flight for April because I didn't know what else to do.

TWENTY-FOUR

WITNESS

I've got some great snaps from that April. Nasir and I spent five memorable days at Big Milly's, our first holiday together, Nasir's first holiday ever, and my one holiday of the year since it was all I could afford.

Some great snaps. The weather was divine, the sea was dazzling, the fishing boats were picturesque, the clifftop bar was out of this world. Five truly memorable days. For all the wrong reasons.

The holiday was a mammoth disappointment from start to finish. From *before* the start, because we'd had weeks of tortuous negotiations deciding what to do. I wanted an adventure, to go exploring, ideally to see Ghana's famous sea turtles (my favourite animal). Nasir wanted to hunker down in Joska Lodge – or Big Milly's if he really *had* to go to a beach – somewhere familiar, where he felt comfortable. I can make a holiday anywhere by the sea, I thought, so that's what we did.

But we were on two separate holidays. At Big Milly's, I swam, sunbathed – T-shirt over bikini – took photos of fishermen and told myself I was having a magical trip. Nasir plugged into my iPod, chatted with anyone from the Upper West and responded to non-stop messages from whoever in Lawra.

There were nice moments. We played pool one night, had a couple of cocktails, talked about Bie, talked about the charity. Then, out of nowhere, we were arguing and back in Accra a day early. Nasir got what he wanted, the air-conditioned room in

Joska Lodge, fried rice and chicken from a stall, Nigerian films on the TV. And I got on another flight with a heavy heart.

In Ramsbury, I uploaded a photo album onto Facebook. There were a lot of fishing boats, which tells its own story.

'Ma call pog.'

Relations improved after the holiday and as Nasir broke off from one of our twice weekly catch-ups to announce *I call my woman*, I could instantly visualise him, smile on his face, sitting on a blue plastic chair outside the house, and it gave me a strong sense of belonging.

Everything hung on those chats. When I passed my Master's exams, he was the first person I wanted to tell and his proud *well done my wife* made being apart manageable. But another time, he revealed that Kendey had been in town for Bie's birthday (which I was devastated to miss) and I felt very far away and a bit ridiculously jealous.

On the matter of the wedding, Nasir was as good as his word and once I was in Lawra for the summer we began planning it. I had this notion of offering UK guests a two-week *experience* in which they'd meet Bie and Shilea, observe our amazing work and witness us getting married in bright matching outfits. Nasir approved, pleased I wanted to show him off, and it didn't occur to either of us that using our nuptials for a donor engagement opportunity might be slightly odd. In my head, it was a joyous vision, a fusion of everything that was important to me.

We set about finding the perfect location, though in the end the decision was made for us. Only one church in Lawra could provide the legal marriage certificate we'd need for the next relationship milestone – a UK visa for Nasir – and so we dutifully attended the pastor's home for the 'marriage counselling' required before he'd agree to hold our wedding.

'Are you committed to each other?'

We nodded enthusiastically, Nasir clenching my hand. 'Yes, we are very committed, to each other and to Bie.'

On cue, Bie leapt across the sofa (naughty by Ghanaian standards) and the way we dealt with him assured the pastor we were a team, a family.

'And will you be attending Church?'

We nodded again. It was all going well.

Of course, he could have asked some different questions. *Where are you going to live?* That would have been an interesting one. It was a question my parents had delicately asked when I'd finally told them of the engagement, and I would have said to him what I'd said to them. *We'll work it out.*

I'm not sure what Nasir would have said. We never discussed it, not explicitly, though we were making plans to build a house in Lawra, on a piece of land the Chief had offered. On the way back from the pastor, we swung by the empty plot.

'The living area would be here.' Nasir paced out a massive room. 'The kitchen, here. And there, the first bedroom.'

I could see it. The walls hung with Ghanaian prints, the floor strewn with Bie's toys, in the kitchen, a cafetière. I envisaged people in and out all the time – the usual Lawra crowd and visitors from England – and I liked the idea of investing in it together, being a family in a house we built ourselves, securing something for Bie, who was running around in the dust, already at home.

We dressed smartly that Sunday and went to church, a sprawling white building still under construction. Hundreds of people, also in Sunday best, congregated with what I'd describe as a new age vibe. Soon, there was wailing, much shouting about the hand of God and then the actual hands of the pastor, coated in olive oil, being laid on faces and arms all around us. Not what I was used to in low Anglican Ramsbury.

Fortunately, the touching stopped before he reached us, a microphone was passed round and people were called on to give themselves to God.

'And why are you here today?' the pastor asked Nasir.

He summoned his most solemn voice. 'We are here to give ourselves to the Almighty.'

After the service, the pastor told us he was willing to conduct our ceremony, on three conditions. First, Nasir must be christened. Second, he must take a Christian name. Third, we must pay for the building of the church's urinal.

We beat a hasty retreat. Nasir might have been willing to be christened. We might even have considered a donation to the toilet fund. But the prospect of changing his name on all his documentation months before the wedding and a visa application was a total no-no. Giving yourself to the Almighty was one thing – Ghanaian red tape was something else.

We put marriage plans on the backburner and focused on our latest batch of SBOs. This time, we made a conscious decision to prioritise skilled tradespeople, where we expected our money – invested in equipment – to have the most impact.

Hayford, a carpenter, lived in the shadow of the Chief's Palace and Nasir wound the motorbike round its boundaries to his small workshop. Faded photographs of his work were pinned on the wall, evidence of talent and a previously successful business.

'Stunning,' I said, studying the images of chests, beds and stools. 'They're works of art.'

'From before my accident.' He touched the dark glasses he wore to protect the socket where an eye used to be. 'Terrible accident, machinery exploded in my face. I sold everything to pay the medical bills. Now, with ATE's help, I have bought what I need to work again.'

It was all laid out for us to inspect, wood piled under a shelter, a shiny array of tools and a mobile phone sitting in its box, with phone credit, ready for orders.

'This is excellent.' Nasir checked the items against the shopping list Hayford had signed with his contract. 'We wish you good luck in your new business.'

'Thank you. I am learning to be a carpenter with one eye, but I think it is a good eye and I can still make my art.'

We left Hayford's with a song in our hearts and set off for Abigail's, where we expected her to be weaving newly bought threads on a newly mended loom. Instead, she was sitting on the ground outside her compound, next to a cloth crowded with bottles of soft drinks and packets of sweets.

'What's this?' Nasir drew up next to a small boy who was buying a cola. 'Abigail, how did you pay for these goods?'

'My grant.' She thrust out her chin. 'With my profit, I will get a better loom.'

Over an agonising couple of hours, Nasir extracted the full story. Abigail (encouraged by her brother) had spent her grant on confectionary and was selling at a loss, assuming the money she took was profit. It was a disaster, and an absolute breach of the contract she'd put her thumbprint to.

'Abigail, I hope you understand,' explained Nasir carefully, 'that because you have not done what you have promised, things cannot continue. You must return any of grant you have not spent.' He sighed. 'And because these products were bought with funds from ATE, we will have to take them away.'

She fell apart, grabbing at his hands, bawling what I presumed were apologies and promises not to break the rules, begging for another chance. It was too late. Nasir went into the compound and emerged, followed by Abigail's mother, with a carton of sweets under his arm.

'I will call a nyaaba. There is a lot to take away.'

The mother now joined Abigail in pleading and pulling at Nasir, until he showed the older woman the shopping list her daughter had signed and the clause stating we would confiscate everything if she misused the money.

'The mother is saying she knew nothing of this. She didn't know the money was from ATE. She says if she had, she wouldn't have let this happen, and I believe her.'

It was a bleak afternoon, us removing piles of stock, Abigail realising she'd blown possibly her one chance, her mother inconsolable, her sister sobbing by the still-broken loom.

As the nyaaba drove off, Abigail gave us the last unspent cedis from the grant. Though we'd done the principled thing, I was grateful to hide the tears behind my sunglasses, aware we were partly to blame.

That night, Nasir and I thrashed out a new procedure, introducing a 'family witness' into our application process, a senior family member who would co-sign the contract, oversee their relative and try to stop them making a life-ruining mistake.

The business owners weren't alone in benefitting from a family witness. I craved one – two actually – and soon they were arriving, in the form of Mum and Dad, via a flight to Tamale and a long dusty drive during which the car broke down, Nasir stressing on the phone to the driver all the way.

I was standing on the veranda, Bie on my hip, as their car pulled up. Nasir fussed with the suitcases and I handed out pieces of mango, so pleased they were there, so proud to demonstrate my happy domestic scene. I wanted to prove, from the off, that marrying Nasir wasn't a mad idea, that it was a rather splendid one, for me and for ATE.

I also wanted to show them how much the charity had evolved in the eighteen months since they'd last visited. We held some brilliant SBO training, assisted by a recently recruited army of 'consultants' who gave the entrepreneurs the one-to-one attention they needed. And, because some things are slow to change, Mum ran a lively role play session on understanding profit and loss.

Just after my folks came, we moved house. I say *we*, Nasir and Kanyiri did the moving, all I did was drop Bie at school and take Mum, Dad and Shilea for breakfast at a tea shop by the roundabout. As we sat at the high counter, savouring oniony omelettes stuffed into sweet bread, the contents of the house rolled by on nyaabas, Kanyiri sitting atop.

I watched my Lawra life pass before my eyes. Boxes of stationery and stuff for workshops, the last of TBC's wheelchairs, the precious fridge, Nasir's T-shirt-filled suitcases, the toys I'd brought Bie from the UK, my summer clothes, now permanently there. In the third nyaaba, I spotted Karen's old flat screen TV.

'Be gentle! I sweated blood getting that here.' Kanyiri gave a thumbs-up. That TV was what the boys watched their beloved football on and he would have protected it with his life.

After breakfast, we strolled ten minutes to the new place where Nasir was orchestrating the unpacking like a maestro.

'Mum and Dad, let me take you to your room.' He led them through the living area to the left wing of the building, where there were three sizeable bedrooms, a shower and loo. In one of the rooms, Kanyiri was unpacking his few personal effects, having decided to move in with us now his mother and youngest brother were back from the south and the family home was a bit cramped.

I headed to the master bedroom on the other side of the property. It was enormous, with a bed roomy enough for everyone to stretch out, a large bathroom (with walls!) and a bath Bie would adore. Off the same corridor, Bie had his own room, ready for whenever he wanted it.

'You've done well here,' said Dad, as we sat on the veranda sucking water sachets. Nasir had negotiated a good price, far cheaper for the charity than paying for volunteers to stay in a lodge.

'Congratulations,' said Mum. 'We can do some great work from here.'

That summer, there was a kind of party atmosphere around the house, around ATE, around us. Kanyiri's brothers would cycle over on Kakpe's 'TBC' bike, little Nyanekpeng on the crossbar, occasionally accompanied by their mum. Nasir was attentive with my parents, and after work we'd go for drinks, enjoy Nasir's delicious meals around the dining table and relax on the vast flaking leatherette sofa, invariably with the football on.

I have some special photos from those weeks, my favourite being one of Mum sitting under our mango tree, Shilea next to her, Bie on her knee as she read to him. My Mum, my dog, my boy.

'This is where I grew up.'

Nasir swung his bike, Dad on the back, Bie on the front, past the Ghanaian flag and under the grand white arch of the Chief's Palace. I followed behind with Mum, Shilea running alongside.

'See there?' Nasir pointed upwards, to where residents were walking on the rooftops, silhouetted against the sun. 'This is where we sleep in very hot weather.'

We weaved through a maze of bustling alleyways and it felt like a secret realm, a town-within-a-town, separate from the rest of Lawra, a-buzz with people, everyone related to the Chief (and each other), many in traditional clothes.

'Good evening, Sister Sarah!' waved one of the many people I knew from around town, as we whizzed past.

All around were animals and smells and noise, family members greeted us, pigs dined off rubbish and children played by open drains. It may have lacked sanitation and been overcrowded, but the Chief's Palace was dynamic and alive.

We walked through an iron gate to Nasir's family compound. His stepmother Georgina, a beautiful woman in her forties, left her steaming pot and greeted us warmly while Karlley, all charm and hospitality, offered seats under the enormous mango tree. Shilea, who was a regular at the Chief's Palace, played with the dogs. It was a lovely family scene, the parents of the groom welcoming the parents of the bride.

Karlley sent Nasir's half-sister Emmanuella out for Clubs and we sat in the shady courtyard and drank to health and happiness, like you do when people are getting married. My parents, after some initial doubts, had embraced the idea and presented us with a roll of luscious purple cloth from the Zambo weavers, to be tailored into traditional outfits for the big day. Until then, the wedding had been this strange thing, disconnected from the rest of my life. That was the moment it became real.

After Mum and Dad left, I opened my laptop and created a save-the-date invitation. I can't imagine what the twenty people I emailed it to thought, given I'd hardly mentioned the engagement to anyone and not all of them even knew I was with Nasir. Though honestly, I didn't worry about that. I could picture the whole thing and I wanted to act quickly, while the image was vivid in my mind.

TWENTY-FIVE

FINE

You People.

It wasn't the first time Nasir had called me that since I'd officially become Chief Executive of ATE. There'd been a formal recruitment process, and though perhaps it came as no huge surprise I got the job, it was a turning point in the development of the charity, as well as my own development as a thirty-year-old living off her parents. OK, my salary (for three days a week) was made up largely of a monthly donation from Mum and Dad, who'd segued my allowance into a standing order, but still. Chief Executive. Reporting to the Board of Trustees. Nasir reporting directly to Dad to try and avoid any conflict of interest.

Which was why I'd just told Nasir that, before we opened our next kitchen, I wanted to research feeding programmes at junior high schools (JHS) and draw up a proper strategy.

'Sarah, Sarah,' he sighed, as if he'd explained it so many times but maybe, this time, I'd get it. 'Sarah, what you people don't understand is we need to arrange things here. First, I must take the head teacher at Karbo JHS for a drink, show respect.'

Yes, things had certainly changed since the spontaneous early days of ATE, when we'd both acted purely on instinct. Now, with more at stake, we needed more procedures and I had become not only his fiancée, but also *You People.*

Of course, procedures *could* be frustrating, but (as I was learning from my Master's) they were necessary. For Nasir, though, they cut against his natural way of working. So, he'd say *we need eighty school uniforms* and would be climbing on his bike to put the order in with the tailor, while I'd be consulting my spreadsheets to check the school uniform budget.

We found our way. The trustees approved an extra £60 for uniforms and Nasir *then* liaised with the tailor and seamstress. I prepared an annual strategy on JHS feeding *and* we took the head teacher for a drink.

One evening, at Home Touch, our new favourite spot, Nasir clinked for beer and made his pitch to him.

'Other NGOs fail because they do not connect with the community. They give the money and they withdraw. We are always here, we weigh and measure the children, we monitor their attendance, we make sure they can learn. The thing is ...' He paused for effect. 'The thing is, an empty sack cannot stand.'

I had to smile. Nasir was confident and passionate, knowledgeable and persuasive, taller, somehow, and more attractive, a far cry from the *small boy* of 2012 who'd be more likely to fetch the Clubs than order them. And knowing we'd made this journey together, I didn't feel like You People. I felt like Us.

Though the work relationship had changed (slightly), I was very much of the mind that the personal relationship would be *fine*. I was thrilled when the paperwork for our plot of land came through and trips of sand, bags of cement, piles of stones began arriving. Those materials, on that land, were solid and a sign of our investment – financially and emotionally – in the future.

The other significant marker for me – tangible evidence the relationship could exist beyond my sporadic appearances in Lawra – was for Nasir to visit the UK. Off went the visa application, along with the £200 fee and a ton of documents, and I trusted that would be fine too. Either way, I would be over for a personal trip in November and again from December to February for the opening of the new kitchen, a family holiday and our wedding.

Although I was now earning, all my cash was flowing into Ghana, be it the visa, flights, hotels, house and, of course, emergencies, of which there was always one. And despite Nasir now having two jobs and a burgeoning income, I never saw him put anything aside for the Ghanaian equivalent of a rainy day. If anything, quite the reverse. There was a lot of buying beers for other young men and paying for *their* emergencies, I suppose as Felix had done for Nasir back in the day. It was another *it's how things work.*

'Sarah, Sarah.' Sigh. 'What you don't understand is that I buy them a meal today and if I need anything tomorrow, they will be there for me.'

In fact, I *did* understand, because my Master's had covered *social capital*, a sort of informal 'insurance' that supported people in crisis, if never quite allowing them to escape the vicious circle. For the skinny young man with a music stall, it had been a safety net, a lifeline. For the Nasir he'd become by 2014, with his growing responsibilities, saving something in the actual bank might have been a better approach. Sigh.

To be fair, it wasn't completely one-sided. At Home Touch, an official from the Ghana Education Service might wander over to shake *our* hands and buy *us* a drink. At Lawra hospital, for a discussion about donating the last wheelchairs from the container, we were given the VIP treatment. And when we drove through town, people would call out as the motorbike whizzed past, *barka, barka, thank you for the feeding, thank you for my grant, thank you for SNAP.*

One afternoon, the three cooks from Karbo Primary came by the house and presented us with thirty eggs – an incredibly generous gift – as a token of their thanks. We didn't do it for the thanks (or the eggs) and it wasn't only us doing it. I can't lie, though, we both had big enough egos to enjoy the accolades.

The prospect of going home that August was hideous. Long-distance relationships are tricky and the thought of leaving this newly attractive man triggered a wave of insecurities. After all, with me away, he was practically a single guy, with an extra swagger, an enviable income, a property, a fast bike, a burgeoning collection of shoes, at least one admirer I'd clocked giving him a smile and a constantly pinging new smartphone that I thought he was a bit too private about.

'Maybe I shouldn't go,' I teased one night at the spot.

'Then stay.' Nasir was very straightforward about these things. 'And if we have to, we eat grass.'

He'd used that phrase before – and it was just a phrase, he didn't mean we would literally *eat grass.* What he meant was if I couldn't fundraise and we both lost our ATE salaries, we'd be *fine.*

'Of course I can't stay.' I mean, how could I tell him *my* fine included that salary, along with interesting work, opportunities and travel? That my fine did not involve chewing even metaphorical grass? 'But we're OK?'

'Sarah, I have said. Now, you make me talk too much.' He clinked his Club against mine. 'I think I want another beer.'

My other tricky long-distance relationship was with Bie.

We'd had such a gorgeous summer and it broke my heart to go, knowing I'd miss him more than I could ever express, knowing he would miss me too. I made a wallchart pinned with photos, marked when I was coming back, and spent hours with him looking at the pictures, promising him I wouldn't be away for long. Promising him, reassuring myself.

Nasir and I had a couple of surprisingly agreeable nights in Accra, which made heading to the airport even more horrible than usual. We sat in the taxi, me clinging onto his hand, traffic throbbing, rain drumming, radio blaring and I had this gnawing feeling everything was slipping away so I clung on tighter and the traffic throbbed harder and the rain drummed faster and the music blared louder. It wasn't all in my overheated imagination. The traffic jam *was* getting worse and soon we'd been sitting in it for over an hour and time really *was* slipping away.

Then Phil Collins came on the radio, singing about one more night, singing about how he can't wait forever.

'I have to go.' Nasir pulled his hand away.

'Go where?'

'My bus is at seven, I need to get back for Bie.'

He grabbed his bag, reached for the door and was gone. And I was left with the driver and Phil Collins. I spent £30 on beer, croissants and gifts at the airport and none of it made me feel fine.

Same old, same old. Shower, cheese, Sauv Blanc and then I hit the fundraising with raw-crazy energy. Nasir kept things going in Lawra and there were messages, calls, an occasional snap of Bie and frequent requests for money, *the boys need this, the TV is broken, I need the fare to Accra for the visa.* It was just about bearable, but I was desperate to get back, to feel it was real again. Evenings spent flicking through photos, Nasir looking great, consoled me a little and also not at all.

I was working in the ATE office when Nasir rang from Accra. He'd gone to the British Embassy to find out if he'd got his visa and was alone, stressed from travel, and it was a *no*. Even though we weren't surprised, we were gutted. Nasir coming to England, to Ramsbury, would have made things more real.

Not that I knew what was real or what I really wanted or where I really wanted to be. This beautiful mess of a relationship – straightforward and so very complicated, involved and so discrete, committed yet so vague – both pained me and suited me, in the sense I didn't (as yet) have to make any difficult choices.

How could I? I wanted both of it, I wanted all of it. And I wanted none of it.

I wanted to go to the ball. Late September, and I headed to London to meet my sister before the flight to Dublin for my second Gamma Ball Rally. As I sat outside the Pret near Karen's office, my phone rang.

'Sarah? Sarah?'

'Hi Nasir.'

'Sarah, you need to send money.'

And there it was. I'd only recently transferred a hundred pounds, Nasir having informed me he'd spent his salary on stones for the new house and had nothing left for food. I'd been angry with him for not telling me sooner and he'd been angry with me because *I can't talk to you about money*.

'There has been a special situation …'

Thoughts of a medical crisis leapt into my head. 'Everyone OK?'

'You won't understand.' He hesitated. 'I have been taken to the juju man.'

He was right, I didn't understand. To this day, I still don't.

Apparently, someone (he didn't say who) had paid the juju man to put a curse on him (he didn't say why) and he needed to pay the juju man to take the curse away (he didn't say how).

I didn't mind pouring my money into Lawra if it was for the children, for health care, family emergencies, I totally got that. But the idea my precious salary was subsidising the juju man, no way. I remembered the basket weaver who'd given him her grant to kill a chicken and cure her HIV and Nasir and I had agreed about that, or I assumed we had. It wasn't about beliefs (and I'm not one to judge anyone's faith). It was about priorities.

'I'm sorry, Nasir, absolutely not. No.'

'This is the problem, I can never talk to you about money.'

He then asked me to send something *for the boys,* which felt like another way for me to pay the juju man. Time, I decided, to cash in that social capital.

'Take Bie to the family compound for food, Kanyiri can go to his mum.'

'Sarah, what you people don't understand ...'

'I don't understand, but it's not about that. It's about us and about sharing financial decisions and about sharing problems.'

I braced myself for another round of *you people.* Instead, silence.

'Nasir?' Now I was seriously worried. 'Nasir?'

'The trouble with the curse ... it has made me do things ...' His voice hardened. 'I will not say.'

My heart went cold. You know, that cold dread you get when you suspect the person you trust most in the world is not telling the whole truth and your life is hanging by a thread. The very worst of my insecurities flooded over me and I was drowning. Drowning …

Somehow, I pulled myself free.

'I can't do this now.'

I put down my phone, wondering what the hell had just happened. And when Nasir messaged me a few minutes later –

this is who I am if you don't want to be with me don't

– I hesitated only momentarily before sending a one word reply.

Fine

TWENTY-SIX

OFF-ISH/ON-ISH

Off

If I was looking for signs I'd made a terrible mistake, I wasn't getting any. If anything, the cosmos was rewarding me. I was met at Dublin Airport by a swish corporate car, whisked to the luxurious Powerscourt Hotel and upgraded to a balcony suite with technology popping out of hidden cabinets, free mini bar and even a decanter of red wine. I mean, I do prefer white, so the cosmos slipped up there I suppose, but as I laid in bed with a pipe of Pringles I felt at peace with my momentous decision and it seemed the universe felt the same.

My phone bleeped and I ignored it because I knew who it was and what it was about and I didn't want to deal with *that* before my speech. I wasn't being cold-hearted. I wasn't even being strong. All I was doing (not for the last time) was the next thing that needed to be done. I flicked Pringle crumbs from my marshmallow robe and slipped into a tight blue dress.

In the lift, my phone bleeped again and instinctively I checked it. Nasir had sent a photo of Kanyiri holding up his excellent exam results, along with four words:

Good luck for tonight.

With that, I headed into the ballroom where the Gamma Ball ralliers donated a mind-boggling fifty grand, enough to transform hundreds of lives. The cosmos was doing its thing.

I cancelled my flights for November, focused on work and threw myself at life in Ramsbury. I saw friends, resumed Ceroc dancing and rejoined my choir, no longer feeling that push-pull, less conflicted, more solvent, able at last to buy a round in the pub with my modest salary and the refund from my flights.

Nasir and I still spoke constantly, civilly – about the charity and Bie, *not* the other stuff – and soon I was yearning to get back out there. Glamorous balls and nights in The Bell are one thing, but nothing trumps a lunchtime at Karbo, a singsong at SNAP, handing a grant to someone who wants to transform their life or having Bie in my arms.

I ignored my confused feelings and got packing.

Off-ish

Five of us went in January 2015 for the exciting launch of the second ATE kitchen. Me, Mum and Dad, Luke Hodgson (ATE's new assistant and son of Stephen, our office-donor) and trustee Susan Suchopar. Safety in numbers.

I flew out early and spent three chilled days on Cape Coast with VSO friends Leela, Alice and Ellie. Leela was working for a charity in the south and Alice and Ellie still had their flights for my now-cancelled wedding. I hung out at the spectacular Ko-Sa Beach Resort by day and drank cocktails at Leela's by night, liberated to be in Ghana without Nasir angsting all over the place.

Now I was the one waiting in Arrivals for UK visitors, I was the one fighting off over-eager taxi drivers and, at the bus station, I was the one giving the stern lecture.

'Split your money. I put mine in a sock and have a few notes in my wallet for robbers. Don't catch their eye and don't be a hero.'

I found my seat, shoved in ear plugs and dived under a sarong, satisfied I'd done a very fair impression of Nasir laying on the scare tactics.

When I stirred a few hours later it was pitch dark. Mum leant across the aisle. 'You missed it.'

'Missed what?'

'Bandits. There was a hijack ahead and ...'

'God, is everyone ...?'

'We're fine. The driver had to reverse a mile down the road to escape. It took forever.'

'Why didn't you wake me?

'You couldn't have done anything.'

Which was true. Though I couldn't help thinking Nasir would never *ever* be caught asleep on the job. He was certainly on top form when we finally arrived in Lawra, the perfect host, helping everyone settle in, carrying my bags through to 'our' side and tactfully depositing them in Bie's bedroom.

That first night, after Clubs at Home Touch and a bowl of the delicious sen sen Nasir knew was my favourite, I headed to bed. A few minutes later I was joined by a sleepy Bie and we cuddled as the ceiling fan spun relentlessly above.

'Ben Obby Irry Lar Keppy Moany.'

We spent the first week weighing and measuring the two hundred students of Karbo Junior High, where we were about to open another kitchen. It was chaos, children everywhere, shoes and sandals everywhere, names and numbers shouted from all directions as we tried to get them to stand correctly for their vital statistics to be taken. A few were nervous of stepping on the scales, fearing they'd break them. If only. After years of deprivation many were not merely thin, they were physically undersized.

'Is there a Ben Obby …? For some reason, I'd taken on the job of calling pupils forward and had comically overestimated my Dagaare. Peals of laughter filled the classroom until Nasir commandeered the clipboard.

'Benobe-irelaar Kpemoanye, please come here.'

A boy stepped up and Mum demonstrated how to stretch out his spindly arm before running the tape measure around the top of it. 'Fourteen point seven centimetres, upper arm.' An upper arm no thicker than my wrist.

'Hello, Sister Sarah.'

It was my friend Judith, from the Tuori days. I gave her a hug, not needing the scales to tell me how thin she'd become since joining a school with no feeding programme. Her ribs dug into me. The same was true of my favourite cow-boy Jeremiah, his handshake strong as ever, his smile charming, his face hollow with dry season hunger. I grabbed the list from Nasir and ran my finger down the names. Celina's was on it, but she wasn't there. Maybe the new kitchen would draw her back, I lived in hope.

At the end of that week, the kitchen served its first lunches, Judith, Jeremiah and the others queueing for groundnut stew. They, at least, would have full stomachs and the chance to learn, to complete school, to build a future.

On the way home, Nasir took us to the main crossroads east out of town.

FIGHTING POVERTY
ACTION
THROUGH
ENTERPRISE
IN LAWRA

It was our new sign, rising from the dust, fifteen feet tall.

I gulped down a tear, recalling those early walks with Nasir when we didn't know each other well and had counted NGO boards as he told me of the corruption and lack of community links that led so many to fail. And now, as we posed in front of our own sign, Luke taking photos, I silently vowed, *we will do better.*

Later that day, Nasir posted the picture on Facebook, with the message:

We are big in terms of our work thanks baba God

After a busy week, Mum and Susan headed home. On Saturday morning, with the house a little quieter, Nasir came into my bedroom and handed me and Bie our eggs and bread.

It was an oasis in the desert. Me, Dad and Nasir stood in awe, gazing at the season-defying green patch of vegetables in the middle of the neat, well-ordered compound.

'Please sit,' said Salam Haruna indicating a bench under a welcome awning, and we began the formal process of awarding him a grant.

'I am a vulcaniser. My father taught me the trade when I was a boy and after he died, I took over. If somebody has a puncture on their motorbike, they ring me and I rush straight to wherever they are and fix it. It is a good business but I can progress. With

221

the grant, I can purchase spare parts in bulk and save money and the trouble of travelling to buy them each time.'

Dad, always alert to potential problems, was impressed.

'Please, there is one more thing.' Salam darted inside the compound, returning with a notebook. 'Here I will record what I have spent, what I have charged, what is to invest, what is for my family and what is for savings.' He laughed. 'The last thing I want is to charge less than I paid.'

The broad grin on Dad's face said it all and I'm not sure who looked prouder in the photos, Salam Haruna and his beaming wife, or Dad, in his ATE T-shirt.

For me, too, the trip had been a triumph – and a relief. Regardless of where Nasir and I were personally, the charity was thriving, the family was thriving and we were making it work.

Sarah Gardner is feeling cold with Charles Gardner and Luke Hodgson at Terminal 5 London Heathrow Airport
January 31, 2015

Snow???! Travelling without a jacket was a mistake

Regrets, I had a few, and not just bad packing. Because I knew, on the evenings Nasir and I had gone alone to Home Touch for *a talk* – me still wanting him to explain what the hell had happened, him, frustratingly, still unable to – I knew there had been moments, fleeting moments, when talk gave way to something more and clear lines became blurry. And whilst we didn't do anything *as such*, I'd given Nasir enough to believe and that felt like a mistake.

In Ramsbury, I hit the ground running, scouts, cake stalls, policy-writing, grant applications and what with my social life and my Master's, I never stopped.

Until something happened that made me. My parents were separating.

The very foundation, the safe, secure foundation my life was built on was wrecked, and so was I. Devastated, for myself, for us all. My family was everything, so much of my identity, and then, seemingly out of nowhere, it no longer existed. The night I found out, I cried with my sister, I went to my friend Laura, I called Nasir.

He was comforting, sympathetic, caring, upset both *for* me and *with* me. After all, they'd been Mum and Dad to him for two years. I felt so alone and he sensed that.

'Don't worry, whatever happens, I am not going anywhere.'

On-ish

I moved out of the house, rented somewhere on the high street, got a rescue dog, worked non-stop. It was the most horrendous time. As well as my parents' break-up, my sister left her husband of nine months and our dear grandfather (Mum's dad) passed away. With things falling apart, I was utterly lost, broken, clinging to Karen, Nasir always there.

In the midst of the nightmare, I wrote a blog.

Catching up

London, UK

Jun 9, 2015

Since my last entry, in January 2014, life has changed. I write on my way to a meeting with DFID (Department for International Development) about female genital mutilation. These days I frequently do things I'm convinced I'm not qualified for. I'm stretched to my limits and learn every day. It's a privilege, but I am exhausted.

Today I left my UK dog, Chico, with a friend and soon I'll leave him for 5 weeks when I go to Ghana. This ridiculous canine situation is representative of my life. I'm split between two places, never completely happy in either and with great responsibility at each end. The division of myself is painful and can feel isolating, but it brings such joy. I have two homes, two communities where I feel safe and valued. Lucky me. I think.

Sx

Can I go back and give that girl a hug? Two homes? Truthfully, I wasn't even sure I had one.

In July, I flew to Ghana, desperate to attach myself to Nasir and Bie, to surrender myself to Lawra and my other life, to dive into the work.

Our house was full of cheerful productivity, our evening drinks at Home Touch a living tableau of the parts of my life that made sense. There, round the wobbly plastic table, were Gabriel and Adeline – both now consultants mentoring our small businesses – and their adorable toddling twins.

There was Makum. There was Luke and Kanyiri, usually kicking a football. And there was Leela Shanti, who had been volunteering with us since May, her talented presence feeling like a real validation of our work. And a comfort for me, because I needed a friend.

The final person at the table was, of course, Nasir, clinking bottles and swilling my glass, confident, in control, having been ably overseeing the charity's activities on the ground. All the pieces of the jigsaw fitted, everyone was doing an outstanding job, everyone got on. It was what I'd craved, a marvellous distraction from the family shit, a huge Lawra hug for the girl whose world was shaken to the core.

Workwise, Nasir and I were as one. Like on the evening we were visited by Margaret, the teacher from Bie's school who I'd introduced to SNAP a couple of years before. Margaret had become a fantastic Committee member and we'd all been distraught when her daughter Joyce had died that August.

'Sarah, I have a question for you and Nasir.' She looked determined, despite her grief. 'SNAP has changed my life. I have become a different parent and others have changed too. They were told their child would never talk and now that child speaks. What I am asking is, although I have lost my Joyce, I would like to remain on the Committee. SNAP showed me my daughter deserved to be loved and I want to encourage other mothers to know the same.'

'That's OK, isn't it Nasir?'

'Yes, I think it is good.'

I handed her an envelope. 'These are for you.'

It was a few photos of Joyce I'd printed and brought with me, aware Margaret had none of her own. Precious images of mother and daughter, she carefully examined each in turn, occasionally brushing her face so her tears wouldn't dampen the paper.

The charity was flying that summer. We had a fruitful meeting with the Paramount Chief. There was a bumpy drive out to farmers Francis and Betty, who had used a second grant to buy another acre of land. And we got a thank you present from carpenter Hayford, though I didn't love riding with a live cock hanging from the handlebars.

The doomed bird hung around on the veranda for days until Kanyiri wielded the large kitchen knife and Nasir cooked it for the party we threw for Luke's birthday. We presented him with a traditional Ghanaian smock and Leela and Nasir created an alcoholic concoction in an immense bowl. We danced through the night, the boys in their smocks, me in a slinky blue number. It wasn't quite my Gamma Ball dress, but I felt pretty fabulous anyway, relieved, after all that misery, to simply let go.

The moment I got on the plane to London, I thought, *shit.* What had I done? I mean, I'd told him, *we are not together,* that I believed in us a family if not as a couple. I'll be honest, though, not all my actions, not on every night, backed up that claim. Nasir, I suspect, took my protestations about the relationship with a pinch of salt. By Ghanaian standards we *were* together and for him it was a waiting game, waiting until I decided what I truly wanted.

After I got back, he posted a picture on Facebook, him with a trendy haircut and sexy shades, me with a glorious smile. No message, only the picture, but it needed no words. We just looked so bloody happy.

On?

Mum and I went to Ghana in November and met up with Nasir and Bie at Big Milly's for a relaxing holiday and definitely separate rooms. My birthday present from Nasir was four seedlings (two mango trees, two orange trees) to be planted at the corners of the plot of land we still owned and that he was still building on.

Leela moved in with me in Ramsbury and we worked together on ATE's first ever application for funds from a charitable body – the Commercial Education Trust – which we won. At the Gamma Ball Rally in Amsterdam we raised a phenomenal £70,000. We had a barn dance in Ramsbury Village Hall. I put my Master's on hold.

In Lawra, the Paramount Chief generously gifted Nasir a piece of land for a dedicated ATE office. Nasir was interviewed on the radio and got our message out across the whole district.

He was in touch with me every day too, my loyal support at the end of what had been – personally, at least – a pretty awful year. When I went to Ghana in January 2016, I had, indeed, made a decision. Well, not exactly a decision but I'd stopped resisting what I now accepted as my inevitable destiny. I was tired of fighting it, tired of trying to be in Lawra and not be with Nasir. I loved him and I loved Bie, who I'd parented as much when we hadn't been together as when we had. They were my family and I wanted to be with them. We were on.

TWENTY-SEVEN

THE PRODUCTION

We were on in another way too. As in, we were always 'on'. In Lawra, it was never just me, Nasir and Bie. Never. Hordes of people came from the UK and we were forever on duty, arranging transport, food, lodgings, entertainment, managing the crowd. I was in my element but it was intense for us as a family, being available, presenting a positive image for ATE, serving up *an experience* without sugar-coating the reality of life in the Upper West.

And answering questions. So many questions. Once, coming out of my bedroom, hair still wet from a bucket bath, I was met by three visitors queuing – queuing! – to ask me one thing or another, including how to tell if an egg was boiled. *Same as in England,* I'd snapped, though I'd done enough hiding behind the louvres to know how easily you can lose your sense of self in Lawra. Even so, a boiled egg?

Thankfully, my guests that January were a great bunch, a revolving door of them for a full-on six weeks. Housekeepers, hosts, impresarios, we were, undoubtedly, putting on a show. Fortunately, Nasir and I were good at that.

Nasir, Ghana Operations Manager

'Life here is about surviving. Things are hard. People can't even get some food a day to eat. ATE is more or less giving a support to people for them to determine their future. The passion of what ATE are doing, it's like I'm part of it and we have to do it.'

The ATE Film

'This is the ATE team meeting.'

Nasir kicked off proceedings in our shiny new office, built from old metal container sheets and hot as an oven. The Lawra gang was used to it, as were the consultants and locals who constantly popped in to the green-gold-red painted structure. I was glazed in sweat.

'We welcome Chair of Trustees, Charles Gardner, and also Dr Nick Maurice, who will run the very important project funded by Commercial Education Trust.'

I glowed with pride. Nick was a Wiltshire legend – GP, international development pioneer and one of the first ever VSO volunteers in the 60s – and we were honoured (and nervous) that he'd agreed to conduct the evaluation of our small business programme.

Nasir shuffled his papers. 'We are also about to open our third kitchen. So today, we have a full agenda.'

He wasn't kidding. I mopped my brow and prayed the meeting wouldn't last long.

John Bosco, Head teacher, Dowine JHS
'Every morning each person is eager to bring a bowl and to be fed. It's quite amazing. Just for the few days of this feeding we have seen the children are attentive. That is the main thing ATE is coming to do. It's not just feeding them but letting them go higher.'
The ATE Film

Our convoy of motorbikes headed eastward out of Lawra and twenty-five bone-shattering minutes later we were at Dowine Junior High. The smell of possibility was in the air, along with beans and gari, another staple.

'Good morning, Miss, how are you?' A passing pupil radiated the same striking confidence that had impressed Nasir and me a few months before. The students, the PTA, even the mango tree in the courtyard, had seemed especially vibrant and we hadn't hesitated to choose Dowine for our next kitchen. I put it down to John Bosco, the magnetic head teacher, who was now emerging like a hero through a billow of smoke.

'Mr Nasir, Madam Sarah, let me show you our kitchen.' He led us to the side of the structure, where a cook was pushing wood through a low hole in the wall. 'Many school kitchens have no ventilation and are very smoky. I have scoured the district for ideas and the result is this tunnel allowing firewood in and fumes out.'

'That's clever,' said Nick, who'd seen a few smoky buildings in his time. We peeked inside to see three cooks stirring a bubbling pot, breathing clean air.

'Thank you. And that is the good news. The bad news is the children did not bring their bowls.' A group of pupils hurried past. 'Now we are cooking, they go to collect them.'

It brought me up sharp. So much had changed for me and the charity since that first lunch at Karbo Primary, yet for most children in the Upper West it was still the case that if a stranger promised them food, they didn't believe it until they smelt it.

After the two hundred children were fed, the cooks gave us bowls of food to try, and we all sat on a step and tucked in. The beans were delicious and this time Dad didn't need to make an emergency exit.

Take a break, I suggested when we got back, and my guests gratefully disappeared for showers and naps.

Although I had a million things to do (and virtually a spreadsheet for each of them), I was determined to make time for Bie and rushed off to collect him from school before retiring to our wing for homework, play and a bath.

At five, Bie and I wandered over to the spot behind our house, accompanied by Kakpe (who'd recently moved in with us) along with Shilea and her puppy Oscar (the rice and beans having finally failed). We positioned ourselves under a mango tree, closely followed by our revived guests and eventually Nasir, who made a toast.

'Today is the day ATE arrived in Dowine.'

Then little Oscar barked and everyone laughed.

Gabriel N-Yoh Maanibe, Senior Consultant

'Upper West Ghana is, even within country-wide, neglected in the first place. It is considered as the last born of the country. And, by its location and climatic conditions, it is easily forgotten. It's neglected, that is the word.'

The ATE Film

Whilst it wasn't exactly a tourist hot spot, we always gave visitors a jaunt round Lawra, including the one national landmark, a windowless, single-storey building where Ghana's first president was once briefly imprisoned by the British.

'Our father, Dr Kwame Nkrumah, was angry with us in Lawra,' explained Nasir. 'They say he arranged a curse and that is why life here is difficult.' He shrugged. 'I can think of other reasons.'

We spent the rest of the afternoon boating down the Black Volta, scouring for crocodiles and passing the odd wishful man panning for gold. No crocs or gold were seen, although Nasir insisted both were there to be found, if you looked hard enough.

Adeline Domboor, Consultant

'So many people have ideas but they don't have anything to do with these ideas because they don't have funds. ATE has come to lift those dreams, it has come to give them hope and they are making it now, making it better.'

The ATE Film

The BizATE evaluation was an enormous piece of work and Nick spent two weeks interviewing dozens of small business owners, consultants, staff and members of the public. The process culminated in a final feedback session and rally at the community centre, attended by over one hundred people.

'Out of my profits I am able to provide for my family.'

Vulcaniser Salam Haruna was one of several Lawra role models we'd invited to tell their story. 'I can afford the basics of life, educational costs, water and electricity. I give great thanks to ATE for what they are doing for businesses. God should keep on blessing them, so they can keep on doing this work.'

I threw Salam Haruna a grateful smile, as Nasir opened the floor.

My income has trebled since ATE backed my business. I have respect in my community.

I need an apprentice to build my enterprise.

What can you do for dry season farmers who try to grow when times are lean?

Working as an ATE consultant has enhanced my job prospects. I feel better about myself.

It was uplifting – and challenging – stuff, and we promised to consider an apprenticeship scheme and a dry season project. Of course, we overran massively and Kakpe had to collect Bie and the twins from school. With children and dogs playing in a corner, we held a short ceremony where I presented certificates of achievement to the consultants and Nick gave a prayer and closing thoughts.

'Never doubt,' he said, quoting the legendary anthropologist Margaret Mead, 'that a small group of committed people can change the world. Indeed, they're the only thing that ever has.'

The whole room rose in spontaneous rapturous applause. Later, back in Wiltshire, Nick would write a favourable and motivating report that formed the basis of our future BizATE work. Meanwhile, the rousing response from our consultants and SBOs was enough.

Karlley Albeboure, Senior Consultant

'A lot of people are now pointing fingers because they have seen from the outside the benefit people are getting, so more people want to come to ATE. ATE is not working for the individual, it's working for the community and it's working for the country, Ghana.'

The ATE Film

Soon, a whole new group descended on us, along with a whole new situation to wrap my head around. Arranging it so Mum came the day after Dad left was a sad legacy of all the heartache, but the second she, Karen and Ross (Karen's new partner) climbed down from the mid-morning coach, I couldn't have been happier. Bie – familiar with family pictures on my laptop – immediately threw his arms round Karen. It was the perfect arrival scene.

Our other guests were Asif Noorani and Graham Tilley, two experienced film-makers who had kindly volunteered to produce a fundraising film. Nasir ordered nyaabas to take the luggage and camera kit back to base and I led everyone to the tea shop, excited – and a little apprehensive.

On the one hand, I was delighted Karen was finally in my Ghanaian home, meeting my Ghanaian family, understanding my life in Lawra. On the other, here were people with cameras and shot lists and questions, asking us to talk to the world. Exposure, on every front.

After a day of settling in and filming at the market – causing quite a stir among stallholders and shoppers – we had dinner at Junction View, a place near town. As the sun went down, friends and family converged – Kakpe on his bike, his little brother Nyanekpeng on the crossbars, Makum, Nasir's brother Prosper – and we ate jollof rice and drank Clubs and Malta Guinness for the boys and it was wonderful. When Bie wasn't playing football with Nyanekpeng and the dogs, he was draped across me or Karen or Mum, my two families merging, evolving, healing.

'I need the loo,' I pronounced after two Clubs.

'Shall I come with you?' said Karen, but Bie had already grabbed my phone and my hand, leading me off to the urinal by the light of the torch.

'Look after Sarah,' called Nasir.

'I will,' he replied from the darkness.

Walking home later, Asif said something I'll never forget.

This is about family, isn't it?

It was the first time anyone had put it into words and now Asif – who probably didn't know Nasir and I were even together

– had just got it. Though it wasn't on their shot list, it was obviously the scene I'd wanted on display.

Peace Zobasegh, mother of Blessing

'When I gave birth, she was OK, she could talk, she could walk, she could eat, she could do anything by herself and I could work. Then she had this convulsion. Now I do everything for her. Because I go to SNAP meetings and see many parents having such children, I always feel happy and know I am not alone.'

The ATE Film

One evening, the crew invited me to watch some footage. I wasn't sure what to expect, hating the awful pity-messaging poverty-porn films often made for other charities. From the first shots of the Zambo weavers, I was blown away.

This was the people of Lawra, demonstrating skills, speaking for themselves, magnificent. Charismatic John Bosco, astute Salam Haruna, ambitious Francis, spirited Peace.

'They're incredible, so resilient. Empowered.'

'You'll like this too.' Graham whizzed through shots until settling on a close-up of Nasir.

Nasir: Shall I say it now?

Asif: Yes, explain the philosophy behind the feeding programme, the way you said it the other night.

Nasir: OK. What I can say is this. An empty sack cannot stand. That is a saying. You get up and push this child to school, the stomach is empty, whatever you say it will not enter. First of all, you have to make the sack stand, then you can carry it.

Graham hit pause.

'Good, isn't he?' said Asif. 'I love that line.'

'Me too.' I said. 'Me too.'

Weighing, measuring, under-mango-tree-drinking, filming, feeding, fire-fighting, boat up the river – still no crocodiles – and before I knew it, the week had gone and my visitors were packing for home.

'Is Oscar OK?' asked Mum, as she handed me her unused DEET. 'He's limping.'

A sick dog was the last thing I needed, what with another guest about to arrive, but Shilea wasn't particularly concerned, so I decided not to be either. Dogs – and people too, to be honest – constantly had minor injuries that failed to heal in the heat or humidity or dust. Even Shilea's ear (despite all our efforts to treat) was a perpetual mess of pus and flies we now simply lived with, and I assumed whatever was bothering Oscar would be the same.

I waved goodbye to family and film crew, promptly welcomed Stephen Hodgson and was guiding him under the mango tree for the requisite Club when I noticed the puppy had more than a sore leg. He was foaming at the mouth.

When Nasir came a few minutes later, he looked at Oscar, now convulsing under my chair in a cloud of dust, and grimaced. 'Snake bite. I'll get the vet.'

Kakpe took Stephen and Bie home, followed by Shilea, tail wagging, cruelly uninterested in the plight of her offspring. I managed to push some paracetamol down the puppy's throat, vaguely acknowledging my evening of impressing Stephen had slipped away. Poor Oscar screamed and I sobbed and when the vet said there was nothing to be done, it could only end one way.

'I am sorry,' said Nasir.

'I know. Please kill the dog.'

Nasir made the interminable walk to the house and emerged with the large kitchen knife and a ghastly expression on his face. He wasn't squeamish about killing animals – I'd seen him dispatch the odd chicken and even bash a goat over the head with a stone after it strayed onto family land and ate the crops – yet, as he stood over Oscar with the knife, the puppy trusting him enough to let him come close, Nasir turned away.

'I can't do it.'

I loved Nasir so deeply in that moment, knowing he'd allowed Shilea's puppy into his heart, that we had that in common. Nasir put down the knife.

'I will call the meat man.'

It was horrific. The meat man arrived, draped in chains like a gruesome, bloody character from a movie. He smelt of death, his energy was death. And Oscar sensed it, using his last strength to limp into the bush. While Kakpe burned the grass around the house – to chase the snake away, for fear its next victim might be a child – we searched for the terrified puppy. After a couple of hours, we admitted defeat, the meat man retired and we went to bed. Outside, Oscar wailed all night and I held Bie in my arms, my hands pressed against his ears, wishing the ceiling fans were loud enough to drown out the screams.

Next morning, the meat man returned, Oscar was too weak to run and the meat man did what the meat man does. At least our puppy was no longer in pain.

And I accompanied Stephen to the tea shop for egg and bread. What else could I do? The show must go on.

After breakfast, we dropped in on carpenter Hayford and as he told Stephen how he'd lost his eye I knew that mourning a puppy in Lawra was tremendously indulgent. And I didn't care. My family had suffered a loss and I needed to retreat to our wing, draw heartbroken Bie and guilt-ridden Nasir close to me and mourn that loss.

But Stephen had travelled a long way and I wanted to give him the old razzle dazzle. So, after some brilliant meetings with small business owners, I put on a nice dress, sat under the mango tree and ordered our Clubs.

Despite everything, the trip ended well, with Stephen running a stirring SNAP group and six more businesses getting grants. As a family, though, we were knackered. It had been a gruelling few weeks, on best behaviour, on display, always 'on'.

Then, at last, we were 'off'. We had an idyllic holiday at the Ko-Sa Resort in the south, where Bie had the time of his life and the two of us spent our days frolicking in the sea. Nasir – who hated the water – guarded the towels and waited for us to drown. In the evenings, we drank cocktails while Bie played and then dined in the restaurant on pasta and Ghanaian food. Something for everyone and everyone happy.

Nasir and I were finally on the same page. I'd given up on romantic dates and we just went for it as a family. And we talked more realistically about our expectations, what the future would look like, how things could work. Plans emerged about me splitting my year between the UK and Ghana, about us having more holidays, about me adopting Bie. About our next production.

And by production, I mean that Nasir and I wanted a baby.

TWENTY-EIGHT

OVATION

I mean, I wasn't getting any younger. And we'd been so together – as co-workers and co-parents – that after four years of playing at being in a relationship, I was ready to get serious. I duly got a period tracking app in advance of my planned summer in Lawra and, meanwhile, we kept talking.

'Hello from Karbo Primary.'

Nasir's face beamed out over WhatsApp video. He'd taken to calling me at lunchtime, waving his phone at pupils with bowls of banku or jollof, children from my old neighbourhood who'd never gone to school before the kitchen opened. Or he'd ring from an SBO visit and I'd be chatting to Hayford, him in his workshop surrounded by furniture and dust, me in Swindon.

I did a quick jaunt to Lawra in April, when we completed the foundations of our new house, the symbolism of which escaped me at the time. In England, the charity moved into donated premises in Ramsbury and Leela and I decorated the window with posters and Zambo cloth, glad to have a visible presence in the village that had made it all possible, and I totally got the symbolism of that.

There was a genuine sense of having *arrived*, people popping in – including the growing number who'd been to Lawra as volunteers – saying hello or buying tickets for our next fundraising push, the highly anticipated Ramsbury premiere of *The ATE Film*.

Come the night of the screening, it was pouring with rain.

Inside the Memorial Hall, we set up displays, put out chairs and as I brushed down my lemon-coloured dress, I told myself this was exactly where people would want to be on a wet Saturday evening in May. And, of course, because Ramsbury is Ramsbury, it was. They flooded in.

'Sarah,' called Mum, 'John's here.'

By the door, people were shaking off brollies and coats, yet John was somehow drier, taller and more dashing than any of them and I couldn't have been more honoured that he'd agreed to host our event.

Let me explain. I'd met John at the Memorial Hall launch in 2013, and then next morning, when he'd come to the house with a small fluffy dog, a standing order and a request to treat the information on the form as *highly confidential*. I promised I would and googled him immediately. Apparently, our new donor wasn't just Dad's contact from the tennis club. He was Sir John Sawers, chief of MI6, the Secret Intelligence Service. To me, James Bond. Three years and a monumental amount of support later, James Bond (now retired from MI6) had agreed to introduce *The ATE Film*.

A moment in the lemon light

Ramsbury, UK

May 27, 2016

I had the best night of my life. The ATE Film Premiere was THE evening. To me, ATE suddenly felt more recognised and appreciated than ever before.

The room was packed, Sir John said some incredibly generous words and soon everyone was captivated by the people of Lawra, their raw honesty and charm and hope.

I could scarcely bear to watch my own interview, as I talked about how it all began with a little boy called Kojo. That loss remained vivid, the impact of it profound. In the hall, you could have heard a pin drop.

The audience hung on every word as Francis, John Bosco, Peace and Margaret spoke about lives that had changed because of ATE. And when Nasir, authoritative and handsome, told Ramsbury – as he had once told me – *an empty sack cannot stand*, his wisdom and integrity shone through.

When the film ended, applause rang to the rafters. I felt so deeply connected to Nasir and Lawra and the work, wanting to treasure each second of this once-in-a-lifetime experience. Then John invited me to address the audience and as I walked nervously to the front, people began to stand. By the time I reached the lectern, the whole crowd was on its feet. My sweaty hand tightened around the paper on which I'd written my speech and I turned to face everyone. And I mean *everyone*.

Makum, my SNAP co-conspirator, cheering her heart out having scheduled a vacation to coincide with this night. Leela, an enduring support and inspiration, hovering to one side. Karen, a couple of rows back, and all my friends (and partners), who'd kept me sane and replete with wine over the years. Dee Anderson and many others who'd been to Lawra as volunteers. And Mum, without whom ATE would never have got off the ground (though not Dad, too difficult).

My eyes scrolled through rows of family and friends: John Haw, my Gamma connection, and his son Charlie, who gave up his trainers; Luke, Stephen and Janet Hodgson; David Willetts, our champion at the Commercial Education Trust; Nick Maurice, our insightful evaluator; Peter Maple, Susan Suchopar and my distinguished trustees and Asif Noorani, who had produced the breathtaking film. Lurking at the rear, Ian Smith, once again generously providing the bar.

Everywhere I looked were neighbours who'd bought cakes at village fetes or sponsored someone or knitted toys for the children of Lawra. People who'd been there from the start, people connecting for the first time, all of them clapping, quite a few sobbing.

I put my crumpled speech onto the lectern and breathed deeply.

'I have written something ...' Chairs scraped as the audience sat down and Karen gave me a tear-drenched smile. 'I've written something ... I'm not going to read it. Everything that needs to be said has been said in the film, by my fantastic team and the people of Lawra.' More applause.

'All I want to say is, *thank you.* Because of you, we can do this vital work, getting pupils into school, giving dignity to disabled children and their families, offering people a chance to improve their lives. For all this, thank you.'

I suppose there was more applause. It's a blur, the rest of the evening, a haze of congratulations and hugs and wine. Later, I messaged Nasir, though it was impossible to convey the reaction using mere words, and I just wished he could have been there.

'What a night,' said Makum, before wafting off to chat with Luke or Dee or one of her many friends in Ramsbury, and I was heartened that such strong bridges existed between my two homes, heartened for if – when – Nasir came.

That Nasir, he's an impressive chap, I heard more than once and I was so proud of him and what he'd done for his community and proud that my community in Ramsbury had taken him to their heart. Nasir, my co-worker, my co-parent, my partner, had won over Ramsbury on the greatest night of my life.

On the eve of my six-week Ghana trip, Leela and I had a quiet night in. Anyway, one thing led to another, it happened so fast, there may have been wine. And before we knew it, we'd agreed to buy a property together.

Next day, we viewed a three-bedroomed former council house in Ramsbury, fell for it instantly and I put in an offer on the way to the airport. It was such a rush that I didn't even tell Nasir until I was in Ghana.

'Good for you,' he said, and (until it came up in our next argument) we discussed it no further. I felt satisfied to be putting down roots, in Ramsbury and Lawra, laying foundations for my family.

We got to work on that – the family part – straight away, with a three-pronged campaign. First, we looked into me officially adopting Bie, which was a ton of red tape. Secondly, we lured Bie out of our bed with a star chart and the promise of a new bike. Thirdly … well, you can imagine what thirdly involved.

Except, after one month, it hadn't worked.

'What if I can't? What if I'm not able to? I'm not even sure I'll ovulate again this time, then it will be November or Christmas and …'

'Sarah, it is one month. Please, calm down.'

He wasn't wrong. And I didn't *need* another child because my heart was already full of love for Bie. So I stopped worrying about my period, opened my spreadsheets and focused on the next thing.

A teenage girl in stripy top and purple tights snagged with holes waved shyly from the side of the road.

'Good morning, Janet,' called Nasir, as the girl skipped off through waist-high maize, guiding us to her home in the rural community of Faalu, 10 km east of Lawra. This girl bristled with life, yet when we got to her compound, it was hushed.

'We have let her down as parents,' her mother confided. 'She is clever and wants to learn but we have no money to pay for school provisions and she has dropped out. I am desolate, I am ashamed, I am …'

'Mother, please …' Janet turned to us. 'I don't mind about school. All I have ever wanted is to be a hairdresser and when I heard about your scheme on my father's radio I thought maybe my dream can come true.'

Janet was one of fifteen young women who'd applied for our inaugural apprenticeship scheme (VocATE) and I was impressed, by her excellent English, her passion, her modest self-belief.

'Janet, if you want to be a hairdresser, we will make that happen.'

Nasir ran over the details, how we would purchase hairdressing tools, pay upfront fees to the apprentice 'master' and monitor the arrangement to ensure Janet was well-trained and well-treated. If she passed her apprenticeship, we'd help her establish her own business.

He spoke directly to the mother. 'It is important the family are in agreement because you must support her for two years of training and one year of work before she begins to earn.

To show you are sincere, we ask the parents to make a small contribution towards the fees.'

'We can save. We will do anything to benefit her.'

A month later, we placed Janet at the stridently named *God is in Control* salon in Lawra and (through our partner, Village Bicycle Project) supplied a bike for her commute. She was one of ten apprentices we set up that summer – hairdressers, seamstresses, weavers – and the day we presented her with her tools and handed the fee to her master, she was bursting with excitement. Though I often struggled to get Ghanaians smiling in photographs, that day I had no such problem.

One balmy evening in August, Francis cycled from his Kuoli farm to a park in the centre of town for the Ghana premiere of *The ATE Film*. Seeing him, in the same burgundy shirt he'd worn for the filming, I was struck by the *realness* of it, that our incredible film was about to come face-to-face with the actual people who were in it.

Francis was joined by others, gathering for their own moment in the spotlight: John Bosco, smart in a sweater vest; Peace, elegant and dignified; Margaret, sparky and dedicated; clusters of youths, mostly Karbo JHS pupils; our own staff and consultants.

'Welcome to the screening of the film for Action Through Enterprise.' The minute Nasir stepped in front of the hundred-strong crowd, they were spellbound.

Eyes fixed onto the screen, hung from the side of a truck, as images of *their* town and *their* community brought *their* story to life. The film's soundtrack – played, of course, through Nasir's speakers – filled the night with evocative music and beautiful words, interrupted only by the odd whoop from a consultant when they spotted their own faces projected against the dark sky.

I glanced at Nasir. He and Gabriel had first viewed the film over FaceTime and they'd loved it, loved the Lawra voices, loved seeing themselves, intelligent and eloquent, on screen. But this was something else, in front of the home crowd, where everyone truly knew the size of the challenges and the magnificence of the results, and it was there on his face, that he got it, how significant this was.

When our logo appeared, on this occasion there was no standing ovation. Just stunned silence. People were speechless, awestruck by what they'd accomplished and that their stories had been heard, in Lawra and in the UK. Then a murmur of approval drifted across the park, soft in the night air.

As we were packing up, Peace and Margaret wandered over and Peace seized my hand.

'Sarah, this will make all the difference for my family. If anyone says anything bad about my child, I will tell them, *watch the film from ATE and learn something.*'

Margaret nodded. 'This is an important night for the future of Lawra. We have problems here, and I am extremely honoured to be part of the solution.'

I couldn't have asked for better reviews. Then Nasir's dad Karlley gave his son an exuberant handshake and put the cherry on the cake. 'The impact this has given to people will stay with them forever. You are a big man in Lawra.'

Once everyone was gone, that big man walked hand-in-hand with me to Home Touch, where he ordered beers and a Malta for Bie, carefully swilling my glass.

'That was a perfect night,' I reflected. 'Watching everything, everyone, on screen, in Lawra.'

'I think it is a very good night and a very good summer.'

Images of awarding grants and launching a new SNAP group and picking a school for our fourth kitchen and handing out sewing machines to apprentice seamstresses danced through my mind.

'It really is. And we're not standing still, we're growing and getting better. There's so much hope.'

A few days after I got back to Ramsbury, Leela and I exchanged on the house. The following week, I felt a bit queer during a meal out with a friend. I bought a pregnancy test and later that night called Nasir to tell him the news. We were having a baby.

TWENTY-NINE

IMPREGNABLE

I didn't stop for eight weeks, moving house, recruiting a manager for the Ramsbury office, doing another incredible Gamma Ball (in Frankfurt and in a less slinky dress) and trying not to throw up. Something had to give and I withdrew, regretfully, from my Master's.

The three-month scan was overwhelming, especially when my phone bleeped with a picture of Nasir, who was on the bus coming to meet me in Accra. Next day I flew out with the photo of our baby in my bag.

I'd walked into the hot chaos of Accra Airport many times, but had never been so grateful to see Nasir. I crawled into the taxi, put my head on his knee and fell asleep, relieved, at last, to be under his protective wing.

'Can't we go any faster?'

We were on Nasir's motorbike travelling to Gombele JHS, where our fourth kitchen was due to open in January. Which, given the speed Nasir was driving, was probably when we'd get there.

Gombele was an hour from Lawra and a few decades behind in development. No decent roads, no electricity, no running water and predominantly subsistence farming. That day, we drove past child after scrawny child walking not to school but to fields or to market and it was evident the kitchen could not come soon enough. It wasn't the only thing.

'Nasir, I need you to go faster,' I shouted.

'This is not a safe road,' he shouted back, if anything *de*celerating. 'Especially in your condition.'

I was the most coddled pregnant woman in Lawra, yet as we slogged along the dusty track, my bladder feeling every slow-motion jolt, all I wanted was Nasir to put his foot down and get me somewhere I could have a massive wee. At the school, I made a dash to the urinal, enlisting someone to guard the entrance. Pregnancy had *not* made squatting any easier and nobody needed to see that.

Afterwards, I waddled over to what I expected to be a building site and was in fact the finished kitchen, the motivated PTA having completed work ahead of schedule. We chatted with the teachers about how to reach out to local disabled children and potential SBOs, I made another visit to the urinal and we were off.

Having a pregnant-with-his-child white woman under his care sent Nasir's anxiety levels through the roof. He worried about everything, the work, the travelling and – because I was off the tablets – the malaria. He got our internal walls sprayed with insecticide, stockpiled DEET and whisked me away from the spot after one Sprite to avoid the worst of the mosquitos.

The TRC positively fizzed with them the day we launched our Dry Season Farmers project and I could see Nasir weighing up whether to send me home. He'd already banned me from going to their distant farms – *dangerous road, many bandits* – though it was less bandits and more long-journey-no-loo that made me accept his decision. Now, sitting in the TRC, I flicked away a mosquito, sprayed DEET and gave him a defiant stare as the session began.

'My name is Clement and I am a farmer in the village of Baazing.'

Clement exuded the gritty determination needed to take on Lawra's toughest farming challenge, defying the yearly shortage of food by growing crops outside the rainy season. He faced searing heat, rock hard soil, untethered goats eating his crop and risk of fire from hunters flushing out prey. And if that wasn't exacting enough, Clement was blind.

'I lost my eyesight in 2003. I was working in a field, looked up and the sky had turned white. Except the sky wasn't white, it was blue. It was glaucoma and I am now totally blind.' He gave a winning smile. 'But disability is not inability. My lack of sight is *not* the problem.'

There was a hum of agreement from the other farmers, many of whom were also blind.

'The real problem,' said Ken, the enthusiastic consultant we'd appointed as their mentor, 'is they are not permitted to use communal clean water wells, which are for drinking. They must find other water, usually far, far from their land. The work is backbreaking.'

More agreement, and the farmers began suggesting things we could provide: specialist boring equipment to dig their own deeper wells near their plots; water pumps for those by a river; watering cans, water tanks and wheelbarrows; even wellington boots to stop feet rotting in damp ground.

'I have been close to giving up,' said Moses, whose one-acre farm was on the banks of the Black Volta. 'My wife and I spend our days carrying heavy buckets, it's very tiring and we cannot make any profit. A pump to bring water will change our lives.'

'That is what we like to hear,' enthused Ken.

'Thank you, but I have another problem. What can we do about the hippos?'

We added robust fencing to the shopping list.

It was a constructive session, during which it became clear Ken would need to be hands-on for jobs they couldn't do like reading instructions on fertilisers and fixing machinery. The dry season farmers, though, were strong-willed and supremely able and I couldn't wait for the day I'd see their flourishing farms.

But not that day. That day I was content to drink my Sprite, eat Nasir's chilli pasta and be in bed by 8.30.

A week in, we went to hospital for a scan, Nasir negotiating to come in with me, which was unusual for Lawra. There were no mod cons – I laid directly on a cold metal table – yet the moment we saw our precious baby, I recognised the love in Nasir's eyes and it couldn't have meant more. That afternoon, I sat on the veranda with Bie and we read my old copy of *Baby in the Family* (given to me by Mum before Karen was born). Bie was thrilled to become *senior brother* and I could sense us all moving into position, ready to welcome the newest member of our family.

'Close your eyes.'

It was the morning of my birthday and when Nasir led me into our bedroom, placed a small box in my hand and asked the question, I said yes. I was thirty-three and with my scan photo and my sparkly ring, I felt like I had it all.

After a sober Ramsbury Christmas, I was back in Lawra at the start of 2017 for the opening of the Gombele kitchen and our pared-down nuptials. Gone was the idea of staging it as a charity event, gone was the big church, we just wanted to be legally married and be a family.

Truthfully, the wedding was as much about red tape as hearts and flowers. The visa (so Nasir could be at the birth) and Bie's adoption were both more achievable with a marriage certificate. So we booked Ko-Sa for a beach ceremony at the end of my stay and I prayed I'd be able to squeeze my fast-expanding belly into the dress I'd brought for the occasion. Meanwhile, I hauled myself round Lawra, Nasir trying to protect me however he could.

'Sarah, the camboo is here.' He'd taken to ordering a motorised tricycle taxi whenever he couldn't drive me. 'You will be careful.'

Being pregnant definitely changed things. As well as discovering the location of *every* urinal, I found myself treated differently by other women, my pregnancy giving us a shared experience, letting me become, at last, one of the girls. I felt it that morning, in the camboo with an equally pregnant Edith, girls on tour, off to meet some of the entrepreneurs she mentored in her role as co-ordinator of our Dowine hub.

'Ladies, we are here,' declared Ken, who drove the camboo as a sideline when he wasn't working for ATE. We stepped into Dowine market square, fringed with shops, family compounds and a few makeshift stalls selling pito and food. Edith led me to a small structure, where Christina, one of our SBOs, was painstakingly braiding a customer's hair.

'Business is going well,' she told us. 'At Christmas, some days I had fifteen clients, dawn til dusk ...'

I had to laugh. Not only was it fantastic she was busy, it was so bloody normal. Women in a hairdresser's talking about the Christmas rush.

We piled into the camboo for our second appointment,

Ken regaling us with the progress of the dry season farmers, *the land is lush, the watermelons are large, they have enough water to last til April,* and with each bump on the road I hugged my own watermelon and pondered that I, too, knew a little something about growing things.

I was looking forward to catching up with Cecilia, a seamstress I'd first met a year ago when Edith had gathered together some budding SBOs. Shy Cecilia had hidden at the back and when asked *what equipment do you need, what will it cost, what will you charge,* she didn't have a clue. I wasn't sure about granting her, I didn't think she was ready, but Edith, Nasir and Gabriel disagreed. *She's got potential.*

Now, as we arrived at her workshop, Cecilia was happily operating her sewing machine, surrounded by posters of dress designs and hangers with outfits ready for collection. She was thriving.

'Look at you,' she said as I lumbered towards her. 'Congratulations, when is the baby coming?' She picked up her own toddler, who'd been playing by her feet. 'It is a blessing.'

We lingered a while, talking babies and profits and frocks, Cecilia showing off her latest creations.

'Sarah, I want to tell you how thankful I am. I pray ATE reaches every needy soul as you reached me.' It was a heartfelt wish from a woman who had transformed her life, and credit to the others, who'd believed in her all along.

After farewells and nipping to a nearby dwelling to use the urinal – embarrassing, but needs must – we set off in convoy with John Bosco, who'd come on his motorbike to guide us to our next location.

'O be song, o be song.' We drove through the outskirts of

Dowine to the soundtrack of John Bosco greeting neighbours and parents, *fine, fine*. He knew *everybody* – and all their problems – including the young woman who lived in the traditional compound where we stopped.

'The girl is sixteen and should be taking exams this year. Since she has become pregnant, she no longer attends school. If you can persuade her back I think she can do well.'

Edith and I nodded, we understood our mission. The two fat ladies were on.

Inside the compound, the family was despondent.

'She has been teased at school and won't go anymore,' the mother told us as the daughter hung her head in shame. 'After the baby is born, she will work on our farm.'

I turned to the girl. 'I understand and it is hard. But you deserve to finish your education, to have a future for yourself and your child.'

'You still have choices,' said Edith, 'however impossible it seems. With help from your family, your mother, aunty, sisters, you can go to school later, when the baby's six months old. That's OK, isn't it Master?'

'Of course,' said John Bosco.

'If the whole family commits to that,' I added 'so will we. We will pay your exam fees. If you need new uniform, we'll buy it. We'll do what's necessary to keep you in education.'

'Barka, barka,' said her father, but the girl dipped her eyes and cradled her bump.

Instinctively, I cradled mine. 'Edith and I are both working, our babies won't stop us doing what we want. And I know I'm privileged and lucky to have a good man and a job. But what we have in common, the three of us, is we are women who want our place in the world.'

'You can have that,' said Edith, 'and we will be here for you.'

I think we got through, with our message of family support and female empowerment and before we left, the girl and her family agreed she should be in school. Edith and I marked the end of a fruitful trip by gorging on bean cakes and pure water in the village square and then, of course, I needed to spend a penny so John Bosco kindly let me use his facilities.

My days of being an unmarried mother-to-be were numbered, and soon Nasir, Bie and I were boarding the bus to Accra. Our Lawra wedding guests – Nasir's dad and stepmum, his brother Prosper, Ken and our Gombele manager, Ernest – were travelling by trotro via Kumasi. Makum, sadly, couldn't make it and Kanyiri and Kakpe were at school. Gabriel was studying in the US and Adeline couldn't travel alone with the twins.

From the UK, Mum was coming (not Dad, who was in Australia). Karen was trying to get pregnant so passed, Leela and Nicola were pregnant so also passed and Laura would never come so I didn't ask. There was one other absentee, the girl who'd been with me and Nasir forever. I'd had a fantasy of Shilea running on the sand as we said our vows, though strangely, when I'd broached the subject with Nasir, he passed.

We spent a day in Accra buying rings – plain gold bands engraved *Nasir and Sarah 2017* – and suits for Nasir and Bie.

'Sarah?' Nasir put his finger in the pocket of a dark blue jacket and pulled out a piece of pink fabric attached to some cardboard. 'What is this?'

I explained it was a fake handkerchief and he fell about

laughing. Nasir loved clothes with all the trimmings so we bought the ensemble on the spot. We found a matching suit for Bie and got a fake hanky made for him too.

Reuniting with our guests at Ko-Sa was glorious. I'll never forget Nasir's stepmum, Georgina, heading straight for the sea, almost transfixed, and lying flat out in it, savouring what was probably the first time her whole body had been submerged in water. I knew it was a huge deal for my Lawra family to be there and nothing said it better than Georgina, giggling in the waves.

On the morning of the wedding Mum presented me with a pile of cards and I had a happy cry reading messages from my loved ones who couldn't make it. At three, she eased me into the cream ASOS maternity wedding gown she'd brought with her (six months pregnant, I'd inevitably outgrown my original outfit) and, along with the bouquet of fabric daffodils sent by Leela, I looked positively bridal. Mum – stunning, in a long Ghanaian dress – held my hand and led me through the resort to my wedding.

On the beach was a bamboo gazebo draped in flowers, banana leaves and balloons, right by the sea. The guests were seated in a semicircle, Karlley resplendent in flowing robes, Georgina dazzling in white lace, the men smart in Dagara smocks.

Nasir and Bie, in their matching suits and pocket squares, stood chests puffed out. Nasir guided me onto a chair before sitting himself, Bie took his place between us on a tiny stool and I slipped off my shoes. Barefoot and pregnant. Not exactly how I'd maybe envisaged it, yet, somehow, ideal.

It was much more than I'd expected, much more than a legal formality. The registrar brought enough Christianity to give proceedings a sense of importance, we solemnly exchanged vows and rings and in the fading sun on a Ghana beach, hot sand between my toes, Nasir by my side and Bie holding my flowers, we tied our knot.

Next day, the Lawra contingent headed north, Mum joined us for a holiday that was over far too quickly and soon we were in a taxi bound for Accra. Bie slept the whole way and I hugged him close, feeling both bonded and consumed by guilt because I wouldn't see him for six months, until after the baby's vaccinations. It was the longest we'd ever been apart and I was dreading it.

We had a final day at the Golden Tulip, a four-star hotel where you could pay to hang out by the pool. Mum's treat, except it wasn't much fun knowing we were about to say goodbye, knowing that even with the marriage certificate, we might still fail to get Nasir's visa for the birth.

It was a sad farewell, Nasir and Bie leaving for the night bus, Mum and I for the airport. Having been used to an upgrade, this time it didn't come and I squashed my pregnant frame into the economy seat and tried not to think of the daunting prospect of running the charity and having the baby, perhaps without Nasir.

I was right to be daunted. Within a month, I was in hospital, bleeding heavily and alone.

THIRTY

THE RAMSBURY CHILD

I missed Bie terribly.

'When can we start the adoption?' I asked Nasir on one of our first calls.

'Sarah, Sarah,' he sighed, head already spinning with the paperwork for his visa application. 'You know you have to be in Ghana for that to begin.'

'I'm sorry.' I felt awful, as if I was choosing one child over another. The Ramsbury child over the Lawra child, the unborn baby over Bie. But I was heavily pregnant, trying to cram my work in before maternity leave and much as I wanted to jump on a plane and throw myself at the intricacies of international adoption, it couldn't happen for months. 'I'm sorry ...'

'It is only a delay ...'

Except it was more than a delay. It was a decision and it broke my heart. And added to the stress. Being away from Bie and Nasir, running the charity, fretting about the visa, it was all pressure. Then, seven months into the pregnancy, I started to bleed, thickly, heavily, and a cold, deep panic took hold.

'Come in immediately,' said the lady on the emergency number and soon Mum was driving me the half hour to hospital. I'd already rung Nasir and although he'd been calm and kind, he was as terrified as I was. Half an hour. Plenty of time for our baby to die.

And you're just waiting. Waiting to be taken through, waiting to be hooked up to a monitor, waiting for your baby's heartbeat. Waiting to be told the bad news.

At last. A loud, healthy throb.

'Sounds normal,' said the doctor. 'I'll have a feel around.'

She diagnosed a one-off bleed and because I'd stopped bleeding, sent me home. Not home exactly. I stumbled through a talk at Aldbourne Memorial Hall that night – fittingly entitled *To Ghana with Love* – grey-faced, barely able to stand. And next morning, between my legs, gushes of blood. Mum and I had another mad dash, again the baby's heartbeat was strong and again I was sent home. When I rang the emergency number on the third morning, *I'm bleeding, a lot,* they told to me to bring an overnight bag.

'The placenta might be separating from my uterus,' I updated Nasir. 'If it does, the baby can't get oxygen and they have to get it out urgently. Like, within three minutes.'

'That is OK, it will be OK.'

He seemed so sure, I wished he could have been there, comforting me, holding my hand.

'Any news on your visa?' We'd submitted a compelling application, including marriage certificate, pregnancy notes, GP letters, testimony from people who'd been to Lawra and could vouch for Nasir.

'Nothing. Will ... tomorrow ... I ...'

'Nasir ... Nasir?' The phone signal was rubbish and the hospital Wi-Fi was expensive and rubbish. 'I'll call tomorrow.'

With a cannula in my bruised hand and a monitor strapped to my abdomen, I pressed on with work, replying to emails, delegating to Leela, confirming meetings and praying the bleeding would stop, my baby would be safe and I could go home to my own bed and my own internet. In the middle of the third night, with the bleeding getting worse, the nurse gave me a steroid injection.

'In case we do an emergency C-section, it will encourage baby's lung growth and give it the best chance of survival.' She smiled kindly. 'It might not come to that.'

I googled *likelihood of dying from placental abruption*, took a selfie to record how completely wrecked I was and checked in with Nasir about the visa. Still nothing. Family and friends rallied and there was a constant stream of people at my bedside, Karen especially, pregnant now herself and always with armfuls of chocolate. That night, they woke me again for another incredibly painful steroid jab.

And each day that passed was another day in which my placenta hadn't abrupted, more time for the baby to grow, less time for Nasir's visa to come.

I've had enough of this, I said to myself on the fifth day. Laying strapped to machines, I felt useless and increasingly concerned that Foreign Office red tape was getting even more protracted than my poor old placenta. I reached for my phone.

'I'm literally about to have a C-section and need my husband here,' I bawled hysterically to whoever answered at the office of Claire Perry, my local MP. 'No-one will tell us anything.'

Two hours later they called back. The fact I'd used my middle-class outrage to elicit an answer did not in any way curb my feeling of total and utter relief. We'd got it. Nasir was coming to Ramsbury.

That wasn't the only relief. After seven days in hospital, the bleeding stopped and I was discharged. On the way home I bought some premature babygrows, just in case.

I had a draining few weeks, speaking at school assemblies,

running staff meetings, in and out of hospital for check-ups. Eventually, they gave me a date for the baby to be induced – ten days after Nasir was due – and I counted down the clock until my husband and then my baby would arrive.

Nasir was freezing. I could see that from my seat outside Costa Coffee as he emerged into Arrivals at Heathrow Terminal 5. Freezing, in his wedding jacket (minus fake hanky) over his one jumper, he was knackered after a tortuous journey via Accra and Lisbon and currently experiencing the biggest culture shock of his life. He'd never been on a plane before, never left Ghana before, never experienced an unusually cold English spring or been in a car with me driving before. Now, here he was, freezing, in the passenger seat, cruising down the M4 in my Nissan. In stunned silence.

Though I'd been desperate for Nasir to come, I was also nervous – scared even – about how it would be, and I wondered what was going through his mind on that drive into chocolate-box Ramsbury. Not that Nasir was familiar with the concept of a chocolate box, he had absolutely no point of reference. Then, as I pulled off the high street, we spotted someone who'd volunteered in Lawra, they *good morning*-ed us and things became weirdly normal.

That evening, Leela made jollof rice and tried to persuade Nasir of the benefits of hand luggage, having discovered he'd done the flights with nothing more than his passport slipped into his pocket. Then, after supper Nasir and I collapsed into bed.

'Got enough room?'

I knew he didn't. We were used to a super kingsize in Lawra

so my basic double was a squash. And despite grabbing every spare blanket, he was cold. Earlier, as he'd rummaged through his bag to retrieve a vast container of groundnut paste and a bag of gari flour, I'd registered how skimpy his clothes were.

'I should have bought you some pyjamas.'

'It's OK, Sarah. I am fine.'

He didn't seem fine, and I never did discover what was going through his mind. We didn't talk about that stuff, we hardly seemed to talk at all, certainly not on that first cold, constricted night. As ever, we got on with the next thing and in that sense, we were on familiar ground.

The following morning, I drove Nasir (shivering despite a borrowed thick jacket) to Swindon Tesco Extra. For a minute, he appeared overwhelmed by so much food, so much variety, in one place, but soon his hands were on red peppers and tomatoes and chillies and the trolley rapidly filled.

'Sarah, can we go there?' In the clothes section we picked up jeans, jumpers, pyjamas and anything warm. Later, his gloved hand in mine, we wandered down to The Bell where he enjoyed a much-anticipated Guinness and I enjoyed the sight of him in his new baby-blue pullover, chatting with well-wishers, in my spot.

We had a hectic ten days. Dad took us to Reading to buy Ghanaian food, I did my handover with the ATE officer manager, Sarah Livesey, who was covering my maternity leave, and we ran a fundraiser in a scout hut where Nasir captivated the crowd. In the house, he heroically tackled an IKEA changing table without reading the instructions and painted the spare bedroom.

For a man used to being in control, off on his motorbike

whenever he fancied and understanding how everything worked, those waiting days must have been difficult. He tried to make the best of them, exploring Ramsbury, popping to the village shop to buy beers with some of the £100 I'd given him, embracing the Wi-Fi to watch Nigerian films, speaking daily with Bie and catching the traditional British cold. Meanwhile, the induction drew closer.

I finished work on the Friday and went into hospital on the Monday, with the vague notion I'd have the baby and be home by tea. Instead, they inserted a pessary (to 'ripen' my cervix), gave me a big ball to bounce on and told Nasir to go because nothing was happening that night.

'Thank you. I think I will stay.' He was being protective, but also – without his own transport – he was trapped. We spent a sleepless night, him sneezing in a chair, me proclaiming every slight twinge as a contraction. In the morning I was relieved to see Mum and Karen, grateful for the distraction and the offer to ferry Nasir around for however long it took.

'Could you get me some crisps?' It was the morning of the third day and Nasir was eating leftover fishy rice for breakfast. Although I'd been told *nil by mouth*, I was so determined to have a natural birth I decided the order didn't apply to me and wolfed down an orange and a family bag of cheddar Kettle chips.

I was brushing crumbs off the bed when the midwife announced she was about to break my waters. After two days of waiting and bouncing, I felt ridiculously unprepared and once she'd done the deed I panic-washed, conditioned and dried my hair.

I needn't have bothered. Apparently, an oxytocin drip and

pethidine painkiller do not land well on an orange and a bag of crisps and my hair took the brunt of it as I threw the lot up. My breakfast wasn't the only thing I lost. I was petrified, out of control, screaming.

'Nasir!' He patted my back and held out a cardboard bowl. 'Please don't divorce me!'

The labour was nearly as fast and hard as the vomiting. My body went into overdrive and I felt blood pouring from me. 'I'm bleeding out!' I shouted – too many episodes of *Grey's Anatomy* – and the midwife assured me, despite the heavy blood loss, that I wasn't going to die.

'Now, Sarah ...' She waved a pair of scissors. 'We need to get baby out on this push or we're going to have to cut you. Can you push?'

'I can't!' I yelled, regretting those antenatal classes I'd missed whilst in Ghana. 'I don't know how to push!'

'Sarah, come on.' Nasir was steady and reassuring, in the midst of what felt to me like terrifying chaos. 'Concentrate and push the baby.'

This was far from the serene ethereal-music-massage-oil labour of my dreams. I was covered in blood, coated in sick, pumped full of drugs, strapped on my back, more frightened than I'd ever been, clueless. And then, in one (frenzied) hour and three minutes it was done and she was there.

There are no words for how I felt. Miraculous, love, joy, none of them get close to it. She was perfect and I was now hers.

'Hello, Aviella.' Nasir stroked his daughter's cheek. Aviella was the name we'd chosen for a girl, viel meaning *lovely* in Dagaare, aviella meaning *it is lovely, all is well.* It suited her completely.

Over the next hour, we worked out how to breastfeed while

Nasir took photographs. Not of mother and baby – of the placenta.

'What are you doing?'

'The placenta is very important to my people. Usually, we plant it with the crops.'

'Can I see?' After the whole hoo-ha about it abrupting, I was genuinely interested. To my untrained eye, it looked immaculate. Almost a shame it wouldn't end up on his land.

There was never a beautiful photo taken of me and Aviella those first few days, though I have got a series of selfies, her clamped onto my engorged boob or asleep on my chest. I spent two days on the sofa, breastfeeding, cuddling her, completely physically connected. On day three, I had a massive cry (hormones!) and did some hoovering.

Nasir came into his own. He was a confident, collaborative parent, selflessly taking Aviella when I needed a shower or a wee, bringing her back when she needed me. Although I was weak (having lost a dangerous amount of blood), I wanted her close all the time and Nasir also did that instinctively. Instead of putting her down for a sleep, Nasir would sleep with her. He could change her nappy while I floundered and was gentle with her tiny limbs as he slipped them into premature baby clothes.

'Sarah, I don't like this for her,' he told me that first night home when I put Aviella in a Moses basket. 'She should be in bed with the mother.'

I agreed. But I wanted to try *what you're supposed to do*, particularly given the size of our bed. 'Can we see how it goes?'

He shrugged. 'You do what you want, you know what I think.'

Of course, he was right. It didn't work for Aviella and it

didn't work for us, and we soon bought one of those cribs that attach to the side of the bed – for extra space – and all slept together, like we'd done with Bie.

It was Bie's sixth birthday a week after Aviella was born and that was tough, watching the WhatsApped video of the party, everyone singing *Happy Birthday*, far, far away. I felt for Nasir, sharing the agony of being torn between two places and apart from a child.

'Nguri, nguri, Aviella, sleep, sleep.' One evening I stood by the bedroom door watching him sing a Dagara lullaby. As he held his daughter, tiny in his steady hands, her eyes were wide and bright, gazing at her father. 'Aviella, Aviella, your eyes are like lights. You are my light.'

It was pure, unshakeable love and I found it comforting. While everything was new and intimidating for me, Nasir took it in his stride. He cared for his baby, watched his movies, didn't flinch at my milk-laden breasts or battered, ripped body and cooked mounds of pasta, and that was all I could have asked.

Tempting as it was, I didn't spend the entire time watching Netflix, eating Nasir's fried eggs and breastfeeding. We'd walk round Ramsbury or go to Mum's, Nasir proudly pushing Aviella in a second-hand pram. On the odd occasion Nasir popped out on his own he'd often meet someone who recognised him, usually from the film screening.

'Did they say their name? What did they look like?' I'd ask.

'I'm not sure,' he'd say. 'They had brown hair.'

He had the opportunity to go further afield when he was invited to London to address the Commercial Education Trust, our BizATE sponsors. It was a huge deal, not least because

Nasir had never been on a train before, let alone London Underground. Mum, Aviella and I saw him off at the station, Nasir in a white smock, waving through the train window, off into the unknown. I was reassured that film producer Asif was at Paddington to escort him to the meeting, less convinced I could cope with Aviella for a whole day without him.

I only needed to be half-worried. Nasir triumphed, in a setting as far from his normal life as he could have imagined, a grand period building with a swirling staircase, walls lined with paintings, air chinking with coffee cups. He talked about Lawra in a way I never could and (according to Asif) held the mostly older, white, male CET board in the palm of his hand. As for me and Aviella, we survived. But I was beyond relieved when Mum dropped Nasir home.

One Saturday evening in June, as we laid in bed watching TV, Aviella snuggled between us, my phone rang.

'Sarah!' shouted Asif, 'Guess what?'

It was the call we'd been waiting for.

In London, the cream of British-Ghanaian society was gathering for its big night – the prize-giving ceremony of GUBA, the *Ghana UK-Based Awards*, where ATE was up for Charity of the Year. Of course, it would have been amazing to attend, to admire Nasir in his traditional smock, to squeeze myself into a dress and go to a glittering party. It wasn't practical though and we'd sent Asif on our behalf.

'Can you hear me? It's quite noisy here.'

'Yes,' I whispered, Aviella still asleep. 'How's it going?'

Nasir pulled the phone towards his ear and we listened together as Asif broke the news. ATE had been recognised by the Ghanaian community. We'd won.

The following week, Asif delivered the weighty gold trophy and presented it to us in the garden, where we popped something fizzy and toasted GUBA and toasted Aviella. It was a proud day for us, doting parents and award-winners, a welcome validation, a positive sign for the future. Anything is possible, I thought, watching Nasir chat with Asif, holding his own on my turf as I had fought to hold my own on his, his daughter in the crook of his arm, a glass of Prosecco in his hand, our prestigious GUBA on the mantelpiece.

A few days later, with a suitcase bulging with new jeans and T-shirts and a nearly empty carry-on bag because he still didn't quite understand what should go in it, Nasir climbed into a cab and headed to the airport. After four weeks of Nollywood and nappies, of caring for our beautiful girl, of Nasir caring for me, of being together day and night, it was time to separate. For Nasir to be with our child in Lawra. And in Ramsbury, for me and Aviella to go it alone.

THIRTY-ONE

TERMINAL 5

Over the next few months, we spent a lot of time in Heathrow Terminal 5, me, Aviella and Nasir. I had a favourite café in Departures and one in Arrivals, I knew where the best loo was, which shop sold baby food pouches, how long it took to get to the gate.

It was the café in Departures where I ended up fighting for my marriage. But that's a way off and there were thousands of miles to be flown before then.

August 2017, T5

Aviella and I had a laid-back summer, going for coffee in the village, hanging out with my pregnant sister, popping in to the ATE office because I couldn't keep away.

Despite my fears about coping alone, Aviella slept well, she never cried – literally the first time I heard her cry was when she got vaccinated – and by the power of my breast milk I could pretty much send her to sleep on demand. That was the plan, sitting in Terminal 5 before the flight to Accra: pray she'd drift off in one country and wake up in another, and if she didn't, stick my boob in her mouth.

Accra Airport was the usual commotion, but Aviella was rested as I handed her to a delighted daddy, introduced her to an excited senior brother and then tightly held that brother, my Bie, after six lost months.

We stayed at Big Milly's, not quite ready to attempt the night bus to Lawra. It was bliss. Nasir hung out with Aviella, Bie and I swam, and later we'd relax in our air-conditioned apartment, safe from mosquitos, ordering food and beer while Bie played with his little sister. We started (with Kendey's permission) to begin the process of me adopting Bie. More paperwork, yet, watching our children asleep in each other's arms we felt ready to take on the world and all the red tape it could throw at us.

Back at Accra Airport, after a fantastic one-week trip, I was bereft. Missing Nasir and Bie, missing Nasir's helping hand, wanting to turn to him as I shuffled bag and sleeping child and tried to buy a sandwich. At Heathrow, after seven days of closeness, I put Aviella in the car seat of Mum's Fiesta and she screamed the entire way home.

November 2017, T5

I bought a book at WH Smith. Having juggled motherhood and the charity since September (when I finished maternity leave), the prospect of extra childcare and even five minutes to myself with a paperback felt like luxury.

Don't get me wrong, I'd wanted to work. I missed it, the charity needed my fundraising and I needed my full salary. It was hard, though. Hard to hand over my content baby to Mum or the childminder, hard to be the mother I wanted to be, present and available, whilst running a strategy meeting or doing a school assembly. But I wasn't willing to sacrifice the way I was parenting for ATE and I couldn't sacrifice the charity for Aviella. Both had to be equal for everything to work.

So, I worked in the Ramsbury office when I could and if Aviella cried she was brought to me. Although some evenings my breasts ached with milk, breastfeeding was integral to our ability to be in Ghana – the journey, the health risks, the impracticality of formula – and I couldn't dream of giving it up. I recalled the women of Lawra, working in fields, carrying produce to market, teaching in schools, often with babies on their backs or boob out, child feeding at the front. Bie, such an independent, happy boy, had been mothered that way and it's what I wanted for Aviella.

Doing it in Ramsbury, however, was not easy and I looked forward to giving the village of Lawra a chance to raise our child. I slid my book into my bag and carefully headed to the gate, praying Aviella wouldn't wake.

She slept on the flight but not the night bus, the ear-splitting Nigerian films being the loudest thing she'd ever heard. She wouldn't go to Nasir, so I stood in the aisle trying to soothe her and ignored the glare of other passengers, who'd never seen a baby make quite that much fuss.

There was a welcoming party in Lawra – Bie, Prosper, Kanyiri, Kakpe – and then one of them took Aviella, and that was how it was. Aviella would be off, ridden round on a bike or motorbike, laughing, unstressed and when she wasn't, when she wanted me, she was delivered back. Like those first baby weeks with Nasir, it was organic, intuitive, all these young people so at ease with a small child it made my heart sing.

One afternoon, Peace, Patience, Margaret and John Gandaa came to the house to present us with a pile of baby essentials on behalf of SNAP. We'd received few gifts, despite it being an important part of the culture and us having handed out numerous baskets of nappies and baby lotion over the years. I think people assumed we were too rich to need anything (we weren't). Anyway, it made the SNAP Committee gesture more touching, as was their pleasure in greeting the newest member of the ATE family.

Aviella came everywhere. At the SNAP meeting, she was passed round the mums. At the workshop for the next batch of dry season farmers, she was with Kanyiri. Once, I found him flat on his back outside the TRC, asleep on a table, Aviella in the carrier on top of him, also asleep, guarded by Shilea.

And on the day Nasir and I toured rural schools to identify our next kitchen, Aviella came along in her carrier, my arms and pashmina around her, Nasir driving even more cautiously than ever.

The ride to Biro was dirt and cows for miles and when we arrived there was nothing there, just a few buildings dotted around an arid landscape and a small, newly opened JHS that was so quiet it seemed abandoned.

Then, hope. Along the front of the school was a carpet of delicate purple flowers. I was blown away by their beauty and that someone cared enough to nurture them in the dust.

'I am very pleased you came.' Madam Irene Lieku was the passionate, persistent (and perhaps green-fingered) head teacher who'd written us an emotive letter about building a kitchen. 'This is exactly what Biro needs.'

She led us along the veranda, past empty desks, through deafening silence to the one occupied classroom.

'This is the whole school?' asked Nasir, registering ten girls and two boys clustered round one battered textbook.

'I am afraid so. We have a high rate of child marriage for girls and the boys travel south to find work. But these are good students.' A flicker of pride crossed Irene's face. 'And they are all here.'

It was a no brainer to select Biro as our fifth kitchen. And Aviella was there, from day one, an ATE baby through and through.

Work was great, family was great and I had a life again. I could wash my hair, go running, play with Aviella in the inflatable bath we'd bought, go to spots and drink actual beer. Nasir was an amazing father and our support network was trustworthy, loving and vast. I was more productive and got more sleep than I'd done for months. Aviella was happy.

'Why don't you stay?' asked Nasir one evening, walking back from Home Touch. 'I think you should stay.'

'I've been thinking that too,' I said, and this time I almost meant it. *We can always eat grass.* Except grass still wasn't an option, not for us or for the thousand people ATE worked with, not for Bie and not for Aviella.

The journey from Lawra to Ramsbury was torturous. The fourteen-hour night bus, the 10.30 pm flight, everything more challenging now Aviella was getting bigger and my bum was getting sorer with her weight on me. I couldn't even distract myself with the in-flight meal because there's no room for the tray with a sleeping babe in arms.

She woke the instant she was strapped into the Fiesta. It turns out breastfeeding in a car seat is physically impossible and we stopped off in Reading for a break from the howling. Sitting in a corner of the M&S café, trying to be discreet with Aviella on my breast, I thought wistfully of Lawra, of me and Aviella and that easy, comfortable ride to Biro on Nasir's bike.

At home, I looked at the pile of dust-red clothes and at my crying baby and at my phone buzzing with emails and at the state of my hair, and wondered how I would manage until December.

December 2017, T5

The week before Christmas, Aviella and I collected Nasir from the airport and within hours he was braving the cold in the warmest coat we could borrow, wearing a Santa hat and rattling buckets for ATE's Christmas appeal. It was the beginning of a magical fortnight.

I needed it. Since my return, I'd crammed the usual Christmas fundraising into the daytime and spent my nights holed up with Aviella in bed or whispering with Leela on the landing, waiting for our babies to doze off. For me, the arrival of both Nasir and Christmas promised respite – and fun.

We threw a party for ATE supporters, held in our house so the children could attend. Karen and I had taken to dressing Aviella and her new baby Rossy in matching Christmas outfits and Nasir – ever the fan of ornamental clothing – highly approved of Aviella's reindeer onesie.

He wore his traditional smock that night and gave a moving speech, thanking guests, promising to use their donations wisely. The Prosecco flowed, much of it in my direction, and when Aviella stirred, Nasir tended her, which I couldn't have appreciated more.

He swung the trolley into Tesco's booze aisle. 'This is a lot.'

I peered at satsumas and chocolate and cheese and thought, *yes, I know.* We both knew – were achingly aware – the money

I was about to spend on Christmas could feed the twelve Biro pupils for months. Then Nasir grabbed some beers, because of course, whilst he cared about Biro, he also relished that stacked trolley overflowing with treats. Why shouldn't he? The other shoppers did, and Nasir had had few enough treats in his life.

My family and I made a huge fuss for his Christmas Eve birthday, with candles, presents and home-made curry. A plateful of cake on one knee and Aviella dressed as a robin on the other, he leant towards me with a whisper.

'This is the best day I have ever had.'

After everyone left, we finished our Christmas wrapping, Nasir handing me strips of Sellotape. It was five years since we'd bonded over communication fans, five years of friendship and common purpose, five years of ATE and of us. We'd come a long way and our Christmas was the pinnacle of that achievement.

But it wasn't perfect. Because that bed wasn't any roomier, my salary didn't go any further between us and things were pretty stretched. Nasir had brought no money and no gifts, so everything was on me, which was fine since it was his first English Christmas. Though I would say, he earned a fair salary and had seen me leave enough presents for Bie and the boys to know the score. Maybe I should I have told him. Maybe he should have asked. I'm pretty sure he found the situation a little uncomfortable too, a little disempowering. So not idyllic, not entirely.

On New Year's Eve, we went to London for the day. Nasir was so cold I bought him a sweatshirt from the London Eye shop, emblazoned with a trendy Union Jack, extremely expensive. Despite that, he was grumpy all day, his knee hurt from a recent football injury, it poured with rain and the spell was well and truly broken.

January 2018, T5

It was a relief to fly to Ghana, the three of us, to arrive in Lawra and into the arms of our boys and Shilea. Lawra was the one place things made sense, where our children could be together, where Nasir felt solvent, where I could work when I wanted, without guilt.

We had momentum that winter, after a year of modest growth for the charity. Nasir even drove that bit faster to Gombele, where hub manager Ernest had lined up prospective businesses for us to sponsor.

'This is Amatus,' Ernest announced as we entered the shady area outside a small, tidy house. 'He is eighteen and has already established an enterprise selling pomade body cream.'

Amatus showed us containers of Vaseline, wax, oil and perfume and boxes of bottles and printed labels. 'I sell at the market in Kumasi. One day I want to have staff and a factory.'

We were impressed. I put Aviella on the ground (where she became transfixed by a passing chicken) as Amatus told his story in clear, measured English.

'After my father died six years ago, we lived in a violent nightmare. My uncle stole everything, our home, our possessions, and left us only with beatings along the way. We were alone, my mother and two young brothers, and no-one stopped it. There was no money and no food and I had to decide, go to school or go to work. I decided to do both.'

Using the one thing the uncle had not taken – his father's fishing equipment – Amatus fished the river by night and attended school by day, squeezing in other backbreaking labour such as loading lorries, often without food.

'My teacher recognised my work, my efforts to be somebody, and gave me a loan for my business. Now, I must repay him and I can't do that unless I sell up, and then there will be no business left.'

He was humble, clever and impassioned and of course we funded him. I'm not going to sugar coat it though, Amatus was an angry young man, furious his family had been left to fend for themselves at the hands of a brutal relative.

'We are not an isolated case and no-one is fighting against this. If I can be successful, I will lead the fight and I will try to change society.'

'Amatus,' I said, 'I *know* you will.' Then I noticed Aviella had crawled off and ran over to remove a lump of goat poo from her mouth.

Aviella grew, the charity grew and several auspicious developments around that time cemented our position in Lawra:

- We negotiated a partnership with Lawra Municipal Assembly to use some land in town for a purpose-built Inclusion Centre, where we would house our office, workshops and a SNAP play scheme. Structural engineer Stephen Hodgson designed it and work began on bringing it to life.
- We collaborated with the Ghana School Feeding Programme, proudly sharing our school kitchen so they could provide lunches while we did breakfast instead. Releasing money for vulnerable rural schools – where we could have more impact – felt like an important strategic decision that moved forward how we operated in Lawra.
- We opened the kitchen in Biro and appointed hub manager

Evarist. In Dowine, Prosper replaced Edith (who'd decided to be a teacher). Impressive Kaamil Issahaku came to lead the SNAP programme and expand our disability casework.

New businesses, new kitchen, new staff, new premises, lots of visitors. Things were busier and harder, more work, somehow more Aviella, possibly less Nasir. One evening, as I cooked for guests, oversaw Bie's homework and tried not to step on the baby, I remember wishing my husband would make an appearance.

Overall, though, a rewarding winter, topped off with the best news ever, which I announced on Facebook with a picture of me and Bie:

Sarah is with Nasir
7 February 2018

Out celebrating with this gorgeous boy who today became my legal son. Couldn't be prouder xxx

Yes. Having submitted our careful application in January, we got confirmation from the Lawra authorities of what we'd wanted for so long. I'd adopted Bie.

March 2018, T5

It all turned to shit as soon as we got to England. Aviella went from forty-degree heat and sitting on Uncle's Prosper's lap at dinner to freezing weather and a high chair and she didn't much like either. Then she got a nasty sore throat and temperature. I dialled NHS 111.

'Has the child travelled anywhere she might have picked up

something?'

Where do I start? I thought. *Malaria? TB? Goat poo?* I burst into tears, sobbing that I'd killed my child. In the end, though, Aviella was fine, and the worst was yet to come.

'I have received a letter,' said Nasir on one of our calls. 'They must see you in person about the adoption. The court in Wa.'

'But we've got the adoption.'

'The problem is ...' and he read the letter. It was long-winded, steeped in bureaucracy, every word a heartbreaker. I had not, it told us, officially adopted Bie.

Talk about bad timing. As the authorities in Lawra were processing our certificate, the law in Ghana changed, making adoption legal through regional not district courts. Our adoption was null and void. Which was how I felt inside, especially since I wouldn't be in Ghana again until August.

'I'm sorry, I can't get there.' I hastily worked out the dates, the cost, the flights. Could ATE manage without my fundraising push, could I really do a fourth trip in eight months, could Aviella handle the dry season heat? It was the Ramsbury child over the Lawra child again and it did not feel good.

Not much did. I was struggling with money and childcare, I wasn't sleeping because Aviella breastfed all night, Nasir and I talked less and argued more. Then Mum invited me, Karen and our families for a cottage break in Cornwall and, at last, there was a bright spot. It was short-lived. At the end of March, I collected Nasir from the airport, he took Aviella in his arms – and from that moment on he completely ignored me.

In Cornwall, he refused to speak, refused to look at me and now, if Aviella stirred in the night, he rolled over and went back to sleep. One morning, I woke to the familiar smell of fried eggs wafting round the house. Remembering the many eggs he'd made me over the years, I hoped his dark mood had lifted. But no. He ate his breakfast alone, my family awkwardly making coffee around him.

All I'd wanted was a father who would take his child so I could have a shower or share an hour with my sister and a bottle of Prosecco. And if it sounds small to moan about having a shit holiday, then you've probably never been a single parent. Because when you're on your own with a nine-month-old and a taxing job, there is *nothing* bigger than someone frying you an egg.

It was more than a shit holiday, though, much more. Rejection, humiliation, it was – at that point, at least – the worst week of my life.

'Why's he always on his phone?' Karen asked, but I didn't know. The adoption? The juju man? Money? Family pressure? A girlfriend?? Or was he just checking the Manchester United scores? When I asked it was like poking him with a stick.

'Don't question me, don't make me talk. You make me talk too much.'

That's all I got out of him the whole week. With nowhere to go and a gammy knee playing up in the cold, it was as if he was trapped, wounded, angry. And I was shattered and confused.

On the last day, I had a migraine so bad I couldn't move and when Mum drove us home I sat with my head between my knees, Nasir staring blankly, unspeaking. At a service station, he went to the loo and I managed a few words.

'Mum, I think my marriage is over.'

Next morning, although I didn't want to be with him for another second, I reluctantly drove Nasir to the airport, in silence, deciding what to do. In the end, I decided to fight for my marriage.

'Do you want breakfast?' I was surprised when he said yes and a few minutes later, over airport coffee, I began.

'Nasir, I love you, but we can't live like this.'

He rubbed his knee and said nothing.

'Come on, talk to me.'

'You make me talk too much.' It was the old tune, yet quieter, mellower. 'I think I have been struggling.'

'It's tough, being split between two places.'

'Yes, being split, maybe that is the problem. The work, the family, everybody thinks I can solve all their problems. It's too much. And you always want to discuss feelings. You question me. You don't trust me.'

'I want to, it's just …'

'There are things you don't understand but I will fix them, I promise. Next time will be different.'

I *didn't* understand. I *was* terrified, terrified our family would be broken, so I accepted his promises and decided not to ask more questions, fearing his reaction, fearing the answers.

After he left, I sat there in Terminal 5, wondering if I'd done the right thing. But he was my husband and my partner in the charity and the father of my child and the father of my Bie and I wasn't ready to give up on any of that.

THIRTY-TWO

SNAPPED

Things got better and they got worse. We ricocheted between countries and homes, somersaulting from good times to bad, believing in a future together, then doubting it, sinking *and* swimming. And I think he felt that too.

Of course, something – someone – was bound to snap.

"Biro"

the one when the husband ruins it

I'll set the scene. Because the next few months can be summed up that way, in scenes, flash frames almost, of the charity, the family, Nasir and me. And one of the most vivid snapshots happened one day in Biro, when it all went well until it all went wrong, as it did that whole summer.

Aviella and I had flown to Ghana in July, travelling with Nasir, who'd come to the UK for a training course. He'd been true to his word, there was no repeat of the holiday behaviour and I reached Lawra upbeat and keen to get working. In that spirit, I set off one morning with Aviella and hub manager Evarist for the long drive to Biro.

Biro was proving to be our toughest gig. There was little commerce, scarcely anyone had marketable skills and (for the first time) we'd struggled to find applicants for our business grants. Evarist had spent weeks cajoling and mentoring a few potential candidates and now, as we pulled up outside a small dwelling surrounded by maize and an explosion of red chilli peppers, I was hopeful.

'Aviella, don't go far,' I called, my now toddling daughter already off with the children, playing among the chillies.

After a chat with new business owner Vincent about his plans to trade guinea fowl, I did the pep talk and presented the customary fan of cash. There was a yelp of glee from the children and one of Vincent's daughters ran over, Aviella wedged on her hip, gappy grin on her face.

'They are who I am doing this for,' Vincent smiled. 'I pray with this grant I will proceed in life. I wish my girls can be nurses and the boy be a teacher. A family of professionals, I would like that.'

Vincent was educated and proactive, his children were bright and beautiful, his garden was growing and whilst he lived simply and with no electricity, he had similar dreams for his family as I had for mine. 'Let's make that happen,' I told him, and the children ran off, laughing.

While he and his supportive wife put signature and thumbprint to the contract, another boy – about twelve years old, dirtier, thinner, shabbier than Vincent's children – wandered across from a herd of emaciated cows.

'The boy wants to attend school,' said Evarist, after a brief chat. 'But his family say he must work. He has asked us to speak to them and I said we would.'

And that was Biro. For every Vincent, looking to the future, there were dozens of children without one. Determined to give this cow-boy a chance, we promised to drop in after our next appointment.

Though the ride from Vincent's house to Melita's compound was short, the mood in the dusty, lifeless courtyard couldn't have been more different. Melita, fragile and nervy, led us to some wobbly plastic chairs, observed from a distance by her sullen husband and a woman half-covered with a piece of fabric. Behind Melita, clinging to her skin-and-bone arms, were her children, watchful, wary, one practically naked, a beaded belt slung below a hugely distended stomach. Aviella ran to examine a pile of groundnuts, yet none of the children joined her, there was no playing, no gappy smiles, no laughter. Only the unmistakeable stench – wafting from the husband – of something dodgy being smoked.

Truthfully, we'd been in two minds about whether to grant Melita at all. Her petty trading in groundnuts was on the cusp of viability and in Lawra or Dowine we wouldn't have considered her. In Biro, with so few applicants – and impressed by her resolve in tracking us down at the school and attending workshops – we wanted to give her a chance.

Take this opportunity seriously, be honest with us …

The usual speech, but something was wrong. The atmosphere was wrong. Specifically, the husband was wrong.

He didn't greet us, he didn't stand by his wife's side to encourage her in this new endeavour, he just glared, hunting catapult swinging from his belt, one hand behind his back, hiding the source of the distinctive smell.

If you make a good profit, tell us. If things go badly, we'll help …

Words said many times before, but as I glanced from Melita to her brooding husband, I hesitated.

Er … we want you to be successful, we want to celebrate with you …

Evarist got out the inkpad for the thumbprints, first Melita, then the husband, who slumped onto a chair next to me, close enough to smell his home-brewed akpeteshie breath and the illicit joint he flicked away. I immediately wished Nasir had come with us to this new, out-of-our-depth place, as he usually did when we handed out grants.

You must support your wife, if you misspend the grant, we will reclaim it …

The husband shifted in his chair, impatient, fiddling with the catapult. He didn't want the speech, that much was clear. He wanted the money. The threat, the sense of menace, was palpable.

'Sarah,' said Evarist, under his breath, 'we must go. Now.' He put his hand on Melita's arm. 'I'm sorry, we can't do this today.'

I grabbed Aviella and we made an immediate exit, shaken, knowing we'd messed up. We were still shaking when we arrived at the skinny cow-boy's farm and politely offered the money for school fees and uniform. His grandfather, plainly drunk, just laughed.

'His job is here.' He indicated a deep, stinking pit in which several skeletal cows were crammed. 'Those animals are more valuable to me than that child.'

It was a sad journey back to Lawra, plenty of time to think about the tears streaming down the boy's face and the confusion and fear on Melita's when we left her with no money and an angry husband. Plenty of time to consider how much we had to learn about this rural location, where cows could be worth more than a child and where a poor woman's one chance to better her family's life could be crushed by a man who saw only cedi signs and his next drink.

We stayed in touch with Melita and ended up giving her a

hundred cedis. I'd like to believe she managed to keep them from her husband. Though we never did get that cow-boy into school, we succeeded with lots of other children and by the autumn attendance at Biro JHS had trebled. All that was to come, as was the profit Vincent made, enabling him to buy health insurance for his family and re-roof their house. Our victories in Biro were hard-won and few, yet all the sweeter for it.

That evening, after a long shower, I went to Home Touch with my children and dogs and sat in the last of the sunshine, waiting for Nasir. Waiting for Nasir was something I did a lot of that summer. The summer of Vincent and Melita and the cow-boy, the summer when all the children got malaria but thankfully recovered, the summer when our new house continued to go up but the adoption still evaded us, the summer when joy and despair constantly circled, as they did that day in Biro.

"Car"

the one when we drive to Accra with the lights flashing

Those evenings at Home Touch, I'd listen for the throb of Nasir's motorbike and always be delighted, relieved, when he turned up. And I'd ask where he'd been, and invariably he'd say he was with his new friends.

'I have been having a drink with my friends,' he'd beam, so honoured to be hobnobbing with local dignitaries –

government workers, assemblymen – so awash with whiskey, because that's what he drank with them at Matron's, a slightly posher spot behind our house. In a way, they were Nasir's Gamma Ball Rally, giving him status, glamour even.

Occasionally I'd join them, though mainly I was happier at Home Touch, watching the children chase Shilea, anticipating the rumble of Nasir's bike, faintly aware the trophy spouse had been replaced by the trophy friends.

'One of my friends is driving to Accra,' Nasir announced a few days before I was due to leave. 'He has the use of a big man's car.'

'Is there enough room?' As well as the three of us, there was Asif, who'd been assisting with BizATE workshops, and his wife, Michele, who worked in the media and was interested in writing about me and the charity. 'It'll be a squash.'

'It's a big car, I think it will be fine.'

We drove the whole way with the sidelights flashing, as important men in Ghana often did to get waved through toll booths and police checkpoints. I worried we'd be a target for bandits. Nasir lapped it up.

We didn't get hijacked, but it was pretty horrendous, five adults and a restless baby stuck in daytime traffic for hours. And once we'd paid for the petrol, it cost more than the night bus anyway. As we stumbled into Sleepy Hippo, Aviella and I were ready for bed. Nasir, on cloud nine, went for a beer, alone.

Next evening, Asif googled *Accra cocktails* and we found ourselves on the rooftop Skybar, intoxicated by breathtaking views and super-strong martinis. It was an amazing night, and possibly the only time Nasir and I enjoyed ourselves in Accra that didn't involve fried rice and Nigerian TV. Michele took our photo and we looked glowing and together, the couple I'd always wanted us to be.

That night meant a lot to Nasir too, though perhaps not in the same way. He set up a Twitter account with a photo of himself and Asif brandishing cocktails, and the profile description:

Am very honest person

A few weeks later, Nasir told me he needed £3,000 to buy a car. He had decided he was too good for the bus. We argued about it until inevitably I gave in and sent the money.

"Christmas Morning"

the one when Nasir prefers the cash

The car wasn't the first financial thing Nasir and I disagreed about that year. Back in May, raw from Cornwall and bank account depleted, I'd refused to buy him a flight for Aviella's first birthday, afraid he'd ruin her celebrations like he'd ruined the holiday, resentful I was expected to cough up again. Of course, *he* could have paid but in our relationship, apparently, the money only flowed one way.

In October, I didn't invite him to Karen and Ross's wedding, same reasons. When Christmas came, however, with its promise of tidings and joy, optimism overcame resentment and I duly bought his ticket.

'I will not make a speech,' grumbled Nasir.

We held an ATE Christmas Party, but despite fairy lights, gallons of donated Prosecco and a Tupperware container of cocktail sausages brought by local spymaster Sir John Sawers, Nasir was not in a Christmassy mood.

In the end, he said a few words, topping off a cordial evening, at least for everyone else. You can see it in the photos, guests munching sausages, children running round ankles, me, puffy-eyed, fixed smile, Nasir, in a Lawra smock, skulking beside the baubles.

Because that Christmas, unlike the last, was not magical. There was a troubling undercurrent – both ways – mostly about money. I'd get annoyed when he went to the pricey corner shop after I'd spent a fortune in the supermarket and Nigerian store. He'd be upset when I wouldn't give him the cash. I'd remind him he could have brought his own money. He'd accuse me of humiliating him.

The depressing truth was that since the juju-related break-up of 2014 we never properly talked about money, never found common ground, never made it work without someone being pissed off.

And that brings me to Christmas morning, the three of us in bed, doing presents. This time, Nasir had brought gifts – a pretty dress for Aviella, earrings and a bag for me – which I appreciated. I'd made a big effort for him, a gold necklace engraved *Aviella/ Bie* and their dates of birth. Up his street, I thought, as he unwrapped it with those hands I'd fallen in love with.

'Thank you, Sarah, it's nice. But to be honest ...' he inspected the necklace and sighed. 'To be honest, I would have preferred the cash.'

"Shilea"

the one when we all cry

We were still squabbling about it on the bus to Lawra in January. On the bus because, after all, Nasir had not spent the three grand he'd lobbied so fiercely for on the car he claimed he so desperately needed. Perhaps the money went into the new house, I wondered hopefully, though more likely it went to one of the many relatives and friends who would have been asking for help with emergencies and needs on a daily basis. After all those times seeing newly granted business owners come under the same pressure, I'd like to think I would have understood but, as ever, it wasn't discussed.

In Lawra, I showed him a spreadsheet of our finances, housing, travel, savings, the lot, trying – failing – to engage him in our future. Meanwhile, with Aviella about to turn two and soon needing her own £600 seat on every flight, our commuting days were numbered and decisions had to be made.

It wasn't all bad. Our volunteers set up a library at Karbo Primary, Dad ran the BizATE workshops and the Inclusion Centre was nearly complete. At home, I was occupied with the children and the litter of puppies Shilea had recently delivered.

Nasir, however, was conspicuously absent, probably with his new friends. He didn't say and after a while I stopped asking.

One hot evening in February, after our visitors had left, I wandered down to Home Touch with Aviella, Bie and, for the first time since she'd given birth, Shilea, her swollen boobs dangling beneath her. It was wonderful to see her out again, playing with the children, checking in on me as she had done for seven years.

Later, Nasir appeared and we had a rare drink together before heading home, his brother Richard taking the folded stroller on his bike, the rest of us piling on with Nasir, Aviella up front, Bie and me hanging off the back, Shilea following behind.

And in that moment, if you'd taken a snapshot, you'd have seen a happy family, the children giggling, me keeping an eye on my dog, noticing she needed to offload some milk. Nasir turned onto the main road and we pootled along at ten miles an hour.

And then it happened. The first thing was the roar of a motorbike going about fifty, then the shriek of its drunken rider, then a screech as the bike veered dangerously towards us.

Nasir swerved to the side of the road and before we knew it Shilea launched herself at the speeding bike. I put my hands over Bie's eyes, but Aviella saw everything, as Shilea made impact and somersaulted limply through the air.

When she hit the ground, she didn't move.

'No!' I screamed, then she somehow dragged her damaged body to the side of the road.

'Let's get the children home,' said Nasir.

'You take them. I'm staying with her.'

Richard waited with me while I sat in the dirt, Shilea's head on my knee. She was quiet, not obviously in pain. I was sobbing. Soon, a crowd gathered, watching the white woman weep over her dog.

'Come, Sarah.' Richard hailed a camboo. 'I'll help you move her.'

At the house, I carried Shilea out of the camboo, placed her gently on the ground and stroked her as she faded and died.

Everyone was in pieces. Shilea was our dog, *our family*, and we loved her. Nasir led me inside and held me. Prosper, in tears, took Shilea to the new property, where he buried her. Later, he put a message on social media:

Tonight, we've lost one of our children

Shilea died as she had lived, loyally, valiantly, protecting us. I spent the next fortnight hand-rearing her puppies, not knowing how to be in Lawra without her, missing her so much. Shilea had been there at the start of everything and by my side throughout. Now she was gone, it felt like an end.

"Accra"

the one when Nasir snaps

It was a tragic finale to an uncomfortable trip. Despite the thrill of the work and the joy of the children, Shilea's death couldn't help but feel symbolic, of something ebbing away. The night she died was the most united we'd been for months. It didn't last long.

We quarrelled all the way to Accra, had a grim couple of days and as we were about to leave Sleepy Hippo for the airport, Nasir grabbed my arm and fell apart.

What he said that night, I'm not going to share. It's too private. Not that he *told* me anything, I didn't understand what had caused this awful despair. All I knew was my husband was a mess, my dog was dead and my daughter was witnessing more trauma.

I did what I could. I offered to stay, I offered to go with him to Lawra and sort out whatever the problem was but, with the taxi outside, we agreed he would come to England as soon as possible. It was one flight I didn't mind buying, he seemed so broken.

Three weeks later, as he waited for his night flight from Accra, he called.

'I need to tell you something. It is important.'

He took a breath, and so did I.

THIRTY-THREE

BIG MAN

I think if he'd killed someone, we might have got over it.

But not this.

If he'd told me he'd been unfaithful, who knows? I'd suspected it anyway, perhaps a confession would have cleared the air and we could have moved on.

But not this.

There were a hundred things he could have admitted to that I might have forgiven him for.

But Not This.

'I gave money to a friend. I loaned him some of ATE's money. He was supposed to repay it, but he has not.'

'How much?'

'Fifteen thousand cedis.'

Two thousand pounds.

And in an instant, he destroyed everything.

I hung up.

When he called back, I got both barrels. *I can't believe you're not supporting me. The wife stands by the husband. You are a shit wife.*

'I'll see you at Heathrow,' I told him and then sunk to the floor, weeping for everything I knew I was about to lose.

For the family he'd wrecked.

For the people who would suffer if the charity was ruined.

For all of it.

We drove in cold silence from the airport. At the house, Nasir stormed inside and we didn't speak, didn't even glance at each other, until Aviella was asleep.

'You stole ATE money.' I was determined to be calm. 'And you need to return it.'

'I did not steal. I borrowed. You make me feel small. That is not what a wi …'

'Use whatever word you want. And after all those speeches telling *other* people how to behave. People will think the whole charity is corrupt.'

He glared, as if I was the one in the wrong.

'Nasir, I fell in love with a man who protected me. Protected everyone. Someone humble and kind and decent. What happened to that man?'

'Sarah, you talk too much.'

I went downstairs, where a concerned Leela gave me a hug. When I said I couldn't tell her what was happening, not yet, she quietly, acceptingly, made me something to eat.

It was a long night. Nasir, defiant, in the bedroom, Leela, being kind, downstairs, me between the two, watching my life implode, asking myself – because he wouldn't tell me – how he could have chosen some new friend over everything he claimed to love. Asking myself, *what should I do next?* Aware that whatever I did, and whatever he did, one way or another, we were fucked.

Of course, I could have dug into my dwindling savings, as I'd done for the car, as I'd done for the flight. I could have discreetly replaced the money and kept it between me and Nasir, an awful secret to poison our relationship and our charity forever. I could have rescued Nasir, like he'd rescued me so many times in Lawra. And if he'd done pretty much anything else, maybe I would have. Just not this.

I walked into the bedroom, where Nasir was on his phone, frantic.

'I am trying to sell the house.'

'The house I've put thousands of pounds into?'

'I can't find anyone to buy it, I can't find fifteen thousand cedis. I can't …'

'Whatever happens, I want to be clear. I'm not giving you the money.'

And I stared at him, my husband, and just felt so disappointed.

I had to get away, so I took Aviella and went to Mum's, where I also found Karen.

'Nasir's done something …' Karen instinctively took my hand as I confessed my husband's misdeed. They looked horrified.

'OK, love,' said Mum, 'we can get through this. First, you need to tell the trustees.'

I went upstairs and Aviella screamed in the kitchen. Eventually, Mum brought her up and she clamped herself to my breast as I reported her father and blew our family apart. With that one call, I knew I would never adopt Bie, knew I may never visit Lawra again, knew Aviella's relationship with her brother and dad would irrevocably change. And I did it anyway, because it was the only way to protect her, to protect ATE, to stop us all from being crushed.

At one point, I had to kneel on the floor and stick my head out of the low window to get any phone reception, Aviella still clinging on. Karen told me later how that image, to her, literally represented my life. On my knees, exposed, sucked dry.

I left a voicemail for Dad, chair of trustees, who was in

Australia. That must have been a lovely message to wake up to, his son-in-law, the father of his grandchild, misusing money from the charity his family set up. What an incestuous mess.

I walked to the office and broke the news to a devastated Leela. Nasir had been her friend and colleague too, and through his actions she also faced the prospect of losing her livelihood and everything she'd spent four years working on. We were trying to make sense of it all when we spotted Nasir stalking past the office. Witnessing him, through the window, he was like some irate stranger, separate and apart. My phone rang and I was informed he'd been formally suspended from his job.

And then we spent an interminable week together, holed up in my bedroom, in pieces. Inside, I was hollow where the trust had once been, outside I was raw, my sense of safety and protection ripped away. At some point, sat on the floor amidst his T-shirts and our broken dreams, I told him it was over. For me, there was no other way forward. After all those years and everything we'd achieved together, I was done.

We couldn't help each other, so I held Aviella tight, crying for my family who I might never see, crying for the work I might never do, wanting to blame Nasir for all of it and knowing that I'd also got things wrong, that I had also let people down. I'd told a child I would never leave him, I'd brought another into the world who would never know her father as she should.

And then there was the charity, and all the lives ruined if it collapsed.

My boys, who lived in the ATE property, would they lose their home? Would our twenty staff and cooks lose their jobs? Would a thousand children go hungry and stop attending school? Would our small businesses fail and our SNAP groups fold?

'Nasir, I could move your flight,' I said one day through the grief. 'Why don't you go early? Why don't you just go?'

But he wouldn't. 'This is the last time I will see my daughter. I need to be with her.'

We dragged ourselves out of the bedroom, I made a packed lunch and we went to the park, where Nasir played with Aviella, limping with his achy knee, swaddled in borrowed winter clothes, never quite warm. It could see he was in pain – and not just physically – and I felt for him, I truly did. But I was as embittered and angry as I had ever been, knowing he had brought this on us all and that we were all going to pay.

Nasir never did apologise, not really. There were moments when he would take responsibility, say he was sorry, beg for forgiveness. Though there were more when he didn't, when he was furious with me for not covering for him or with whoever had taken him to the juju man or some other excuse. I'm not sure he even really thought he'd done anything wrong.

A generous supporter gave Nasir the money to pay back and I was thankful, not wanting things to escalate, fearing where that might lead. Once the money was replaced and the drama died down, we settled into a strange, still misery. Like the mood in a house after someone has died, shrouded in sorrow, suspended in time until after the funeral when life, somehow, must begin again.

I remember saying goodbye, the three of us in the driveway because I definitely couldn't face taking him to the airport. I stood there, Aviella in my arms, and Nasir gave us a hug and a kiss and said, *I love you* and I said, *I love you, too.* And he got in his cab and was gone.

He eventually told me what happened with his friend, saying he'd loaned him the cash for an exclusive investment, something about an infrastructure project, something about there being absolutely no risk of him defaulting on the loan. Not that it matters – or perhaps it even makes it worse – but I found out much later that the friend actually repaid the money soon after (and that he hadn't known it was charity money in the first place). So was it just bad timing that had brought things to a head? Or was it, somehow, always going to end like this?

Whatever. Whatever the reasons Nasir had, the excuses, the cultural dynamics, the colonial legacy. The pressures – which I'd totally underestimated – of being married to the white lady, of being that little bit rich, but not rich enough. Whatever had happened and whoever's fault it was and however it could have been different. Whether the girl from Ramsbury and the boy from Lawra could have ever made a go of it. Whether he detonated things because it was all too hard. Whether I let him, because I felt the same. Whatever.

He did it, I think, to impress his friend. And because *that's how things worked*. He'd risked everything to be what he thought was a *big man*. When, to the people who mattered, he'd been a big man all along.

I wanted, at some stage – for Aviella's sake if nothing else – to be able to remember the good stuff, the good times, the good man. Meanwhile, I had a daughter to care for and a charity to save. No-one else could do it, no-one was coming to my rescue and I actually didn't want anyone to. This one was on me.

THIRTY-FOUR

JUST, MAYBE

I got on with it, because it was *the next thing to do.*

And the hardest. Facing everyone. Explaining. Putting things right. It wasn't just the humiliation, though that was overwhelming, it was the loss. Of my beautiful life in that beautiful, challenging place, of my family in Lawra and – still raw and so symbolic – of my dog. More than that. It was the loss of my confidence, my faith in my own judgement, my faith in people. I felt I'd lost myself, my identity, gone. Just gone.

That first morning after he left, if I'd had time to look in a mirror – which I didn't because I was a single parent in a crisis – I would have seen a thirty-five-year-old wreck, battered, exhausted, so different from the naive, optimistic girl who'd arrived in Lawra seven years before with such high hopes and all the wrong clothes. Yet, through the misery and shame, one thing was clear. To do *the next thing* I'd have to summon up that foolish girl, with her unremitting energy and unerring belief that everything would be alright. Was she there, I wondered, deep inside? Broken but not quite beaten. Down but not quite out. She'd better be, I thought. Without her, I had no chance.

Of course, having said this one was on me, it wasn't all *about* me. It never had been.

'I need you to step up, Kaamil, there's no-one else.'

One of my initial calls was to our SNAP project leader, realising the key to everything – my self-worth, my income, my children's homes, all the work – was in ensuring the survival of ATE.

'You're our most senior person in Lawra. I know it's difficult, but for us to go on, I need you to help manage things.' It wasn't an order, more a plea.

'I understand. Of course, I'll do it.'

Over the next couple of weeks, I reached out to every member of staff, in Ramsbury and Lawra, explaining I was fighting for the charity, promising not to let them down, asking them to keep the faith. Without exception, they did, despite their own personal distress. As important – and even more humiliating – I had to face our supporters, and began meeting a few trusted contacts in the hope that if I kept them on board, others would stay too.

One of the first was Nick Maurice, a great friend to the charity, who I met in the local café. I trembled at the prospect of the whole of Ramsbury overhearing my revelation. I ordered a coffee and no cake. Knowing I was about to swallow my pride, I didn't think I could keep anything else down.

'Nasir has loaned out two thousand pounds of charity money without proper authority. The money has now been replaced and there is an ongoing investigation.'

How many times did I end up saying those words? I dread to think. That whispered conversation with Nick was one of many coffees and drinks (along with, eventually, hundreds of calls and emails) and it was the most torrid period of my life. Walking into The Bell and imagining everyone judging me, *what an idiot, poor thing, did she know?* Putting on a brave face as I sat with Sir John Sawers or CET's David Willetts, laying my worst experience out in front of them, being ruthlessly honest, completely transparent and feeling utterly, utterly distraught. And, thankfully, incredibly supported.

Nick was understanding, kind and deeply affected. He knew what a potential disaster this was and could see we were trying to deal with it. Fortunately, the majority of people felt the same. We lost a few standing orders, not loads, and I cancelled too many fundraising events because I simply couldn't bear them. And I did weeks of that, humbling myself by day, holding Aviella by night, grateful for the strength to keep going.

In the end, after it was mutually agreed between Nasir and the trustees that his contract would be terminated, an email was sent to our supporters.

We have made changes to our structure, as well as financial and reporting processes.

The catalyst for these changes was the discovery that a senior member of staff in Lawra made an unauthorised loan to an unconnected person in early 2019. As soon as the trustees became aware of this incident, we ordered a full investigation. The loan has now been repaid in full and the member of staff is leaving ATE. The incident has been fully reported to the Charity Commission.

And with a press of a button, my whole world knew. A few people lobbied for Nasir, hoping there was a way for him to continue with the charity, maybe in a different capacity, for him to have a second chance. I respected their position, but I disagreed. We – me and the charity – needed to move on. I had to be able to assure a Gamma Ball Rally and the Ramsbury cake-bakers and anyone who bought a raffle ticket or took out a standing order, that *your money will make all the difference, your money is safe with me* and know it was the truth. And it was the same for everyone, we all had to believe otherwise the whole thing was over. So Nasir left the charity he helped set up, doing a good handover to the other staff, and ATE looked to the future.

The one time I cried in public was the trustees meeting when they discussed whether to keep paying rent on the ATE house. I was to give factual information only, listing everyone who lived there – *Nasir, Bie, Kanyiri, Kakpe, Prosper* – then listen, mute, impotent, my head screaming *don't throw my boys onto the street.*

'You're doing really well,' said Susan, my ever-supportive trustee.

'Well done,' said fellow trustee Pete Willetts, as I wiped away a tear. But I knew, however sympathetic they were, that the charity had to come first.

In the end, they kept the property on for a few months. Our long-standing treasurer, Andrew Ritchie, went over the figures and it made financial sense given the rest of UK team would be over that summer. From my perspective, it was one less awful consequence to dread. The children could stay.

Somehow, we kept the show on the road. Staff were indomitable, trustees were unshakeable, key funders were unwavering and the fundamentals, the love, the loyalty, the community trust – in both my villages – prevailed, despite everything. And, perhaps a little, because of it.

That spring, under the calm leadership of Kaamil, we opened our landmark Inclusion Centre and launched a new kitchen in Bagri Junction, that first school I visited in 2012. We put the whole organisation on a more professional footing, especially around money. Before, we'd worked on total trust, now our system was based on total *dis*trust and even the smallest transaction was signed off by several people in both Ghana and the UK. Having failed to recognise just how much pressure Nasir was under, this was about more than just protecting our money – it was about protecting our employees. There's no one hundred per cent guarantee, but I was fairly confident it would be hard for anyone to misuse our funds and not get found out, and I hoped that would help them resist in the first place.

All the other UK staff went to Ghana, giving the local team a vital boost, and I spoke to them on the phone constantly – individually – never in a team video meeting. Again, couldn't face it. I was glad Ramsbury was standing with Lawra, but for them to be over there, doing my work, seeing my boys, drinking in my spot … honestly, I hated it.

It was, though, all part of approaching things differently, of unravelling the tangle of relationships at the heart of both what had gone wrong and what had been glorious. The charity no longer revolved around me and Nasir, and not before time. Emerging from our shadow, the staff rose to the occasion and gradually, with careful dedication across two countries, we nursed ATE through its crisis and a more positive future became possible.

With Nasir, not so much. We all know how bitter and twisted things can get when a relationship ends badly, and the pain of our respective betrayals was vivid in the late-night texts and angry calls.

It was debilitating. Aviella scarcely slept, and neither did I, both of us running on empty for months. I threw myself into the arms of my family, who helped us through the darkest times. We had a desperately needed holiday in Greece with Laura, my forever friend who loved me no matter what. We had restorative weekends with new friends Asif and his wife Michele – by then, my collaborator in this book – who knew *everything* and surprisingly liked me anyway. Besides them and a few other close supports, I saw no-one, did nothing, just worked and cared for Aviella.

'Where is your wedding ring?' Nasir asked on one of our more harmonious chats. 'You have taken off your ring.'

After weeks of feeling it burn into my finger, I'd removed the band he'd given me eighteen months before.

'I'm sorry,' I told him. 'I can't …'

'Sarah …'

'We'll always be parents, to Aviella and Bie. We'll make that work.'

I had no idea how. The last thing I wanted was for him to come to the UK, and the prospect of me going to Lawra, to Ghana even, was inconceivable, however much I wanted to see Bie. Too soon. Too much nastiness. Too little trust. Meanwhile, we continued the calls and video chats both of us hated and the children often found difficult. I don't suppose anyone was communicating, not properly, but we were in touch, just, and for now that was as good as it was going to get.

I was in constant contact with Kanyiri and Kakpe, covering their school fees, reassuring them I'd always provide a roof over their heads, backing them however I could. And Kanyiri updated me about Bie, passing on small gifts I sent over, a T-shirt, a football, money for a treat. It drove Nasir mad, *you humiliate me, you insult me.* I didn't care. I was up to here with being humiliated myself and only wanted Bie to know I was thinking of him and to put a smile on his face.

Really, I tried *not* to think about him, not to think about when – if – I would see him, sick at the thought it might be never. So I kept telling him *I love you, I will always love you* and clung even tighter to Aviella.

Can anyone with a van help??!

I was sitting on the street outside my house, surrounded by my possessions and desperately posting on social media. I had never felt more alone.

Leela and I had decided to sell up and get our own places, not exactly because of what had happened, though doubtless hastened by it. More unravelling. Unfortunately, my flat purchase had fallen through and now, as I was about to decamp to Mum's, the removal people hadn't materialised, none of my friends or family were available and so I'd single-handedly boxed up and lugged out everything I owned.

Any help gratefully received!!

Leela had already gone, and it was just me, on a packing case, praying someone on a local Facebook page could bail me out. With the new owners about to descend, a message popped up. It was Nasir.

sorry I'm not there to help

He was being kind, the old Nasir, the Nasir who'd come running when I got trapped at election rallies or was invaded by snakes or termites or vultures. The good man I had been building a life with, the man I'd needed when I thought I needed rescuing.

Another message appeared from someone with a van and

soon I was in Mum's spare bedroom, property-searching online, not having to worry about what would suit Nasir, acknowledging I was finally ready to leave Ramsbury. And, unlike before, this was not a gesture, not for a man, not even for an adventure. Not even because it was the next thing to do. I was doing it for my independence, for me and my daughter to live our lives, connected always with Ramsbury and Lawra, but also, just us. Just us.

We moved into a tiny house in nearby Hungerford and things settled down. I did a few fundraising events and towards the end of the year was able to join a team video meeting, the Ghana staff crowded round one laptop, and it was OK. Aviella began to sleep, which meant I did too. A little, but not all, of my naive optimism resurfaced, a little, not all, of my faith in people did likewise. Somehow – and it was definitely a group effort – ATE had survived and so had Aviella and so had I.

On New Year's Eve, I took a photo of the two of us in matching polar bear pyjamas.

'Night, night, Aviella,' I whispered as she fell asleep. 'See you next year.'

I sat downstairs on my own with pasta pesto and a nice Sauvignon Blanc, feeling at peace and in control. It had been the worse year of my life, yet it had got me where I needed to be to make the best possible future for myself, my daughter and my charity. I uploaded the photo onto Facebook, wondering if anyone would notice the sadness in my eyes or how many more wrinkles now surrounded them.

31 December 2019

Happy New Year

I'm very glad to see the end of 2019! It's been too hard and too sad. I toast the new decade tonight with tremendous gratitude for the wonderful bits of my life, and with lots of hope and excitement for the future. Yay for fresh starts, and for optimism!

Obviously, like everyone else, I had no idea what was coming in 2020.

THIRTY-FIVE

FOLLOW THE STAR

I could write a book about our response to Covid, about how the Lawra team dealt so heroically with the nightmare of lockdown, backed resolutely by our Ramsbury staff and trustees. About how we provided food to vulnerable families and how our entrepreneurs adapted their businesses, such as the seamstresses who sewed countless face masks. There's a book in the way the people of Lawra showed resilience and courage in the face of crisis and how the people of Ramsbury and beyond never forgot their friends in Ghana and donated thousands of pounds to our emergency appeal.

There's a book in it, for sure, but it's not this book. Because, despite 2020 being framed to a large extent by coronavirus, in the end that's not what it was about, not really, not for the charity and not for me. So please do read the Annual Report for a fuller version of our fightback and meanwhile stick with me here, because here – unpredictably and against the odds – you'll discover my hopes for 2020 were not entirely misplaced.

That said, Covid made everything starker, rawer, more profound. The challenges. The decisions. And (yet again) the quest to survive.

Hungerford was a ghost town, that first morning of lockdown. Deserted, dead, zero people other than me and Aviella walking to nursery. I'd been in denial until then, not quite believing this virus would touch our lives. Now, grasping my daughter's hand, it was like being in a post-apocalyptic movie.

It was full-on dystopia at Tesco and the shelves were picked clean. As I paid for my meagre basket, I braced myself and made a call.

'Nasir, I know it's hard, but it's time to pull together.'

'I agree, Sarah. Things are going to be bad.'

'Have you got any food? Is there anywhere to buy food?'

'The shortages are here already and the market has been told to close. The lockdown in Ghana will be very strict. The Government is stopping transport to the north and Lawra will be cut off.'

'But it's lean season ...'

'In Accra, I think they are more frightened of the virus than of hunger.'

I promised to send him some money for food, he thanked me and it was the longest, calmest, most collaborative conversation we'd had in over a year.

Unpacking my shopping, guilt washed over me. About everything. That I'd gratefully received one of the precious places the nursery was still allowed to offer, but was maybe putting my two-year-old at risk by using it. That I'd sent cash to Nasir and Bie when I knew my SNAP families needed it more. That I had, in an act of defiance, purchased quite a lot of Corona beer.

So many clashing priorities, so many horrible choices, so many ways to get it wrong.

Grainy faces popped up on my computer screen, to vanish seconds later.

'Hello, Sa ...'

'Prosper, are you there?'

'..........'

'Kaamil, you need to turn on your microphone.'

'Sarah ...'

'Prosper?'

'Kaamil, Leela here. Click on the microphone with a line through it.'

A Zoom call to Lawra was the telecoms equivalent of nailing jelly to a wall. Everyone, in England and Ghana, was working from home and reception in Lawra was temperamental at best. Still, it was a far cry from my dongle days of 2012.

'We are in full lockdown now,' Prosper explained eventually. 'People have been told to stay indoors and they are terrified. Schools are shut and so, of course, are our kitchens. Many people, many children, are fleeing to Kumasi for work or food. I don't know if they will ever come back.'

'No-one can trade,' added Rexford, hub manager for Gombele and Biro. 'The markets are finished and there is no money anyway.'

'The people I am most worried about,' said Kaamil, 'are the SNAP families. They live on the edge and without our assistance, I fear for their survival.'

It was the triple whammy, Mum's eternal triangle, Education, Enterprise, Disability. All taken out by Covid.

'Can we keep the Inclusion Centre going?'

'No, Sarah. This morning I locked the doors. The Inclusion Centre is closed.'

It was cruelly symbolic and for a moment there was silence. Then Prosper dropped out again and Leela went to put on a new movie for her son. When we reconvened, we decided to make the SNAP families our top priority.

'Can we get them food? Any farmers we can talk to? Could we at least deliver rice and beans to the rural families?'

I saw the terror on their grainy faces. Ghana's lockdown was so brutal and the message from the government so grisly, that the prospect of going into people's dwellings felt to them like a suicide mission.

'We will do our best,' vowed Kaamil, before his connection was lost.

I washed and straightened my hair, applied make-up to my blind-panic face and sat in my living room, smart from the waist up. I pressed record.

'As Covid-19 rips through the UK,' I said into my laptop, 'fear, stress and sadness touches all of us. When the virus reaches Lawra, there is no doubt it will have disastrous consequences ...'

This had to work. With fundraising cancelled, we needed the emergency appeal to feed SNAP families, to pay our Ghana staff, to ensure the charity stayed alive.

As I finished, a photo arrived on my WhatsApp from Prosper, of him and Kaamil, colourful face masks and plastic gloves in place, handing over a bag of rice to a family in Biro, and I was so proud of them I can't tell you. ATE soon became, to the people of Lawra, an emergency service, delivering food, paying for medication, checking on school pupils and mentoring businesses and farmers, the staff stepping up because their community needed them to.

Through their endeavours, we discovered the beating heart of ATE. No longer a dysfunctional family dominated by two individuals in a flawed relationship, we were now an organisation to celebrate, a group of talented people that got stuff done. For me too, after a crushing year of shame, there was new confidence and conviction. Alongside Leela and our fantastic newest UK recruit, Tara Colsell-Hawes, I helped the Ghana team navigate unknown waters, we raised a staggering £30,000 through the appeal and kept things going when they could have fallen apart.

Covid barely reached Lawra in 2020. There was a handful of reported cases and after a couple of months people stopped wearing masks, markets began trading, schools brought back their exam years and the district (sort of) returned to normal. The grave legacy of a harsh lockdown, however, was evident.

Even when schools fully reopened, the mass exodus to the south meant less than half the students materialised. Those who did had no shoes, like in the old days. We worked exhaustively to locate missing pupils, offering free uniforms and books, and I cherished those calls from Rexford to say ten young people had rejoined Biro JHS. Some, though, were lost forever.

It was horrendous, of course it was, yet I witnessed the absolute best of my colleagues over there and in the UK. In the face of adversity, we did essential work, work no-one else was doing, work that saved lives and gave Lawra a chance to recover, a chance to rebuild.

It wasn't just the charity and it wasn't just Lawra that needed to rebuild. Since the awful events of March 2019, my relationship with Nasir – father of my children and still my legal husband – had been wretched. But the pandemic – and plain old passing of time – took a bit of heat out of things. Our weekly video chats stopped being traumatic and became (let's not get carried away) merely uncomfortable. Nasir and Aviella communicated slightly better and Nasir tried to call when Bie was around, me breaking into a huge smile, as I'd always done whenever I saw his lovely face.

As the UK settled into a quieter, simpler way of life, I was able to regain a little balance. Somehow the smallness, almost the *dullness* of it all, gave me space to focus on what was important. After the turmoil and break-ups of recent years, Mum, Karen, Ross, me and the children regrouped, spending hours on the phone or running round Hungerford Common, finding pleasure and love in each other's company.

Whilst I know the 2020 lockdown was an ordeal for many people, for me it was an opportunity to build my nest with Aviella. I made friends with my new neighbours, sharing Coronas over the garden fence if weather allowed. Our house had a makeover and I painted walls, planted flowers and gave Aviella the pink bedroom of every girl's dreams. It wasn't always a ball, cooped up alongside a child with a big personality. Overall though, and to my surprise, it was grounding, nourishing, life-affirming.

One Friday, with Aviella at home and me not officially *at work*, my phone rang.

'Hi, I'm from The Fore and I'd like to interview you about your recent grant application. Sorry to spring it on you, are you available now?'

'Erm ...' Aviella was playing in a corner, furniture was pushed to the middle of the living room and I'd just slathered wallpaper paste onto lining paper. 'Can you give me five minutes?'

I quickly stuck up the paper and when she called back I was able to answer all her questions before Aviella got bored and insisted we went to the garden to look for bees, our new favourite game since they shut the playgrounds. Luckily, we got the grant, five grand, which was more than we'd asked for. And that was lockdown for me, loving my home, loving my family, keeping the charity running, looking for bees.

We began the search for a Director of Operations with one overriding aspiration. To recruit *from* Lawra and find a qualified person ready to be a community leader in the way a UK manager never could. I was overjoyed when we received an application from a candidate with roots in Lawra *and* in ATE.

My old friend Gabriel N-Yoh Maanibe had been there from the outset, at that first chaotic BizATE meeting when we had to ask them back the next day. Since then, he'd studied development, worked internationally and was now returning with the experience, the insight and, crucially, the passion. With the prospect of Gabriel coming on board, I could sense my own passion for the work rising once more, no longer soldiering on but genuine enthusiasm. It was a relief to know I could feel that way again.

It *was* complicated. Wasn't it always with ATE? Gabriel was not only my friend, he was husband to my friend Adeline, father to my goddaughters, distant cousin to Prosper. And Nasir. So I tried – not wholly successfully – to take a back seat, allowing the trustees to do all the due diligence they could throw at it. In Lawra – where everyone is pretty much related to everyone else – if you want to recruit locally, from the community you work in, that's what you've got to deal with.

Gabriel's appointment was a watershed moment for the charity and for me in particular. He was now the one whizzing round on the motorbike, doing the hands-on work, and I accepted that. Whilst I was across everything, with a key strategic role, I no longer needed to do it all, and I couldn't anyway, and anyway, I shouldn't. The response to the pandemic showed that the people of Lawra didn't need a load of people in Ramsbury making decisions for them when the expertise and dedication was already there. As we looked to the next five years – with ambitious plans to open five more hubs and double the Lawra staff – the charity set up by the middle-class girl with more than a whiff of white saviour about her had moved on and that's exactly how it should be.

Some things, though, will never change. And when I'm with Aviella, the girl born from my love of Lawra, I see a connection, a bridge between two villages that will never be broken. One afternoon towards the end of 2020, she was sitting on the floor in our house, counting coins from her money box.

'I'm putting it in piles,' she told me. 'This one is for the man who lives under the bridge in Hungerford and this one is for the children you help in Ghana.'

My wonderful Aviella, thoughtful, determined, aware of the world. Although she drives me insane at times and single parenting is demanding – even on a good day – in that moment, I couldn't have been prouder.

Actually, I could. Because just before Christmas, Aviella was chosen to play Mary in the nursery's Nativity. She spent hours rehearsing the big song and one cold December morning I walked her to school, both of us humming *Follow the Star* and full of anticipation for the show that afternoon, which was to be screened via Zoom.

As I dropped her off, an image filled my mind, of three thousand miles away and under a beating sun, where other girls attended classes because of ATE. Pupils in seven schools – including Judith, Jeremiah and (sometimes) Celina, my first friends in Lawra – learnt on a full stomach. A hundred business owners – like those strong-willed Zambo weavers – provided for their families. Janet and a dozen apprentices trained. Clement and the farmers cultivated crops in unwelcoming soil. And Peace, Patience and two hundred families with disabled children built lives with dignity and hope. And that was all *us, we* did that. ATE and the people of Lawra and Ramsbury, and the team and the donors, and my family who got the ball rolling and Nasir, whose wisdom and effort helped to make it all happen. And me, whose naive optimism sparked the whole thing and whose unassailable commitment kept it going through bad times and good.

That afternoon, from around the world, we logged on for the Nativity, boxes of excited, beaming faces. There was my Dad, in Australia, and Mum, Karen, Ross and my two beloved nephews in Ramsbury. And in Ghana, Aviella's family (sporadically) turned up in force: Prosper, who'd been a rock for ATE and a rock for me in those two precarious years, festive in his Santa hat; Kanyiri, the impressive boy who'd grown into an impressive university student and, along with his brother Kakpe, an irreplaceable part of my life.

And Nasir and Bie, proud dad and senior brother, thrilled to see Aviella, if only by video, Bie, looking smart in clothes I'd sent him, nine now and still the easy, calm, optimistic – perhaps naively optimistic – boy I've loved with all my heart his whole life, and always will.

And, of course, it's bittersweet. Because even at my most positive, I don't know what will happen to us or how we'd ever be in the same room together or if we ever will. For now, though, it's enough for us all to be there for Aviella, watching her shove the baby Jesus in a manger and sing *Follow the Star,* until there's not a dry eye in the house, not mine or anybody's.

ACTION THROUGH ENTERPRISE:

TEN YEARS AND BEYOND

As we go to print, Action Through Enterprise has been celebrating a remarkable 10th anniversary. Who would have thought, given how it all began, that we'd make it this far? Or bring so many wonderful people – from two continents – together? And have achieved so much? And have the potential to achieve so much more?

Of course, I want to say *I did*! But my wildest dreams didn't get me to where we are now – and where I think we are going. All that, I promise, is for the next book. Meanwhile, here's what we've been up to …

- We've opened more hubs in Lawra, so that anyone in the district can access our programmes should they choose to. We've done this two years ahead of schedule and believe we have a model for development that is high impact, low cost, kind and replicable.

- Whilst continuing our work in Lawra, Action Through Enterprise is now expanding to a whole new location. Nandom, to the north, will be our next exciting venture, with plans to open an Inclusion Centre and launch two hubs in 2024. The groundwork, the building of relationships and listening to local people, has already begun.

- The team in Ghana goes from strength to strength. Gabriel is now Country Director, leading a staff of fifty-one and heading the expansion to Nandom, ably assisted by Kaamil (Deputy Director and SNAP lead), Rexford (Girls to School), Helen, Ernestina and Esther (SNAP) and Charity, Sylvester and Julius (Hub Managers).

- The UK team – of me, Tara (now Development Director), Rachel Barker (admin and finance), Dee Anderson (SNAP) and Michele (part-time communications) and our incredible trustees, led by new chair Nathalie Burdet, work alongside the Ghana staff – forming one glorious team that is stronger because of all our cultures. And we've learned from our mistakes, recognising the pressure our Lawra staff can experience (especially when it comes to money) and providing support as well as rigorous structures and governance.

- Kanyiri and Kakpe both do incredible work for ATE during their university holidays – and I'm really proud to report that Kanyiri is about to graduate with a degree in Medical Laboratory Studies, and Kakpe is taking a BSc in Development Planning. I know they have a wonderful life ahead of them.

- With six SNAP groups, we support more than 400 disabled children and their families, with more groups launching every year. Many previously written-off children are attending school or learning a trade and becoming valued and valuable members of the community.

- In ten years, we have funded and mentored 127 entrepreneurs and dry season farmers – after ATE support, these businesses make five times more profit, their owners can support their family's needs, pay for basic health care and improve their living conditions – a quarter have even built a new home.

- More than forty-five girls are learning a trade as VoCATE apprentices, many (like Janet) going on to run small businesses with apprentices of their own. The effect of our work ripples through communities, and we continue to train young women with great potential – including some who have come through SNAP.

- We provide school meals and other vital resources in eleven schools in Lawra – and have enabled almost three thousand young people to attend school. We are now collaborating with two schools in Nandom, as the first part of our expansion plan.

- A growing number of individual girls are being supported by us to attend Senior High School, so they can transform their lives and become a generation of role models for other women in their villages.

- We opened an IT Suite in the Inclusion Centre, with twenty-eight computers donated by SEGA – and now the people of Lawra are learning the skills so many of us take for granted. Plans are already underway for a similar Centre in Nandom.

- We achieve so much on what's actually a tiny budget. Around £225k a year to raise up a community of over fifty thousand people is incredibly good value, and we've got really good at making the most of our precious donations, brilliant staff and amazing supporters in the UK and Ghana.

- I'm excited to invite you to be part of the Action Through Enterprise story – please donate your time, donate your money, run a marathon, run a cake sale. There are so many ways to support our important work and everyone is welcome to contribute however they can. I would love a by-product of this book to be the growth of Action Through Enterprise, with more people joining us in our quest to tackle poverty and create opportunities in Upper West Ghana.

- Donate at: justgiving.com/ateghana
  - £24 provides a rural girl with sanitary pads for a year, allowing her to attend school
  - £20 a month feeds five children every school day, enabling them to learn and transform their lives
  - £60 buys a bicycle for a family with a disabled child, ensuring they can work, study and be part of the community
  - £300 sets up a small, sustainable business, supporting families to support themselves
  - £700 gives a young woman apprenticeship training, giving her a trade for life.
- Contact us at: admin@ateghana.org
- Visit us at https://ateghana.org

WE COULDN'T HAVE
DONE IT WITHOUT YOU

Our deepest thanks go to:

Everyone who has made Action Through Enterprise possible: the staff and volunteers; the trustees; the collaborators and cheerleaders; the donors. All have contributed to the brilliant small charity ATE is today.

Thanks to the amazing team, past and present, in Ghana and the UK, who have brought the most incredible combination of skills, experience and passion: Prosper Albeboure, Dee Anderson, Rachel Barker, Esther Bekah, Rexford Benon, Tara Colsell-Hawes, Jessica Cruse, Starr Gaanu, Helen Gala, Ernestina Gan, Kenneth Gan, Luke Hodgson, Kaamil Issahaku, Lamissi Karbo, Sylvester Karbo, Edith Kebo, Kanyiri Kuube-isaan, Kakpe Kuube-isaan, Charity Kyekpo, Sarah Livesey, Julius Maaire Walier, Gabriel Maanibe, Nicholas Nawme, Edina Nuokpier, Leela Shanti, Ernest Tangpuori, Dibaar Yirle, Evarist Yirviele and, of course, ATE's very first member of staff, Nasir. It's been more than just a job for all of us and that shows in what we have achieved together.

Thanks to ATE's wise and wonderful trustees, who have carefully ensured we're legal, effective and kind: Nathalie Burdet, Jennifer Congrave, Alice Delemare, Priyanka Devani, Stephanie Green, Nigel Henham, Pete Maple, Nick Maurice, Andrew Ritchie, Suki Ritchie, Susan Suchopar, Peter Willetts and Jacob Winter. With special thanks to Sarah's Mum, Pip

Coid – a founder trustee and enduring advocate for kindness and justice – and Sarah's Dad, Charles Gardner, the chair of trustees for ten years and whose constant belief in the work has made all the difference in the best and worst of times.

Thanks to all the people and organisations who have partnered, collaborated with and been cheerleaders for the charity, particularly: Geoff Anderson; Susie and Alex Anglesey; Lord Ian Austin; John Bosco; Sue Brady, Martin and Eugenia Ephson; Ghana Education Service Lawra, Ghana International Foundation, Ghana School Aid; Chris and Elaine Goodman; Colin Green and IMET 2000; John Haw; Janet and Stephen Hodgson; Lawra Municipal Authority; Mary Karbo; Naa Puowele Karbo III; Sue Kolljeski; Marlborough Quakers; Physionet; Peter Oliver and SEGA; Paul Ramsbottom and The Savannah Education Trust; Roger Raymond Trust; Rotary Clubs and Rotarians across Wiltshire and Berkshire; Epiphany Productions the community of St Mary's Church, Newbury; Sir John Sawers; Steve Sherman; Ian Smith; Graham Tilley and Epiphany Productions; Joe Weeks; David Willetts, John Hillier and The Commercial Education Trust; Jaime Williams, Gamma Telecoms and their Gamma Ball Rally partners; VSO; former colleagues at The Winchcombe School, specially Barbara Bradford, Rhona O'Neill and Felix Rayner; Leahy Winter.

Thanks to ATE's donors – too many to name – who've given time, money, expertise, office space and a fair amount of sweat in running marathons. Every £10 has been celebrated and used to the best of our abilities to make a genuine difference in Lawra. We are so grateful to every single person who has believed in the charity, the team, the mission – your support has been far more than we could have hoped.

And especial thanks to Sarah's former neighbours and the

organisations of Ramsbury, the other village in this story. From The Bell to the Holy Cross Church to the Primary School, you have taken the people of Lawra to your heart and built a connection that strengthens us all.

Thanks to our friends ...

Sarah: I'm beyond grateful for the people who have supported me personally through this momentous decade, especially Nicola Wilks, Laura Ellison and Owen Lucas for endless laughter and love. And to Leela, for being my partner in so many ways across so many years. I couldn't have done it without you.

Michele: to the amazing women in my life, Ambreen Hameed, Keely Winstone, Judith Broadbent and Sally Richards, who have supported me in my work, my writing and basically everything (and for a very long time), and especially Rachel Ford who, as well as all that, helped us get the beginning of the book right.

Thanks to our families ...

Sarah: to my sister Karen who I love to end of the earth, my brother-in-law Ross who arrived in our family at our darkest time and has been a rock for us through it all, and my wonderful nephews, Rossy and Albie, who remind me that life should be lived to the fullest with as much laughter and mud as possible. To my parents for giving me a secure and happy life of opportunity that made it possible for me to have so much adventure and take risks – I know how fortunate I am and am grateful for it every day. And my husband Jon, with whom life exceeds every optimistic expectation I've ever had – I can't believe I've been lucky enough to find you.

Michele: to my husband Asif, whose spirit of adventure and sense of justice first introduced me to ATE, Lawra and Sarah and without whom this book would never have happened. He patiently endured many readings of *To Lawra With Love* and his ever-brilliant insight always made it better. He continues to inspire me and be there for me through our own adventure together. To my Mum, my brother Matt, my Grandma and to my Dad, who planned to buy piles of the book for his nurses but is no longer here to do so. And to my impressive nephews Amaan and Kian, the next generation of ATE supporters.

And finally, with eternal gratitude to each other – for a book we're proud of and a friendship for life.

Sarah and Michele

A NOTE ON THE WRITING

This is Sarah Annable-Gardner's story, from her best recollection of events and people she has met or collaborated with or clashed with or loved during a defining decade in her life.

I believe she has an important story to tell – actually more than one – of how things can change for the better when dedicated people work together; of how a young woman can find resilience and purpose; of how respect and love must never be taken for granted.

Or course, in choosing which moments and people to feature we have had to take difficult decisions. Unfortunately, we haven't been able to mention every incredible person who has contributed to Sarah's life and also the wonderful work of the charity (though we have attempted to redress that in our closing pages).

We want this book to reach the widest audience, to introduce new people to a world that may seem distant and different to their own. To that end, we've tried to make it as accessible as possible. We've represented conversations as they probably occurred – the spirit of the exchange – because obviously no-one can remember every word as precisely spoken over a period of several years. On occasion, we have conflated events or not listed everyone who was there, so the book reads smoothly. However, we have always kept to the essence of what happened and tried never to assume anything Sarah didn't know or see with her own eyes. I've also been able to make use of Action Through Enterprise's invaluable library of blogs and case studies featured on its website.

Where possible and appropriate, we have used people's real names, with their full knowledge, and we'd like to thank Kakpe Kuube-isaan for his kind assistance in informing and liaising with people in Lawra. In some cases, and for various reasons, we have taken the decision to change names, notably Nasir and Bie.

Our whole process has been guided by one principle – that this is a book Aviella and Bie can read when they're older and know it is truthful and from the heart, and I hope we've achieved that.

Michele

Sarah Annable-Gardner is Chief Executive of Action Through Enterprise. She lives in Wiltshire with her husband, daughter and cat.

Michele Carlisle is a TV producer, writer and charity consultant. She lives in London with her husband.

Action Through Enterprise is a dynamic small charity working with communities in Upper West Ghana to alleviate poverty and create opportunities.

Contact us at: admin@ateghana.org
Visit us and donate at: https://ateghana.org

TO LAWRA WITH LOVE

TO LAWRA WITH LOVE

TO LAWRA WITH LOVE

TO LAWRA WITH LOVE

TO LAWRA WITH LOVE